MICHIGAN

WITHDRAWN

Also in This Series

Arizona, Malcolm L. Comeaux

Colorado, Mel Griffiths and Lynnell Rubright

Hawaii, Joseph R. Morgan

Maryland, James E. DiLisio

Missouri, Milton D. Rafferty

New Jersey, Charles A. Stansfield, Jr.

Texas, Terry G. Jordan, with John L. Bean, Jr., and William M. Holmes

Wyoming, Robert Harold Brown

Forthcoming Through 1984

Alaska, Roger W. Pearson and Donald F. Lynch

Mississippi, Jesse O. McKee

North Carolina, Ole Gade and H. Daniel Stillwell

South Carolina, Charles F. Kovacik and John J. Winberry

Utah, Clifford B. Craig

All books in this series are available in paperback and hardcover.

GEOGRAPHIES OF THE UNITED STATES
Ingolf Vogeler, General Editor

Michigan: A Geography
Lawrence M. Sommers

Michigan is truly a "Great Lake State": the two peninsulas, many islands, and 3,100 miles of shoreline on four of the Great Lakes give the state a unique location and a diverse physical environment. The natural landscape is largely the result of erosion and deposition of surface materials during the Great Ice Age. Glacial ridges alternate with till plains and lake bottoms to give Michigan a varied topography and great contrasts in soil fertility.

The book, through the use of text, photographs, and maps (drawn especially for this volume by Sherman Hollander), stresses the relationships between this varied natural resource base and the economic, social, and political geography of Michigan. Emphasis is placed on the demographic character, the historical background, and the natural and human resources that have led to Michigan becoming one of the principal manufacturing states in the United States. The book also looks at agriculture and recreation and tourism, which, along with manufacturing, are the major bases of the state's economic development. The regional coverage focuses on the urban dominance of Detroit. This comprehensive overview of Michigan geography closes with an analysis of some of the major quality of life issues in the state and a short glimpse into the future.

Lawrence M. Sommers is professor of geography at Michigan State University in East Lansing. He is the editor and principal author of *Atlas of Michigan* (1977) and *Fish in Lake Michigan: Distribution of Selected Species* (1982).

MICHIGAN
A GEOGRAPHY

Lawrence M. Sommers

with
Joe T. Darden
Jay R. Harman
Laurie K. Sommers

Westview Press / Boulder and London

Geographies of the United States

Copyright © 1984 by Westview Press, Inc.

Published in 1984 in the United States of America by Westview Press, Inc., 5500 Central Avenue, Boulder, Colorado 80301; Frederick A. Praeger, President and Publisher

Library of Congress Cataloging in Publication Data
Sommers, Lawrence M.
    Michigan, a geography.
    (Geographies of the United States)
    Bibliography: p.
    Includes index.
    1. Michigan—Description and travel.   I. Title.
II. Series.
F566.S67   1984   917.74   83-19791
ISBN 0-86531-093-9
ISBN 0-86531-490-X (pbk.)

Printed and bound in the United States of America

CONTENTS

PART 3
THE ENVIRONMENTAL AND
NATURAL RESOURCE BASES

PART 4
PATTERNS OF HUMAN ACTIVITY

PART 6
THE FUTURE

FIGURES

TABLES

PHOTOGRAPHS

ACKNOWLEDGMENTS

To prepare a geographic analysis of the cultural and physical diversities of Michigan is indeed a challenge, and it requires the input of numerous individuals and the use of a wide variety of sources. This project began over ten years ago when Dr. Edward Fernald, professor of geography at Florida State University, suggested that a joint effort be undertaken to produce a book on Michigan that would parallel his successful text on the geography of Florida. This project served to stimulate a considerable amount of writing and thinking on various aspects of the geography of Michigan, but in 1974, it was set aside to prepare the *Atlas of Michigan,* which was published in 1977. In 1980, the writing of a text on Michigan was resumed as one of the Westview Press geographies of states of the United States. Three colleagues, knowledgeable about various aspects of Michigan, and a cartographer ably contributed to the completion of the manuscript.

Over the period indicated above, numerous individuals have provided invaluable assistance. William Cheek was the first student assistant, followed by Marlia Jenkins and, most recently, Sherry A. Daniely. These individuals collected data, did library work, and helped compile statistics in tabular and rough draft map form. The typing of the many drafts was ably performed by Cheryl Clark, Kim Jaquette, Florence Harvath, and Julie Mathews.

The cartography for the project is primarily the capable work of Sherman K. Hollander. Figures 2.2 and 11.7 were compiled by the Center for Cartography and Spatial Analysis, Department of Geography, Michigan State University, which is headed by Michael Lipsey. Editorial assistance was provided at the final draft stage by Katherine McCracken, Social Science Research Bureau, Michigan State University. Dr. LeRoy Barnett of the Michigan State Archives provided valuable assistance in locating historical photographs.

At Westview Press, I would like to acknowledge Associate Publisher Lynne C. Rienner who encouraged the book; Lynn Arts, the production manager for the volume; and the meticulous and most helpful copy editing of Megan L. Schoeck. Series editor Dr. Ingolf Vogeler provided valuable criticism of the final draft.

The objectives of the book are to provide essential information on and analysis of the systematic and regional geography of Michigan for the student and layman alike. This text, along with the *Atlas of Michigan,* presents a comprehensive spatial view of Michigan; we hope that it also will enable citizens and private and public sector employees to make better decisions for the near and far term.

Lawrence M. Sommers

PART 1

INTRODUCTION

Size, shape, site, and situation are important factors in the geography of any political entity such as the state of Michigan. Large size or area normally results in a variety of physical and cultural characteristics that give distinction to the state as a whole as well as to the smaller regions, counties, cities, villages, and townships. The principal objective of this geography is to determine the significance of the spatial character of Michigan as a whole, as well as of its various composite parts. The state and its parts can be analyzed regionally and systematically or topically. This book will utilize both approaches in order to bring out the unique geographic importance of Michigan.

Michigan has a peninsular shape despite its interior continental location, and the fact that it touches four of the Great Lakes is of major importance. Michigan's long, common border with the Province of Ontario, Canada, also means that the state has an international significance. Chapter 1 analyzes the geographic importance of the uniqueness of Michigan's shape and location.

MICHIGAN'S UNIQUE SHAPE AND LOCATION

Michigan is the third largest state east of the Mississippi River and ranks twenty-third in size in the United States (Figure 1.1). Of the eastern states, only Georgia and Florida are a little larger. Michigan is considerably larger than a number of nations in the world. For example, Portugal and Austria are both smaller than Michigan, as are Belgium, the Netherlands, and Luxembourg combined; England and Wales together are about the same size. Michigan covers a total land area of 58,216 sq mi (150,779 sq km), of which 1,398 sq mi (3,631 sq km) are inland water. The jurisdictional boundaries of Michigan include an additional 38,575 sq mi (99,909 sq km) of Great Lakes water area, or an area two-thirds the size of the land area; if this additional area were counted as part of the total, Michigan would rank eleventh in size. The Michigan coastline is 3,251 mi (5,231 km) long, including 977 mi (1,572 km) of island shorelines. The central and dominant position of Michigan in the western Great Lakes area has led to its being called the Great Lake State (the state's official title is the Wolverine State, after an animal that is now extremely rare).

Michigan's peninsular shape is of major significance. The Upper and Lower Pen-insulas, separated by the narrow Straits of Mackinac, are quite different, partly because of their locations. The Upper Peninsula, particularly the western portion, has much in common with the state of Wisconsin, and there has been some discussion in that area about forming a separate state or becoming a part of Wisconsin. This section is big enough to be a state, but the population and economic bases are limited. The Mackinac Bridge, built in 1957, has made movement between the two peninsulas much easier, and a little more cohesion has resulted.

Because of Michigan's peninsular shape, places in the state may be far apart, especially from north to south. The state's greatest length is 456 mi (734 km), and its greatest breadth is 386 mi (621 km). However, the driving distance between Monroe in the southeastern part of Michigan and Ironwood in the northwestern part is about 620 mi (998 km); from the Ohio line to Sault Ste. Marie is about 390 mi (628 km). Going only 500 mi (805 km) from Detroit would take one east to about New York City; south to beyond Knoxville, Tennessee; and west to Des Moines, Iowa (Figure 1.2).

Location may be considered in both an

3

4

ISLE ROYALE

L. Superior

KEWEENAW
•Houghton
HOUGHTON

ONTONAGON
BARAGA

Ironwood
GOGEBIC   Marquette
               MARQUETTE   LUCE   Sault Ste.
IRON   ALGER Munising Marie   CANADA
                                            CHIPPEWA
WISC.   DICKINSON   SCHOOLCRAFT
                   DELTA   Manistique   MACKINAC

          Iron   St. Ignace
          Mt.   Straits of Mackinac   DRUMMOND IS.
     Escanaba   L. Huron
     MENOMINEE
                                        EMMET   CHEBOYGAN

     Menominee   •Petoskey   PRESQUE ISLE
                            CHARLEVOIX
                                     OTSEGO MONT-   ALPENA
                            ANTRIM   MORENCY
                                     •Gaylord   Alpena•

                   LEELANAU KALKASKA CRAWFORD OSCODA ALCONA
                        Traverse
          L. Michigan BENZIE GRAND City   •Grayling
                             TRAVERSE

                   MANISTEE WEXFORD MISSAUKEE ROSCOMMON OGEMAW IOSCO
                   Manistee•   Cadillac
                   MASON LAKE OSCEOLA CLARE GLADWIN ARENAC
                   Ludington•   Saginaw Bay HURON
                   OCEANA NEWAYGO MECOSTA ISABELLA MIDLAND
                                                      BAY
                                    Mt. •   Midland
                                    Pleasant   TUSCOLA SANILAC
                   MUSKEGON   MONTCALM   GRATIOT SAGINAW •Bay City
                   Muskegon•   Saginaw•
                        KENT   LAPEER
                   Grand•   IONIA CLINTON SHIAWASSEE GENESEE
                   OTTAWA Rapids   •Flint   ST. CLAIR Port
          Holland•   Huron•
                   ALLEGAN BARRY EATON INGHAM Lansing OAKLAND MACOMB
                                                LIVINGSTON
                                                      Pontiac•
          •Over 1,000,000
          •175,000–1,000,000 VAN BUREN KALAMAZOO CALHOUN JACKSON WASHTENAW WAYNE L.
          •25,000–175,000   Kalamazoo   St.Clair
          •10,000–25,000   Benton•   Battle   Ann•   Detroit
          •2,000–10,000   Harbor   Creek Jackson• Arbor   CANADA
                   BERRIEN CASS ST. JOSEPH BRANCH HILLSDALE LENAWEE MONROE
          0   Mi.   100   Monroe•
                                                                    L. Erie
                   IND.   OHIO

FIGURE 1.1. Political map of Michigan.

Welcome-to-Michigan highway sign near Iron Mountain. (Courtesy Michigan Travel Bureau)

between the equator and the North Pole, 45° north latitude, lies just south of Alpena and Gaylord.

The major characteristic of Michigan's relative position is that it is located in the interior of the North American continent. Michigan lies farther south than many parts of Europe and at latitudes similar to those of the southern parts of the USSR and northern Japan. Because of the state's interior position in a large land mass, however, its climate is quite different from those areas, with the exception of that of the southern USSR.

Despite its interior, northerly position, Michigan has milder winters than might be expected because of the moderating effect of the water that surrounds Michigan, especially the waters of Lake Michigan to the west and, to some extent, of Lake Superior to the north. These lakes take in considerable heat during the summer and cool slowly during the fall and winter. The prevailing westerly winds cross Lake Michigan and warm up as they move from west to east, so the winter extremes in temperature are more moderate in southern Michigan

exact, or mathematical, and a relative context. Michigan occupies a mid-latitudinal position, extending from 42° to 48° north latitude, from the southern border to Isle Royale. The longitude range is from 82°30' to about 90°30' west longitude, which puts Michigan in the extreme western portion of the eastern standard time zone—however, those parts of Michigan that are adjacent to Wisconsin use central time as it is more convenient. The parallel halfway

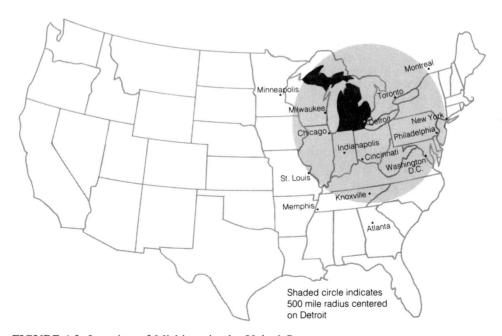

Shaded circle indicates 500 mile radius centered on Detroit

FIGURE 1.2. Location of Michigan in the United States.

than in Wisconsin. Frosts are delayed in the fall and extended in the spring, giving rise to the "lake effect," a consequence of Michigan's location that is important to fruit growers and the winter sports industry.

RELATIVE LOCATION IN THE MIDWEST AND THE UNITED STATES

The eastern point of Michigan is directly north of Tampa, Florida, and the western tip of the Upper Peninsula is almost directly north of St. Louis and New Orleans. The state's location in the north-central part of the country is close to a large part of the nation's population. It is centrally located on the Great Lakes, and there is easy access to the highly industrialized and agriculturally important areas of central and northeastern United States. Many people who live in the warmer southern and interior regions of the United States travel to Michigan for a summer vacation. They are attracted by the Great Lakes, the thousands of inland lakes, and a cooler summer climate. The winter snow also attracts skiers and snowmobilers from the flat and urbanized areas of Ohio, Indiana, and Illinois.

Michigan has become a major international transportation center for waterborne goods. The St. Lawrence Seaway opened up Michigan's harbors to ships of many nations, and trade via the waterways with European countries and Canada is important. The bulk of the material transported on the Great Lakes, however, is heavy products—such as iron ore, coal, and limestone—that are carried between northern and southern lake ports. General cargo, along with coal, forms much of the goods shipped south to north.

Direct air flights are scheduled daily to London, Frankfurt, and other European airports from Detroit's Metropolitan Airport, and Detroit is also a major point of departure for flights to the east, south, and west in the United States. During the winter, there are additional direct flights to Florida, Puerto Rico, Mexico, the Caribbean, Arizona, and California to accom-

modate the people who wish to take advantage of the warmth and sunshine of these areas.

The fact that Michigan is adjacent to the Province of Ontario is significant. Including the water boundaries in Lake Superior and Lake Huron, Michigan has many miles of common boundary with Canada—more than any other state. The points where the two countries are separated only by a river are very important crossing places between the United States and Canada, and in each case an important city has developed on both the Canadian and U.S. sides: Sault Ste. Marie, Port Huron, and Detroit in Michigan; Sault Ste. Marie, Sarnia, and Windsor in Ontario. The St. Marys Falls Canal handled 88,634,900 short tons (80,391,854 t) of cargo in 1978, 98 percent through the U.S. locks and 2 percent through the Canadian. There are important railroad and highway bridges at the three major crossing points into Canada, and there is also a tunnel that connects Detroit and Windsor, Ontario. The adjoining area of the Ontario Peninsula is one of the most populated and productive parts of Canada, and thus the flow of goods and people between the two highly developed sections of Michigan and Ontario is considerable.

Michigan's proximity to Canada has also been significant because many thousands of Canadians have moved into the United States. In 1978, 26,343 Canadians reported as aliens in Michigan, almost 10 percent of the Canadians who reported in the United States. Some Michiganians have moved to Canada, but far more Canadians have moved from there. (The movement to Canada has increased, however, in recent years.) A considerable portion of Canadian industry is partially or wholly U.S. owned, including a number of firms that are owned by Michigan companies, such as the automobile firms. This fact has aided the movement of people and capital into Canada. Canada has become more and more concerned about the potential of U.S. domination because of U.S. industry and money in Canada, and this problem is a major point in the political relations between the two countries and between the state of Michigan and the Province of Ontario.

LOCATION AND HISTORY

The area that is now Michigan has been significant in U.S. history. From the period of the early French explorers through the French and Indian War, the War of 1812, and the recent world conflicts, this area has served as a base for important military and economic operations. Both air and land military bases have been located in the state because of the strategic importance of communication routes such as the "Soo Canal," the large population, and the automobile industry, which can easily be converted to manufacture war material such as trucks, tanks, and other mobile equipment. The St. Lawrence Seaway runs through Michigan-controlled waters in its western portions, and the great circle route—the shortest straight-line distance between the industrial heartland of the United States and the major population centers of the Soviet Union—is via Michigan, Canada, and the North Pole.

PEOPLE, LOCATION, AND PHYSICAL ENVIRONMENT

Location is an important a part of the total environment as are resources and landforms. Escanaba, for instance, is an important port, but its deep, natural bay is only one of many factors, both cultural and physical, that influenced its develop-

ment. Political decisions, the availability of public port facilities, local initiatives, and transportation planning have also had an impact. The economic development of markets and wholesale firms and cultural influences such as people's preferences and organizations also have had an impact on the location of a port at Escanaba. The major factor, however, was that Escanaba is a significant outlet for the important iron-ore resources of the Upper Peninsula.

On the other hand, the port at Detroit occupies an unlikely site if physical features are considered, but the port has been built, deepened, and extended to serve the rapidly growing industry and population of the area. The locks at Sault Ste. Marie are another example of how humans overcame a physical barrier—the rapids in the St. Marys River—to permit the important transport of iron ore and other heavy goods between Lake Superior ports and other Great Lakes and world ports without re-shipment.

The physical environment of Michigan undoubtedly had more influence on the way of life of the Indians than it has on life today. Through activities like lumbering, digging drainage ditches, building highways, and using insecticides, people can greatly alter or permanently destroy aspects of the physical environment. The needs and technical capacities of people are constantly changing, so inhabitants of a given area change the way they use the earth and its resources. Michigan's physical resources and how people have altered those resources to meet their needs will be discussed in subsequent chapters.

PART 2

THE POPULATION

The people who inhabit Michigan are the most important resource the state possesses. The 1980 census put the total at 9,258,344, which makes Michigan the eighth most populous state in the United States, and the average population density was 159 people per sq mi (61.4 per sq km), 2.5 times the national average.

Michigan is typical of the northern industrial states in that its growth slowed considerably in the 1970s. The 4.3 percent increase from 1970 to 1980 contrasts with an 11.4 percent increase for the United States in the same period and with a 13.6 percent growth in Michigan from 1960 to 1970. Large numbers of people have left the northern, highly urbanized states for the Sun Belt, and there has been a decrease in the number of new residents, including aliens, as well.

The population of Michigan is very unevenly distributed. Most of the people live in cities in the southern third of the state—43.7 percent of the inhabitants live in the three counties of Wayne, Oakland, and Macomb—and sparseness of population is a major characteristic of the northern two-thirds of the state. This distributional pattern is closely related to the intensity of manufacturing and associated employment opportunities, which will be covered later in some detail. In 1980, the Michigan population was 85 percent white, 13 percent black, and 2 percent other, including Hispanics.

The nature and significance of population numbers, growth trends, distribution, and demographic and ethnic characteristics will be covered in the next two chapters. The people of the state make up an important part of the geography of Michigan and, together with what they do, are what this book is about.

CHAPTER 2

POPULATION: NUMBER, DISTRIBUTION, AND GROWTH TRENDS

Michigan is the eighth most populous state in the United States and ranks third behind Illinois and Ohio among the twelve north-central states (Table 2.1). Michigan's population of 9,258,344 (per the 1980 census) is more than double that of its neighbor Wisconsin and fourteen times that of North Dakota. In fact, the combined population of the three counties of Wayne, Oakland, and Macomb—4,043,633—is larger than the total population of thirty-six states of the union. Wayne County alone has five times the number of people in the entire state of Nevada.

The population figures of some Michigan counties go to the other extreme. In 1980, eleven counties had fewer than 10,000 people (Table 2.2). Six of them are in the sparsely populated Upper Peninsula, and five are in the northern third of the Lower Peninsula. With 1,963 people, Keweenaw, at the tip of the Keweenaw Peninsula, has the fewest people of any county in the state. The entire Upper Peninsula has 319,757 inhabitants, which is only about one-seventh the number in Wayne County alone, the single most populous county in Michigan with 2,337,240 people. Thus, it is obvious that Michigan is a state of extremes when it comes to how many people occupy

a certain amount of space in its various regions. The distribution of people is closely related to the employment opportunities in the major manufacturing areas; the retail, commercial, and service activities that accompany manufacturing; the intensity of agriculture; and the transportation facilities in the various portions of Michigan. The overall effect during the twentieth century has been an increasing economic dominance of the southern third of the state.

DISTRIBUTION AND DENSITY PATTERNS

The distribution and density patterns of the population were established when industry became dominant in Michigan in the early 1900s, and they have remained essentially the same in gross character since that time. The trend until the 1970s was the increasing movement of people into the urban and suburban areas, but the 1980 census shows some remarkable percentage increases in the predominantly rural counties.

Michigan's 9,258,344 people live in 58,216 sq mi (150,779 sq km), which gives an average density of 159 persons per sq mi (61.4 per sq km). The greatest population

TABLE 2.1. Highest population rank, United States and north-central states, as of 1980

	United States				North Central States		
Rank	States	1970-1980 % Growth	Population	Rank	States	1970-1980 % Growth	Population
1.	California	18.5	23,668,562	1.	Illinois	2.8	11,418,461
2.	New York	-3.8	17,557,288	2.	Ohio	1.3	10,797,419
3.	Texas	27.1	14,228,383	3.	Michigan	4.3	9,258,344
4.	Pennsylvania	0.6	11,866,728	4.	Indiana	5.7	5,490,179
5.	Illinois	2.8	11,418,461	5.	Missouri	5.1	4,917,444
6.	Ohio	1.3	10,797,419	6.	Wisconsin	6.5	4,705,335
7.	Florida	43.4	9,739,992	7.	Minnesota	7.1	4,077,148
8.	Michigan	4.3	9,258,344	8.	Iowa	3.1	2,913,387
9.	New Jersey	2.7	7,364,158	9.	Kansas	5.1	2,363,208
10.	N. Carolina	15.5	5,874,429	10.	Nebraska	5.7	1,570,006
11.	Massachusetts	0.8	5,737,037	11.	S. Dakota	3.6	690,178
12.	Indiana	5.7	5,490,179	12.	N. Dakota	5.6	652,695

Source: U.S. Bureau of the Census, 1980 Census of Population and Housing, Advance Reports (Washington, D.C.: Government Printing Office, March 1981).

TABLE 2.2. Total population of the counties of Michigan for 1940, 1960, 1970, and 1980

County	1940	1960	1970	1980	Percent Change, 1970-1980
Alcona	5,463	6,352	7,113	9,740	36.9
Alger	10,167	9,250	8,568	9,225	7.7
Allegan	41,839	57,729	66,575	81,555	22.5
Alpena	20,766	28,556	30,708	32,315	5.2
Antrim	10,964	10,373	12,612	16,194	28.4
Arenac	9,233	9,860	11,149	14,706	31.9
Baraga	9,356	7,151	7,789	8,484	8.9
Barry	22,613	31,738	38,166	45,781	20.0
Bay	74,981	107,042	117,339	119,881	2.2
Benzie	7,800	7,834	8,593	11,205	30.4
Berrien	89,117	149,865	163,875	171,276	4.5
Branch	25,845	34,903	37,906	40,188	6.0
Calhoun	94,206	138,858	141,963	141,557	- 0.3
Cass	21,910	36,932	43,312	49,499	14.3
Charlevoix	13,031	13,421	16,541	19,907	20.3
Cheboygan	13,644	14,550	16,573	20,649	24.6
Chippewa	27,807	32,655	32,412	29,029	-10.4
Clare	9,163	11,647	16,695	23,822	42.7
Clinton	26,671	37,969	48,492	55,893	15.3
Crawford	3,765	4,971	6,482	9,465	46.0
Delta	34,037	34,298	35,924	38,947	8.4
Dickinson	28,731	23,917	23,753	25,341	6.7
Eaton	34,124	49,684	68,892	88,337	28.2
Emmet	15,791	15,904	18,331	22,992	25.4
Genesee	227,944	374,313	445,589[a]	450,449	1.1
Gladwin	9,385	10,769	13,471	19,957	48.1
Gogebic	31,797	24,370	20,676	19,686	- 4.8
Grand Traverse	23,390	33,490	39,175	54,899	40.1
Gratiot	32,205	37,012	39,246	40,448	3.1
Hillsdale	29,092	34,742	37,171	42,071	13.2
Houghton	47,631	35,654	34,652	37,872	9.3
Huron	32,584	34,006	34,083	36,459	7.0
Ingham	130,616	211,296	261,039	272,437	4.4
Ionia	35,710	43,132	45,848	51,815	13.0
Iosco	8,560	16,505	24,905	28,349	13.8
Iron	20,243	17,184	13,813	13,635	- 1.3
Isabella	25,982	35,348	44,594	54,110	21.3
Jackson	93,108	131,994	143,274	151,495	5.7
Kalamazoo	100,085	169,712	201,550	212,378	5.4
Kalkaska	5,159	4,382	5,272	10,952	107.7
Kent	246,338	363,187	411,044	444,506	8.1
Keweenaw	4,004	2,417	2,264	1,963	-13.3
Lake	4,798	5,338	5,661	7,711	36.2
Lapeer	32,116	41,926	52,361[a]	70,038	33.8
Leelanau	8,436	9,321	10,872	14,007	28.8

TABLE 2.2 (continued)

County	1940	1960	1970	1980	Percent Change, 1970–1980
Lenawee	53,110	77,789	81,951[a]	89,948	9.8
Livingston	20,863	38,233	58,967	100,289	70.1
Luce	7,423	7,827	6,789	6,659	- 1.9
Mackinac	9,438	10,853	9,660	10,178	5.4
Macomb	107,638	405,804	625,309	694,600	11.1
Manistee	18,450	19,042	20,094	23,019	14.6
Marquette	47,144	56,154	64,686	74,101	14.6
Mason	19,378	21,929	22,612	26,365	16.6
Mecosta	16,902	21,051	27,992	36,961	32.0
Menominee	24,883	24,685	24,587	26,201	6.6
Midland	27,094	51,450	63,769	73,578	15.4
Missaukee	8,034	6,784	7,126	10,009	40.5
Monroe	58,620	101,120	118,479	134,659	13.7
Montcalm	28,581	35,795	39,660	47,555	19.9
Montmorency	3,840	4,424	5,247	7,492	42.8
Muskegon	94,501	149,943	157,426	157,589	0.1
Newaygo	19,286	24,160	27,992	34,917	24.7
Oakland	254,068	690,259	907,871	1,011,793	11.4
Oceana	14,812	16,547	17,984	22,002	22.3
Ogemaw	8,720	9,680	11,903	16,436	38.1
Ontonagon	11,359	10,584	10,548	9,861	- 6.5
Osceola	13,309	13,595	14,838	18,928	27.6
Oscoda	2,543	3,447	4,726	6,858	45.1
Otsego	5,827	7,545	10,422	14,993	43.9
Ottawa	59,660	98,719	128,181	157,174	22.6
Presque Isle	12,250	13,117	12,836	14,267	11.1
Roscommon	3,668	7,200	9,892	16,374	65.5
Saginaw	130,468	190,752	219,743	228,059	3.8
St. Clair	76,222	107,201	120,175	138,802	15.5
St. Joseph	31,749	42,332	47,392	56,083	18.3
Sanilac	30,114	32,314	35,181[a]	40,789	15.9
Schoolcraft	9,524	8,953	8,226	8,575	4.2
Shiawassee	41,207	53,446	63,075	71,140	12.8
Tuscola	35,694	43,305	48,603	56,961	17.2
Van Buren	35,111	48,395	56,173	66,814	18.9
Washtenaw	80,810	172,440	234,103	264,748	13.1
Wayne	2,015,623	2,666,297	2,669,604[a]	2,337,240	-12.5
Wexford	17,976	18,466	19,717	25,102	27.3
Total	5,256,106	7,823,194	8,879,862[a]	9,258,344	4.3

[a]Corrected for errors found after tabulations were completed.

Source: U.S. Bureau of the Census, 1980 Census of Population and Housing, Advance Reports (Washington, D.C.: Government Printing Office, March 1981).

densities are in the southern, especially the southeastern, parts of the state; the lowest, in the northern Lower Peninsula and the Upper Peninsula. The densities in and around cities grew rapidly from 1950 to 1970, but the urban areas generally decreased or grew more slowly in the decade from 1970 to 1980. There are also large areas in Michigan where no one lives—portions of the forested, sandy, and swampy regions.

The highest average population density is in Wayne County with 3,863 people per sq mi (1,492 per sq km), and the lowest is in Keweenaw County with 3.6 per sq mi (1.4 per sq km) (Figure 2.1). The great growth in Wayne County took place between 1930 and 1950, which correlates with the rapid growth of the automotive and related industries. The people of Wayne County are largely supported by manufacturing, retail, transportation, and service industries, which do not require a great deal of space for their operation, and the employees are concentrated in housing developments in Detroit and vicinity. This kind of urban concentration requires the import of large amounts of food, energy, industrial raw materials, and other goods from other areas of the state, the nation, and the world. The products of industrial and urban Michigan are also exported nationwide and worldwide; thus, trade is another reason for the concentration of population in southeastern Michigan.

GROWTH TRENDS

Population growth has characterized the development of the United States, and Michigan is no exception. The area was designated as Michigan Territory in 1805 and became a state in 1837. In 1830, the population totaled only 31,639; by 1900, this number had grown to 2.4 million; by 1930, to 4.8 million; by 1950, to 6.3 million; by 1970, to 8.88 million; and by 1980, to

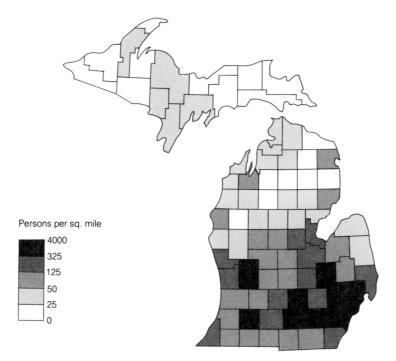

Persons per sq. mile

- 4000
- 325
- 125
- 50
- 25
- 0

FIGURE 2.1. Population density, by county, 1980. (Source: U.S. Bureau of the Census, *1980 Census of Population and Housing, Michigan* [Washington, D.C.: Government Printing Office, 1981].)

TABLE 2.3. Total population of U.S. states ranked by percent of change from 1970 to 1980

States	1970	1980	% Change	Rank
Nevada	488,738	799,184	63.5	1
Arizona	1,775,399	2,717,866	53.1	2
Florida	6,791,992	9,739,992	43.4	3
Wyoming	332,416	470,816	41.6	4
Utah	1,059,273	1,461,037	37.9	5
Idaho	713,015	943,935	32.4	6
Alaska	302,583	400,481	32.4	7
Colorado	2,209,596	2,888,834	30.7	8
New Mexico	1,017,055	1,299,968	27.8	9
Texas	11,198,655	14,228,383	27.1	10
Oregon	2,091,533	2,632,663	25.9	11
Hawaii	769,913	965,000	25.3	12
New Hampshire	737,681	920,610	24.8	13
Washington	3,413,244	4,130,163	21.0	14
South Carolina	2,590,713	3,119,208	20.4	15
Georgia	4,587,930	5,464,265	19.1	16
Arkansas	1,923,322	2,285,513	18.8	17
California	19,971,069	23,668,562	18.5	18
Oklahoma	2,559,463	3,025,266	18.2	19
Tennessee	3,926,018	4,590,750	16.9	20
North Carolina	5,084,411	5,874,429	15.5	21
Louisiana	3,644,637	4,203,972	15.3	22
Vermont	444,732	511,456	15.0	23
Virginia	4,651,448	5,346,279	14.9	24
Kentucky	3,220,711	3,661,433	13.7	25
Mississippi	2,216,994	2,520,638	13.7	26
Montana	694,409	786,690	13.3	27
Maine	993,722	1,124,660	13.2	28
Alabama	3,444,354	3,890,061	12.9	29
West Virginia	1,744,237	1,949,644	11.8	30
Delaware	548,104	595,225	8.6	31
Maryland	3,923,897	4,216,446	7.5	32
Minnesota	3,806,103	4,077,148	7.1	33
Wisconsin	4,417,821	4,705,335	6.5	34
Indiana	5,195,392	5,490,179	5.7	35
Nebraska	1,485,333	1,570,006	5.7	36
North Dakota	617,792	652,695	5.6	37
Kansas	2,249,071	2,363,208	5.1	38
Missouri	4,677,623	4,917,444	5.1	39
Michigan	8,879,862	9,258,344	4.3	40
South Dakota	666,257	690,178	3.6	41
Iowa	2,825,368	2,913,387	3.1	42
Illinois	11,110,285	11,418,461	2.8	43
New Jersey	7,171,112	7,364,158	2.7	44
Connecticut	3,032,217	3,107,576	2.5	45

TABLE 2.3 (continued)

States	1970	1980	% Change	Rank
Ohio	10,657,423	10,797,419	1.3	46
Massachusetts	5,689,170	5,737,037	0.8	47
Pennsylvania	11,800,766	11,866,728	0.6	48
Rhode Island	949,723	947,154	-0.3	49
New York	18,241,391	17,557,288	-3.8	50
District of Columbia	756,668	637,651	-15.7	51
Total	203,302,605	226,504,825	11.4	

Source: U.S. Bureau of the Census, 1980 Census of Population (Washington, D.C.: Government Printing Office, 1981).

9.26 million. Since 1960, the state has continued to grow but at a slower rate. Within the state, some areas, especially the large cities, have seen a rapidly declining growth rate and even population losses, but many rural counties have grown over 25 percent, and one—Kalkaska County— grew more than 100 percent between 1970 and 1980. These shifts in population numbers and growth rates are the result of changing resource exploitation, shifting life-styles, and a new manufacturing emphasis—all of which have significant effects on the evolving character of the various regions of Michigan.

The population increase of the whole state from 1950 to 1960 was 22.8 percent; from 1960 to 1970, 13.5 percent; and from 1970 to 1980, only 4.3 percent. In the 1960s, Michigan was the fastest-growing state in the north-central region, with an annual 1.3 percent increase. Other states in the region averaged less than 1 percent, and in the Great Plains states the gain was even less—with North and South Dakota losing population. People looking for work were moving from the farm states to the heavily industrial and urbanized ones, like Michigan.

In the decade from 1970 to 1980, the rapid growth in the United States was in the South and West, in states with warm climates, new employment opportunities, and amenities for the growing number of elderly people. The fastest-growing states since 1970 have been Nevada (63.5 percent), Arizona (53.1), Florida (43.4), Wyoming (41.6), and Utah (37.9). On the other hand, among the north-central states, Illinois and Ohio had even smaller gains than Michigan, (2.8 percent and 1.3 percent, respectively), and Indiana (5.7 percent) and Wisconsin (6.5 percent) had slightly higher gains (Table 2.3).

The 1980 census shows some interesting shifts in the rate of population growth: shifting from the urban-suburban areas to the counties of the northern Lower Peninsula and a few counties in the urban south like Livingston, Lapeer, and Eaton. These regional changes were beginning to be apparent between 1960 and 1970 but increased between 1970 and 1980 (Figure 2.2). For 1970–1980, several patterns stand out: (1) the Upper Peninsula counties had either losses or small gains; (2) the urban counties of the south show either losses— Wayne with 12.5 percent—or small gains; (3) the largest grouping of counties with the greatest percentage gains (over 25 percent) are in the northern Lower Peninsula; and (4) the large gains in the southern third of the state are in nonmetropolitan areas but close enough to cities like Detroit,

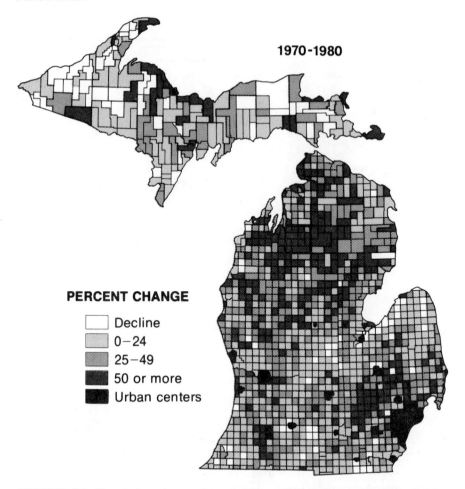

FIGURE 2.2. Population change, by townships, 1960–1970, 1970–1980. (Source: Maps compiled by Richard Groop, and published in Lawrence M. Sommers and John L. Lounsbury, "Impact of Population Growth Trends on State and Local Land Use Policy: The Examples of Michigan and Arizona," *Proceedings of Applied Geography Conferences* 5 [1982], p. 135.)

Grand Rapids, Muskegon, Flint, Kalamazoo, and Battle Creek to draw people from them. Two unusual statistics are a 107.7 percent increase in Kalkaska County, primarily because of a petroleum and natural gas boom in this area, which previously had had a limited employment base; and a 70 percent increase in Livingston County, the result of a flight of residents from Detroit and vicinity to an area where pollution, crime, and urban problems are fewer and many houses are on larger lots in a rural setting.

A number of factors are involved in the

changes in percentage growth in the last decade. Generally, the counties with losses or very little growth are either the economically depressed urban counties with large net migration losses, like Wayne (332,364 people lost between 1970 and 1980) and Muskegon, or the six counties in the Upper Peninsula that have very limited economic bases. The counties that are growing are those that had small populations to begin with, are major recreation and tourist areas with good access via expressway to the bigger cities, have attracted some new small industries (for ex-

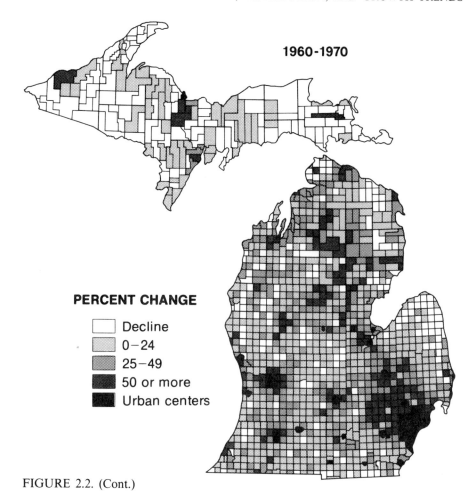

1960-1970

PERCENT CHANGE

- ☐ Decline
- 0-24
- 25-49
- 50 or more
- ■ Urban centers

FIGURE 2.2. (Cont.)

ample, those that process wood products in various ways), and are attracting a growing number of retirees as well as some young families from the urban southern part of the state who want a new life in the rural north.

DYNAMICS OF POPULATION CHANGE

Oakland County is a good example of the dynamics of population change in the predominantly urban portions of Michigan (Figure 2.3). From 1970 to 1980, the population of the county rose 11.4 percent from 907,871 to 1,011,793—a total of 103,922 additional people. The county extremes var-

ied from a loss of 63.4 percent in Rochester to a growth of 233.6 percent in Wixom City. In general, the larger cities in all of Michigan registered losses (Table 2.4), and the rural townships indicated gains. The exceptions like Wixom City are the result of a new industry's locating outside of Detroit—a large automobile plant in Wixom's case. Oakland County is fortunate in that it has many lakes, and many people who live there have converted summer cottages into permanent homes and commute to the surrounding cities to work. Pontiac suffered a loss of 8,564 residents in the 1970s, and Royal Oak lost 15,345. Thus, the population change in Oakland County is a microcosm of the statewide

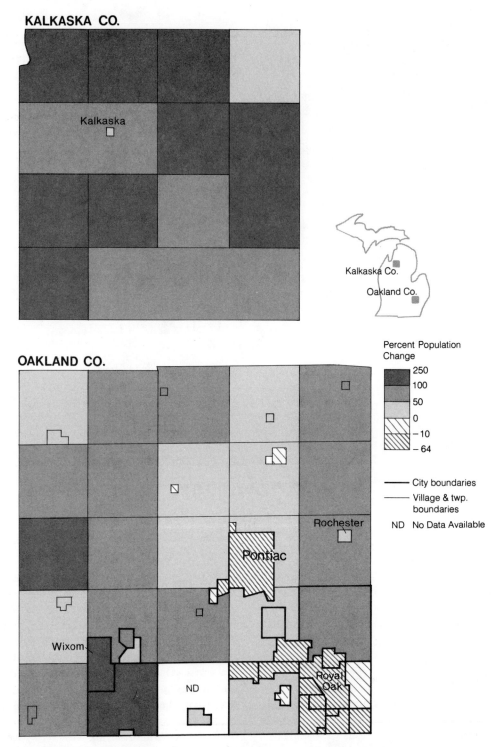

FIGURE 2.3. Population change, 1970–1980, in Kalkaska and Oakland Counties: Percent of change by townships. (Source: U.S. Bureau of the Census, *1980 Census of Population and Housing, Michigan* [Washington, D.C.: Government Printing Office, 1981].)

TABLE 2.4. Population change in cities over 75,000 from 1970 to 1980

	1970	1980	Percent Change
Detroit	1,514,063	1,203,339	-20.5
Grand Rapids	197,649	181,843	- 8.0
Warren	179,260	161,260	-10.0
Flint	193,317	159,611	-17.4
Lansing	131,403	130,414	- 0.8
Sterling Heights	61,365	108,999	77.6
Ann Arbor	100,035	107,316	7.3
Livonia	110,109	104,109	- 5.5
Dearborn	104,199	90,660	-13.0
Westland	86,749	84,603	- 2.5
Kalamazoo	85,555	79,722	- 6.8
Taylor	70,020	77,568	10.8
Saginaw	91,849	77,508	-15.6
Pontiac	85,279	76,715	-10.0
St. Clair Shores	88,093	76,210	-13.5
Southfield	69,285	75,568	9.1
Royal Oak	86,238	70,893	-17.8
Dearborn Heights	80,069	67,706	-15.4

Sources: U.S. Bureau of the Census, U.S. Census of Population: 1970, Number of Inhabitants, Michigan (Washington, D.C., 1971), and U.S. Bureau of the Census, 1980 Census of Population and Housing: Michigan, Advance Reports, PHC 80-V-24 (Washington, D.C.: Government Printing Office, 1981).

flight of people from urban to suburban and nonmetropolitan regions in recent years.

Kalkaska is an example of phenomenal growth from a small population base. The population more than doubled in the 1970–1980 decade—but that means it went from 5,272 to 10,952 people, only about 5 percent of the number of people added to Oakland County during the same period. Kalkaska has only one incorporated village, which grew a moderate 12 percent. The phenomenal growth took place in the townships and it was primarily because of, first, the increased importance of development in the oil and gas industry and, second, the growth in the recreation and wood products industries. Kalkaska's population gain was largely a result of a net in-migration of 4,950 people rather than a change in birth and death rates. Similar population changes have taken place in other counties in the northern half of the Lower Peninsula.

MICHIGAN AS AN URBAN STATE

Although Michigan has large sparsely populated rural areas, the bulk of the people live in urban areas. In 1978, 81.3 percent of the population was classified as urban, and 28.7 percent as rural. "Rural" is defined by the census as places with 2,500 or fewer people. Actually, many of the people classified as rural commute to cities for employment and thus are urban in regard to their place of work. The predominantly urban nature of Michigan is indicated by the fact that 5,688,151 people, 61 percent, live in the eight counties of Wayne, Oakland, Macomb, Washtenaw, Genesee, Ingham, Kent, and Kalamazoo. These counties are 90 percent or more urban.

Figure 2.4 illustrates the patterns of urban development by counties in Michigan. As would be expected, the highest concentrations of urban people are in the area south of the Bay City to Muskegon line and mostly in the southeast near Detroit. These are the areas where the major manufacturing and retail and wholesale activities are located. In addition, Ingham, Kalamazoo, Wayne, and Washtenaw Counties have important universities, and state government accounts for large numbers of employees in Ingham County.

The degree of urbanization in the Upper Peninsula is surprising. Six of the fifteen counties are over 50 percent urban because of the dominance of cities like Sault Ste. Marie, Marquette, and Escanaba in their respective counties and the concentrations of urban people involved in the exploitation

and processing of resources such as iron ore, copper, and forest products. Recreation, education, and services add to the urban base of the Upper Peninsula.

The counties in the central portion of the northern half of the Lower Peninsula, Huron and Sanilac Counties in the thumb area, Oceana County in the west, and Leelanau and Benzie Counties in the northwest each have an urban population of 30 percent or less, but some of these counties had a large percentage of population increase in the 1970s.

Movement from the cities was a major characteristic of the period from 1970 to 1980. All of the cities with over 75,000 people except Ann Arbor, Southfield, Sterling Heights, and Taylor had population losses. The suburban and nonmetropolitan areas have benefited from these losses, and industry as well as other economic activities and housing have shifted from the central

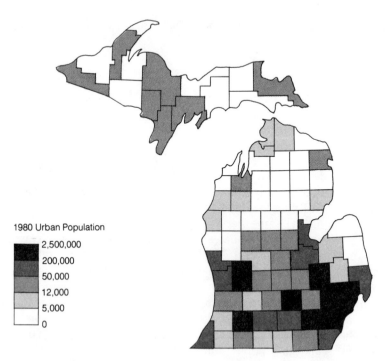

FIGURE 2.4. Urban population, by county, 1980. (Source: U.S. Bureau of the Census, *1980 Census of Population and Housing, Michigan* [Washington, D.C.: Government Printing Office, 1981].)

city. Urban functions have sprawled out into rural and unpopulated areas, facilitated by the development of highways, particularly expressways. These same highways and the automobile have helped the movement of people into the counties of northern Michigan. This urban sprawl is now one of the state's major problems as the cost of energy sources to serve the scattered population is rapidly increasing, and the availability of those sources is increasingly expensive. The next decades should see an even greater concentration of the population, especially in nucleated settlements, in order to reduce energy requirements and to facilitate the development of mass transportation and district heating (use of both waste heat and energy from utilities to heat industrial, commercial, and residential structures).

CHAPTER 3

DEMOGRAPHIC AND ETHNIC CHARACTERISTICS

The demographic and ethnic characteristics of the people of Michigan are important in comparing the state to the rest of the United States as well as in considering regional differences within the state. For instance, the age and sex composition ratios for Michigan as a whole are quite similar to the average for the United States, but counties within the state differ considerably from this average. The birthrate in Michigan in 1978 was 15.5 per 1,000, and the death rate was 8.1 per 1,000. In general, the counties of the southern, densely populated urban third of the state had lower birthrates and lower death rates than the northern, more sparsely populated two-thirds (Figures 3.1 and 3.2), and rural counties tended to have higher birthrates and higher death rates than urban counties. These differences relate to knowledge about birth control, the standard of living, the available health care, and the need for children to work on the farms.

A population pyramid helps to understand the distribution of the number of males and females of various ages in Michigan (Figure 3.3). There are only slight differences between the average age-sex distributions for the United States and Michigan. The dominant trend of both the birth-rate and the death rate is that each was lower in 1979 than in 1970, which means that there were fewer people at the younger ages and more at the older ages in 1979 than in 1970. The average birthrate was 15.6 and the death rate 7.9 per 1,000 population in Michigan in 1979; the corresponding figures for the United States were 15.8 and 8.7. The Michigan population pyramid shows there are fewer people between the ages of 40 to 44 and 45 to 49—people born during the low birthrate period of the Depression in the 1930s. The pyramid also shows a larger number of women than men aged 65 to 79, which is due to the deaths of men during World War II as well as to the higher death rate for men than for women of these ages.

The numbers related to the age distributions have a major impact on various aspects of the economic and social character of the country and state. The number of people between 15 and 65 has a strong bearing upon the size of the labor force, and this factor, in turn, affects such elements as capital availability, family formation, retail demand, housing needs, and savings and investment rates. An increasing older population means more emphasis upon health care needs, retirement homes,

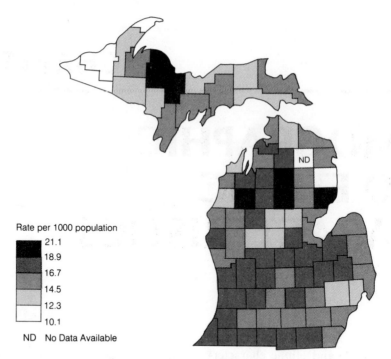

FIGURE 3.1. Birthrate, by county, 1978. (Source: Michigan Department of Public Health, *Michigan Vital Statistics, 1978* [Lansing, 1979].)

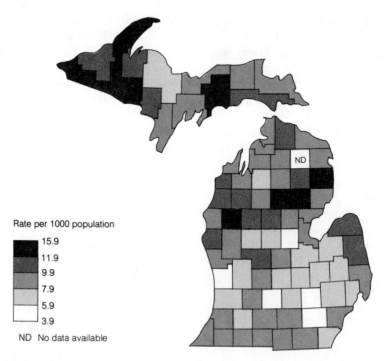

FIGURE 3.2. Death rate, by county, 1978. (Source: Michigan Department of Public Health, *Michigan Vital Statistics, 1978* [Lansing, 1979].)

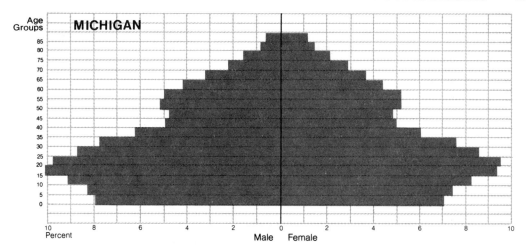

FIGURE 3.3. Population pyramid, 1980. (Source: Based on computer printouts provided by J. Allan Beegle, Department of Sociology, Michigan State University, 1983.)

and annuity and social security costs. A decreasing younger population means less need for schools, teachers, and educational facilities of all kinds.

There are major differences among population pyramids. The counties shown in Figure 3.4 were selected because they show significant population differences between urban and rural regions as well as different economic emphases such as agriculture, industry, forestry, and recreation. In general, the rural counties of the northern two-thirds of Michigan have the highest birthrates, and the urban-industrial counties the lowest; thus, in the northern counties, a higher proportion of the people are younger—compared to the middle-age categories—than in the southern counties. In 1978, Marquette County in the Upper Peninsula had the highest birthrate, 19.9 per 1,000, followed by Missaukee, 19.5, and Iosco, 18.5—both of which are in the rural, northern Lower Peninsula. The lowest birthrates in 1978 were 11.2 in Roscommon and Alcona and 11.7 in Ontonagon, which probably reflect the large elderly population in these counties. The highest death rate was 15.7 in Lake County, and the lowest was 5.1 in Washtenaw County.

Of the counties shown in Figure 3.4, Allegan has the closest to a normal or ideal age group distribution—the largest numbers being for the group of those zero to 25 years old, and the numbers decreasing gradually, with minor exceptions, to the smaller number for the group of those 85 years old or older. Lake County has an unusually large number of senior citizens, which is partly due to the number of retirees who have moved to that county. Ingham County has a large number of 20-to-24-year-olds as a result of the presence of Michigan State University, Lansing Community College, and Cooley Law School. Iron County has larger numbers of residents in the older and younger groups and much smaller numbers between the ages of 20 and 50, which reflects the fact that its youths leave the area for education or employment elsewhere. Wayne County has fewer middle-aged people, which reflects the movement of white-collar management people to the suburban nonmetropolitan counties.

BIRTHPLACES OF MICHIGANIANS

The last three ten-year censuses show more people leaving Michigan than moving into it. The net migration losses were 162,000 from 1950 to 1960, only 27,000 from 1960 to 1970, and as many as 325,000

28

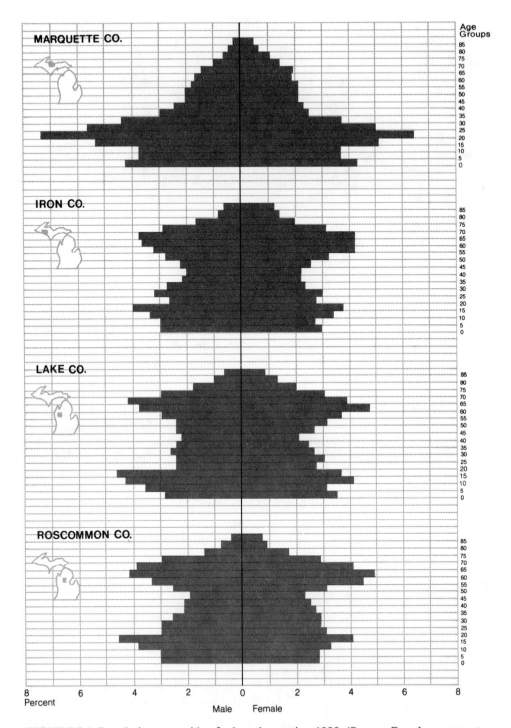

FIGURE 3.4. Population pyramids of selected counties, 1980. (Source: Based on computer printouts provided by J. Allan Beegle, Department of Sociology, Michigan State University, 1983.)

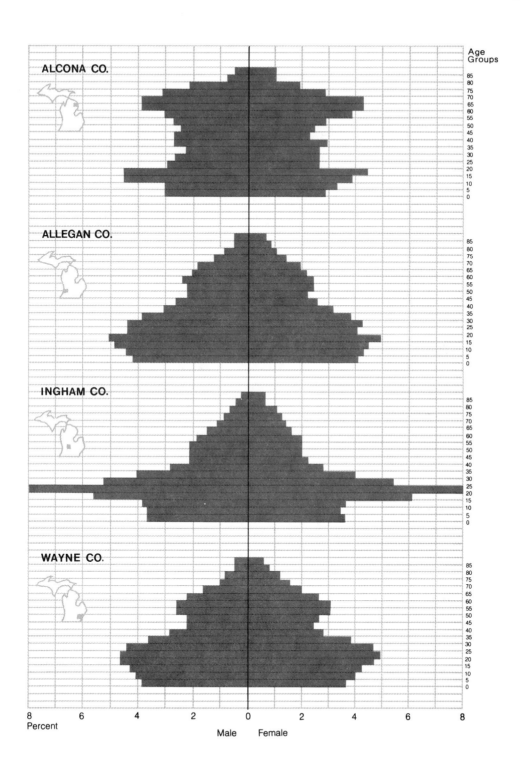

Michigan State University dormitory buildings (*above*) and Agricultural Hall—a major classroom and research building—(*below*). MSU is a significant contributor to employment in Ingham County.

from 1970 to 1980. These figures relate closely to the economic condition of Michigan: The loss is small in good years and grows in the lean years. Too, large numbers of retired people have been attracted to the Sun Belt, and younger people have been seeking economic opportunities in those growing regions of the country as well. In the decade between 1970 and 1980, the urban counties lost the largest number of residents. Detroit alone lost 308,143 people, or 20.4 percent of its population. Many of these people moved elsewhere in the state of Michigan, but large numbers moved out of the state. Many blacks are returning to states in the South, and numerous whites are seeking employment in the fast-growing states, especially in the South and West.

Like the United States as a whole, Michigan is a collection of nationalities from numerous countries. Certain sections of the state are dominated by people of foreign ancestry—for instance, the Dutch in Grand Rapids and Holland, the Finns on the

Keweenaw Peninsula, the Germans in Frankenmuth and Westphalia, and the Poles in Hamtramck. Detroit and vicinity have large populations from eastern Europe—Poles, Rumanians, Hungarians, Yugoslavs, Ukrainians. Most of these immigrants came before 1950 and have become naturalized citizens. As of September 30, 1978, there were 135,522 aliens in Michigan, of whom 19.4 percent were Canadian; 7.5 percent, British; 5 percent, German; 5 percent, Italian; 4.3 percent, Polish; and smaller percentages from a large variety of countries. From each of these peoples, Michigan has gained a bit of cultural heritage, which benefits the entire population. The minority groups—native (from elsewhere in the United States) and foreign-born—will be discussed later in this chapter.

FACTORS AFFECTING DEMOGRAPHICS

Income

Statistics on per capita income provide some significant insights into the differences between the economic characters of various parts of Michigan, as well as between their social characters. In 1979, the average per capita income of all U.S. inhabitants was $8,757, and in Michigan the figure was slightly higher—$9,381. Michigan, with its emphasis upon manufacturing, has a per capita income similar to the states of the industrial Northeast. Michigan's per capita income growth from 1978 to 1979 was 10.27 percent, or slightly less than the 11.61 for the United States as a whole.

Figure 3.5 shows the distribution of average per capita incomes by counties. The high-ranked counties are all south of the Muskegon–Bay City line where extensive manufacturing results in high wage levels. The retail and service sectors in the urban settlements add to the earning power of the inhabitants of these southern urban counties, and suburban counties like Oakland and Macomb rank high because of the large number of white-collar or man-

agerial employees who live there but often work in the many factories and businesses in Detroit or elsewhere in Wayne County. The cost of living will also be proportionately higher in the urban-industrial parts of the state than in the rural sections of the northern two-thirds of Michigan. In 1979, the total annual costs of a moderate standard of living for a family of four in Detroit was $20,821, compared to $20,517 for the United States as a whole. The ten highest 1979 per capita income counties—Oakland, Washtenaw, Macomb, Wayne, Genesee, Ingham, Midland, Kalamazoo, Saginaw, and Calhoun—are all highly industrialized, professional, educational, and urban-retail employment areas. The ten lowest 1979 per capita income counties—Oscoda, Mecosta, Kalkaska, Missaukee, Alger, Ogemaw, Crawford, Lake, Osceola, and Chippewa—are all in the northern Lower Peninsula or Upper Peninsula. The average per capita income of the highest-ranked county, Oakland, was triple that of the lowest-ranked county, Oscoda.

In 1980, the northern two-thirds of Michigan had more counties with 20 percent or more of their population below the poverty level than the southern third did. This fact again points up the difference between urban and rural Michigan. However, if smaller districts were used in the statistical breakdown, cities like Detroit would show large numbers of people below the poverty level in the inner-city ghettos.

Health Care

Health care facilities very closely reflect the population density and particularly the urban density. The largest numbers of doctors, nurses, and dentists are found in the urban counties. Some counties in northern Michigan show proportionately larger numbers of doctors than their neighboring counties because several county areas are served by regional hospitals in cities like Escanaba, Traverse City, and Marquette (Figure 3.6). In 1979, Keweenaw County had no doctors or dentists, and Wayne County had 4,255 doctors and 1,278 dentists. The ratio of

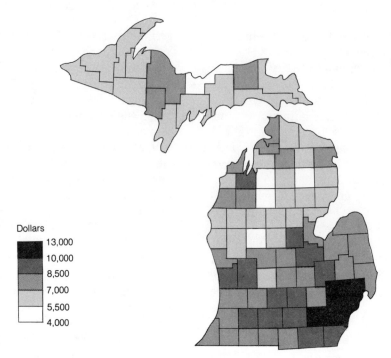

FIGURE 3.5. Average per capita income, by county, 1979. (Source: David I. Verway, ed., *Michigan Statistical Abstract* [Detroit: Wayne State University, 1981], p. 219.)

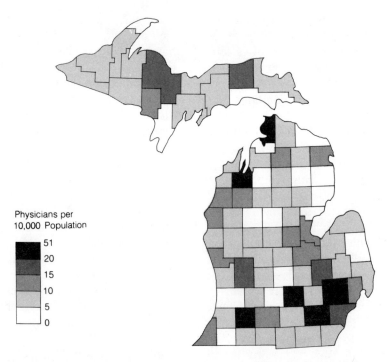

FIGURE 3.6. Physician ratios, by county, 1979. (Source: Adapted from Lawrence M. Sommers, ed., *Atlas of Michigan* [East Lansing: Michigan State University Press, 1977], p. 93.)

doctors, hospitals, and other health care facilities to the number of people served varies considerably in different parts of the state.

Crime

Crimes against persons and property are a heavily urban phenomenon. Thus, one would expect the largest number of crimes to be in counties containing the largest cities in southern Michigan. Wayne County leads the state, with more than 6,250 crimes in 1979 against people and more than 50,000 against property. Additional crime statistics and analysis are presented in Chapter 11.

ETHNIC AND MINORITY CHARACTERISTICS

About 15,000 American Indians lived in Michigan when the French arrived as explorers, traders, and missionaries sometime after 1615. The Indians were primarily members of the Potawatomi, Ottawa, and Ojibwa tribes, and there were small numbers of Huron and Miami. The largest numbers of Indians lived along the rivers and coasts of southern Michigan as farmers, fishermen, and hunters. The French and Indians were conquered by the British in the French and Indian Wars, which ended with the Treaty of Paris in 1763. The British did little to change the economy of the area that is now Michigan, and aspects of both the British and French culture survive today.

The first permanent white settlement was stimulated by Antoine de la Mothe Cadillac in 1701. A few areas were settled by Europeans in the southeastern portion at the Straits of Mackinac, and near the Sault before 1800, but the main settlement began after 1820. The opening of the Erie Canal in 1825 made the surplus wool and wheat of Michigan available to eastern markets and facilitated the flow to Michigan of settlers from New York and elsewhere in the East. The settlement process moved northward in the late 1800s and the early 1900s with the exploitation of lumber, water

power, and then the iron and copper of the Upper Peninsula. With the advent of the railroads and the Industrial Revolution, the ethnic stock of Michigan was augmented by large numbers of Europeans and southern whites. Eastern Europeans—especially Poles, Ukrainians, Rumanians, and Hungarians—as well as Italians emigrated to Detroit to work in the automobile and other large industries. Dutch people settled in the Grand Rapids, Holland, and Zeeland area, and Finns were the major immigrants to the copper and iron mining areas of the Upper Peninsula. German and British settlers and descendants are to be found throughout the state, but certain concentrations exist.

The addition of large numbers of blacks and people of Spanish origin is a more recent phenomenon. The blacks came primarily during the Depression and World War II years to find work in the factories of Detroit and other cities in southern Michigan. Spanish-speaking peoples from Mexico, Cuba, and Puerto Rico came after World War II, and they worked first as migrant workers in the fruit and vegetable districts of the state. Some Hispanics settled permanently in the rural areas, but most subsequently migrated to the cities of southern Michigan. The more recent political refugees from Cuba are found mostly in the cities.

CURRENT MINORITY DISTRIBUTION PATTERNS

Blacks

In 1980, 1,198,700 of the 9,258,344 people in Michigan, or 13 percent, were black (Table 3.1). Of these, 829,868, or 69 percent of the total number of blacks in Michigan, lived in Wayne County—35.5 percent of the population of Wayne County is black. Most of the other large concentrations of blacks are in the urban-industrial cities and counties of southern Michigan. In addition to Wayne, the counties with large numbers of blacks in 1980 were Oakland, 47,962

TABLE 3.1. Number and percentage of major minority groups in Michigan, by county, 1980

County	Total Population	Black Population	Percent Black	Hispanic Population	Percent Hispanic	Indian Population	Percent Indian
Alcona	9,740	6	.06	49	.50	44	.45
Alger	9,225	49	.53	36	.39	194	2.10
Allegan	81,555	1,471	1.80	2,011	2.47	408	.50
Alpena	32,315	19	.06	79	.24	83	.26
Antrim	16,194	15	.09	65	.40	119	.73
Arenac	14,706	7	.05	160	1.09	87	.59
Baraga	8,484	58	.68	37	.44	754	8.89
Barry	45,781	66	.14	420	.92	174	.38
Bay	119,881	1,023	.85	3,162	2.64	604	.50
Benzie	11,205	36	.32	105	.94	143	1.28
Berrien	171,276	24,817	14.49	2,088	1.22	593	.35
Branch	40,188	79	.20	233	.58	102	.25
Calhoun	141,557	13,577	9.59	2,433	1.72	452	.32
Cass	49,499	4,150	8.38	337	.68	256	.52
Charlevoix	19,907	15	.07	62	.31	325	1.63
Cheboygan	20,649	13	.06	60	.29	240	1.16
Chippewa	29,029	369	1.27	91	.31	2,395	8.25
Clare	23,822	8	.03	96	.40	139	.58
Clinton	55,893	169	.30	991	1.77	218	.39
Crawford	9,465	56	.59	49	.52	44	.46
Delta	38,947	12	.03	103	.26	439	1.13
Dickinson	25,341	8	.03	46	.18	37	.15
Eaton	88,337	1,987	2.25	1,616	1.83	264	.30
Emmet	22,992	100	.43	57	.25	595	2.59
Genesee	450,449	78,804	17.49	7,649	1.70	2,696	.60
Gladwin	19,957	1	.005	117	.59	96	.48
Gogebic	19,686	129	.66	60	.30	260	1.32
Grand Traverse	54,899	163	.30	297	.54	394	.72
Gratiot	40,448	36	.09	1,321	3.27	126	.31
Hillsdale	42,071	101	.24	307	.73	77	.18

County							
Houghton	37,872	110	.29	127	.34	76	.20
Huron	36,459	25	.07	396	1.09	78	.21
Ingham	272,437	21,084	7.74	10,523	3.86	1,515	.56
Ionia	51,815	1,642	3.17	907	1.75	188	.36
Iosco	28,349	654	2.31	259	.91	158	.56
Iron	13,635	2	.01	22	.16	60	.44
Isabella	54,110	488	.90	662	1.22	681	1.26
Jackson	151,495	10,840	7.16	1,807	1.19	496	.33
Kalamazoo	212,378	15,846	7.46	2,605	1.23	658	.31
Kalkaska	10,952	3	.03	54	.49	34	.31
Kent	444,506	31,460	7.08	8,742	1.97	2,059	.46
Keweenaw	1,963	9	.46	6	.31	1	.05
Lake	7,711	1,285	16.66	50	.65	50	.65
Lapeer	70,038	163	.23	1,325	1.89	168	.24
Leelanau	14,007	18	.13	72	.51	178	1.27
Lenawee	89,948	758	.84	4,573	5.08	171	.19
Livingston	100,289	478	.48	781	.78	411	.41
Luce	6,659	1	.02	16	.24	254	3.81
Mackinac	10,178	5	.05	30	.29	901	8.85
Macomb	694,600	9,142	1.32	6,638	.96	1,942	.28
Manistee	23,019	47	.20	316	1.37	202	.88
Marquette	74,101	1,270	1.71	489	.66	614	.83
Mason	26,365	178	.68	370	1.40	169	.64
Mecosta	36,961	782	2.12	202	.55	154	.42
Menominee	26,201	6	.02	58	.22	307	1.17
Midland	73,578	566	.77	810	1.10	190	.26
Missaukee	10,009	2	.02	26	.26	34	.34
Monroe	134,659	2,313	1.72	1,803	1.34	255	.19
Montcalm	47,555	112	.24	581	1.22	161	.34
Montmorency	7,492	1	.01	44	.59	19	.25
Muskegon	157,589	19,175	12.17	2,833	1.80	1,120	.71
Newaygo	34,917	555	1.59	680	1.95	142	.41
Oakland	1,011,793	47,962	4.74	14,478	1.43	2,737	.27
Oceana	22,002	42	.19	1,132	5.14	221	1.00
Ogemaw	16,436	9	.05	53	.32	63	.38

TABLE 3.1 (continued)

County	Total Population	Black Population	Percent Black	Hispanic Population	Percent Hispanic	Indian Population	Percent Indian
Ontonagon	9,861	3	.03	16	.16	62	.63
Osceola	18,928	17	.09	106	.56	77	.41
Oscoda	6,858	1	.01	10	.15	30	.44
Otsego	14,993	6	.04	49	.33	29	.19
Ottawa	157,174	632	.40	5,006	3.19	420	.27
Presque Isle	14,267	6	.04	38	.27	40	.28
Roscommon	16,374	0	--	64	.39	51	.31
Saginaw	228,059	35,841	15.72	12,356	5.42	916	.40
St. Clair	138,802	2,804	2.02	2,066	1.49	558	.40
St. Joseph	56,083	1,360	2.42	386	.69	143	.25
Sanilac	40,789	16	.04	861	2.11	95	.23
Schoolcraft	8,575	3	.03	20	.23	351	4.09
Shiawassee	71,140	67	.09	818	1.15	317	.45
Tuscola	56,961	323	.57	1,006	1.77	184	.32
Van Buren	66,814	5,041	7.54	1,499	2.24	468	.70
Washtenaw	264,748	28,323	10.70	4,055	1.53	720	.27
Wayne	2,337,240	829,868	35.51	46,301	1.98	6,667	.29
Wexford	25,102	12	.05	134	.53	85	.34
Total	9,258,344	1,198,700	13	162,398	1.75	40,038	.43

Source: U.S. Bureau of the Census, 1980 Census of Population and Housing, Advance Reports (Washington, D.C.: Government Printing Office, March 1981).

(4.7 percent black); Genesee, 78,804 (17.5 percent); Saginaw, 35,841 (15.7 percent); Kent, 31,460 (7.1 percent); Berrien, 24,817 (14.5 percent); Washtenaw, 28,323 (10.7 percent); and Ingham, 21,084 (7.7 percent). The only county outside the urban south with a large proportion of blacks is Lake County; its 1,285 blacks make up 16.7 percent of its total population. A black recreational community was developed early in the Idlewild area of that county, and it has maintained its unique character as a major black settlement in the northern Michigan lake and forest country.

Increasing numbers and rising percentages have been characteristic of black population trends in Michigan in recent years. The 1960 census showed that the Michigan black population had increased by 275,285 people since 1950, or from 6.9 percent to 9.1 percent of the total population. The 1970 figures indicated another increase of 273,485 and that the proportion had increased further to 11.1 percent. The 1980 total increased only 207,644, and the percentage was then 13 percent of the total. A considerable number of blacks have been returning to the South in recent years because of the expanding Sun Belt economic opportunities and the improving racial climate in that area.

Population of Spanish Origin

In 1980, the census counted 162,398 people of Spanish origin in Michigan, 1.75 percent of the total population. The main concentrations were in both rural and urban areas in the southeastern part of the state. Wayne County has the single largest number, 46,301, but they compose only 2 percent of that county's total. The next counties in order of numbers of Hispanics are Oakland (14,478), Ingham (10,523), Kent (8,742), Genesee (7,469), and Macomb (6,638). The highest percentages are in Saginaw, Oceana, and Lenawee Counties, where Hispanics account for 5.4, 5.1, and 5.1 percent of the population, respectively. In Saginaw and Lenawee, the Hispanics originally worked as migrant laborers in the

growing and harvesting of navy beans, sugar beets, and other labor-intensive crops. In Oceana County, they worked in the fruit orchards, especially picking tart cherries. Mechanical equipment, including fruit pickers, replaced the migrant laborers to a large extent, but many of them have stayed in the county and become permanent residents. Mexican Americans predominate among the Hispanic population, followed by the Cuban Americans. Most counties have some Hispanics, but the northern counties have fewer both proportionately and absolutely.

American Indians

The American Indian population of Michigan numbered 40,038 in 1980, or 0.43 percent of the total population. Two distributions of the Indians stand out: one in the urban counties of the south, and the other in the counties in which there are modern Indian reservations. Wayne, Oakland, Genesee, Kent, Macomb, Ingham, and Muskegon Counties have 18,736 Indians, or 47 percent of the total number in Michigan. The reservation counties— Chippewa County, with Bay Mills Reservation (near Brimley), 2,395; Menominee with Hannahville (near Wilson), 307; and Baraga and Ontonagon Counties, 816— have a total of 3,518 Indians, or 9 percent of the number in the state. In most instances, the reservation Indians have migrated to cities for employment. In contrast to the blacks and Hispanics, many Indians live in the country or in small towns, especially in the northern two-thirds of the state. Baraga and Mackinac Counties in the Upper Peninsula have the highest proportion of Indians in their total populations, 8.9 percent in 1980, followed closely by Chippewa County, 8.3 percent.

POPULATION TRENDS

Ethnic additions to Michigan's population continue to take place but at a lower rate than in previous decades. The relatively

Mexican migrant laborers were extensively used to harvest cherries prior to the development of mechanical pickers. (Courtesy Michigan State Archives)

homogeneous ethnic groups—like the Dutch in the Grand Rapids–Holland area, the Finns on the Keweenaw Peninsula, and the Poles in Hamtramck—are being thinned: The original stock and their children are moving to other areas, and members of new ethnic groups are moving in. Thus, the European ethnic concentrations of the 1930s and 1940s are not as pronounced in the 1980s. The newer residents, the blacks and the Hispanics, tend to still live in more defined regions or parts of cities because of the recency of their arrival and the kind of employment opportunities they have. Their settlement patterns are also affected by past and present discrimination policies against the blacks. The reverse migration trend back to the South will have a continuing impact on the number and location of blacks. The health of Michigan's economy and the resulting job opportunities will have a pronounced effect on the state's power to draw new immigrants and on its power to hold those now there.

PART 3

THE ENVIRONMENTAL AND NATURAL RESOURCE BASES

The environmental and natural resource bases of Michigan differ considerably from those of the neighboring states. There are three major reasons for this: (1) the significance of Lakes Michigan, Superior, Huron, and Erie in the water and climatic environment of Michigan; (2) the geologic sedimentary basin that dominates the underlying rock structure of most of the state, which contains commercially significant amounts of natural gas, petroleum, gypsum, and salt; and (3) the unique surface characteristics that are the result of continental glaciation. The landforms are the heritage of the great Pleistocene Ice Age, and the flora and fauna reflect the fact that Michigan is located in the interior of a large land mass—the characteristics of both are similar yet different in detail from those of the land areas to the east and west of Michigan. The variety of the natural landscape of Michigan presents both advantages and handicaps.

CHAPTER 4

THE SIGNIFICANCE OF THE GLACIAL HERITAGE

The land and water surfaces of Michigan are largely the result of the sculpturing, erosion, and deposition of materials during the Pleistocene epoch. Several stages of the continental glaciation affected the state, but the most important was the most recent Wisconsin stage—its ice retreated from Michigan about 9,500 to 15,000 years ago. Today's water, landforms, and soil characteristics and patterns are related to the nature and results of the glacial processes.

WATER

Water, an absolute essential for human life, is abundant in Michigan both on the surface and as groundwater contained in the glacial mantle and the sedimentary bedrock of the state. As the population has grown, so has the demand on the available water. Many cities, industries, and homes rely on the four Great Lakes that border Michigan for a supposedly inexhaustible supply, but recent studies have suggested that this immense reservoir of fresh-water is not depletion-proof. As the population grows and as the exploitation of resources like coal and oil shale increases exponen-

tially in the Great Plains and western states, the Great Lakes are being looked at as a possible water source for those regions—for domestic use, irrigation, coal slurry pipelines, and the processing of petroleum and oil shale. There are major economic, political, energy, and engineering implications to making water from the Great Lakes available to the largely water-poor western half of the country. Even without this demand, it is estimated that Michigan's future need for water from the bordering Great Lakes may increase fivefold in the next fifty years. Such an increase would have ramifications for industry, tourism, agriculture, and almost all other economic sectors of the state.

SOURCES OF WATER

Michigan has three main sources of freshwater: (1) precipitation, of which there is a fair amount; (2) the Great Lakes, which border much of the state; and (3) the water found in the loose materials that form the land surface of the state and in the underground rock formations. Michigan normally averages 31 inches (78.7 cm) of precipitation a year, which would total about 86 billion gal (325.5 billion l) of water a day. Some of the precipitation seeps into the ground to become a part of the groundwater supply, some is almost immediately returned to the atmosphere by evaporation, and most runs into lakes and rivers that, in turn, drain into the Great Lakes.

The amount of freshwater in the Great Lakes is almost staggering. This water is utilized by coastal communities, and some is piped a considerable distance inland. The Great Lakes bordering Michigan— Michigan, Superior, Huron, and Erie—represent part of the largest inland supply of freshwater in the world as all five Great Lakes account for 95 percent of the surface freshwater in the United States. Some of this water is used directly, some of it seeps into porous layers of bedrock and is distributed far inland. The amount of water actually utilized from the surrounding Great Lakes totals millions of gallons per day.

The people of the state of Michigan use large quantities of water daily. Every 10,000 people in a city use 1.3 million gal (4.9 million l) of water each day and the total use in Michigan is about 12 billion gal (45.4 billion l) a day. This latter figure includes the industrial uses, but for demands such as irrigation and food processing there are no available figures; if there were, the figure would be higher. Water supply needs vary considerably over the state, and in some areas the drain is larger than the supply, requiring the importation of water such as from the Great Lakes. Water is the resource Michigan's industry needs the most of, whether by weight or by volume. More people in the state mean greater requirements for food, industry, and services, which means a greater demand for water. The daily per capita need for water increases with the growth of population and technology. Modern farming, paper processing, and the production of automobiles also demand large amounts of water.

There are water shortages from time to time in parts of the state, not only because of increased demand on the existing supply, but also because of pollution or because water is drawn more rapidly than nature replaces it. Occasional summer droughts cause a rationing of water or a reduction in the amount used for less essential purposes like watering lawns. Potential solutions to such shortages are water conservation measures, building more pipelines from the Great Lakes to interior cities, and keeping the rivers and lakes clean in all parts of the state.

RIVERS

Rivers provide a natural surface drainage and are used for transportation and recreation; in some cases, they also supply fish as a source of food. Unfortunately, rivers and streams are also used on occasion to take away domestic and industrial waste. Michigan has 36,350 mi (58,487 km) of inland streams that carry runoff water into the Great Lakes. The daily outflow of either the Grand or the Muskegon rivers—the state's largest rivers in volume and size of drainage basin—could meet the domestic water needs of the entire state. Rivers in the Lower Peninsula are normally much longer and have larger drainage basins than those in the Upper Peninsula (Figure 4.1).

The rivers that form parts of Michigan's boundaries are also important for transportation. These include the St. Marys River in the Upper Peninsula and the St. Clair and Detroit rivers in southeastern Michigan, between the Lower Peninsula and Ontario, Canada. The St. Marys River flows from Lake Superior to Lake Huron and is controlled by locks built between 1853 and 1855. These locks allow lake freighters to negotiate the 22 ft (6.7 m) of difference between the levels of the two lakes. The Soo Locks on the St. Marys River carry a volume of traffic of about 90 million tons (81.6 million t) per year, an amount that rivals the annual traffic on the Panama Canal when one considers that the Soo Locks are closed part of the year on account of ice. The St. Clair River, the Detroit River, and Lake St. Clair are important links in the St. Lawrence Seaway. The city

FIGURE 4.1. Watersheds of major rivers and tributaries. (Source: Adapted from Lawrence M. Sommers, ed., *Atlas of Michigan* [East Lansing: Michigan State University Press, 1977], p. 41.)

of Detroit is the principal generator of water traffic in Michigan, but ports all along Michigan's coastline contribute to the commerce on the Great Lakes.

Iron ore is the chief product carried south, and coal north, through the western Great Lakes. Limestone, a bulky material used in the steel industry, is carried south through the Great Lakes from quarries such as those at Rogers City in Presque Isle County and Petoskey in Emmet. Manufactured products from all over the world

are shipped through the Michigan ports of the St. Lawrence Seaway. The river portions of the St. Lawrence Seaway in Michigan are normally frozen from late December to early April, which restricts transportation. A demonstration project in 1975 proved that the Soo Locks could be kept open 365 days a year if the amount of traffic and costs warranted continuous operation.

Today, Michigan's rivers are not nearly as important as routes of transportation as they were earlier, but there is a plan to

Rapids in the Presque Isle River in the northwestern part of the Upper Peninsula. (Courtesy Michigan Department of Natural Resources)

build a waterway across the central part of lower Michigan from Saginaw Bay to Lake Michigan, utilizing the Saginaw, Looking Glass, and Grand rivers. This project would require only a relatively short length of canal in the central part of the state, but, of course, the rivers themselves would have to be deepened for any significant development of river transportation. Many of the rivers of the northern Lower Peninsula and Upper Peninsula are of great value today as scenic streams or "wild rivers" and are important for sport fishing for trout and salmon. Certain parts of the rivers are being designated as wild rivers so that their beauty and wildlife can be preserved for the future, even though some landowners along the rivers oppose the idea because they feel that it restricts the ways in which they can use their land to make money. The lawmakers of the state are more and more concerned about private citizens' buying up land in the wilderness or forested parts of the state, which reduces the amount of such land that is available to the general public for recreation.

River Characteristics

Most Michigan rivers are rather slow-moving streams, particularly those in the southern half of the Lower Peninsula. In the Upper Peninsula, there are a number of rapids and thirty-four waterfalls, of which the Tahquamenon Falls, 50 ft (15.2 m) high, are the most famous. Some of the more rapid-flowing and larger rivers have been dammed to create hydroelectric power—for example, the Manistee, Pere Marquette, Muskegon, Grand, Kalamazoo, and Au Sable. The water collects in basins behind the dams and is controlled in order to provide the even flow desirable for the production of hydroelectric power.

The slow flow makes for pollution, especially in the heavily populated southern part of the state, and many industries are big contributors to that pollution. Millions of dollars are being spent annually to improve the quality of the water in Michigan's rivers by reducing the amount of pollution. Progress is being made, but sewage from cities and towns, industrial waste, septic tanks for houses and cottages located on the banks of the rivers, and agricultural chemicals used on Michigan farms are still contaminating the water. However, some rivers, such as the Grand, are now pure enough to let salmon penetrate upstream beyond the city of Lansing.

The beauty of Michigan's rivers and river valleys is one feature that makes the state attractive to tourists. But even in the recreational use of streams there are conflicts, for example, between trout fishermen and people who wish to use the river for canoeing. The state legislature and local governments must decide, through laws governing stream use, what use is in the best interest of most of the people.

INLAND LAKES

Lakes, ponds, and wetlands store a large amount of surface water in Michigan. How many there are varies according to what reference is used, which definition of lake or pond is used, and whether or not a body of water existing year-round is taken into account. The Michigan Department of Natural Resources says there are 11,037 inland lakes, but a study by the Department of Resource Development at Michigan State University registered 35,068 water bodies, 4,401 of which are artificial impoundments, and 6,516 are more than 10 acres (4 ha) in size. The total inland water area of Michigan is 764,160 acres (309,485 ha), compared to a land area of 36,492,160 acres (14,779,324 ha). The highest concentration of lakes is in the interlobate moraine country of southeastern Michigan (the Waterloo Recreation Area), the interlobate moraine area north of Kalamazoo and Battle Creek, the northern half of the Lower Peninsula, and the eastern half of the Upper Peninsula (an interlobate moraine is the terrain that developed between two lobes of the continental ice sheet as it pushed south). The number of bodies of water was much larger in earlier times as many have been drained by people. During the Ice Age, the surface drainage of Michigan was greatly disrupted: Some areas were dammed up, and others were gouged out, which left depressions in which water accumulated to form a large number of lakes.

The lakes not only store water but also have many recreational uses, and like the rivers, the lakes of Michigan are becoming polluted. As pollutants and organic materials decay, oxygen is taken from a lake so that it slowly dies, a process called eutrophication. Some eutrophication is normal, but it is often speeded up unnecessarily when waste products are introduced more rapidly than the water can handle. Concern about preserving the quality of Michigan lakes is developing, and none too soon.

Houghton Lake, in Roscommon County, covering an area of 31.3 sq mi (81.1 sq km) or 20,032 acres (8,113 ha), is the largest inland lake in Michigan. Other large inland lakes having 20 sq mi (51.8 sq km) or more of surface are Torch, Charlevoix, Burt, Mullett, and Gogebic (Table 4.1). Inland lakes are very important for the tourist and resort industry as they supply both winter and summer fishing and excellent opportunities for boating, swimming, and snowmobiling. Many of the lakes are completely built up around their edges with cottages—mostly for summer use, but in southeastern Michigan, permanent residences are frequent. This amount of building creates problems related to sewage and waste removal.

In the northwestern part of the Lower Peninsula, in Leelanau and Benzie Counties, the lakes and forests, as well as the natural beauty of the sand dunes of Lake Michigan, have been incorporated into the Sleeping Bear Dunes National Lakeshore. This development illustrates the conflict between people who wish to preserve the land for use by the general public and those people who have bought land or own property in the area, including land around Glen Lake, the major lake in the park. Current owners will be allowed to retain their property, but as land passes out of the hands of a present owner, the govern-

TABLE 4.1. Michigan's largest inland lakes

	Acres	Hectares
Houghton	20,032	8,113
Torch	18,770	7,602
Charlevoix	17,260	6,990
Burt	17,120	6,934
Mullett	16,630	6,735
Gogebic	13,380	5,419
Black	10,130	4,103
Manistique	10,130	4,103
Crystal	9,711	3,933
Portage	9,640	3,904
Higgins	9,600	3,888
Fletcher Pond	8,970	3,633
Hubbard	8,850	3,584
Leelanau	8,320	3,370
Indian	8,000	3,240
Elk	7,730	3,131
Michigamme Reservoir	7,200	2,916
Glen	6,265	2,537
Grand	5,660	2,292
Long	5,652	2,289

ment will attempt to buy the property so that eventually the whole area will be available for public use.

THE GREAT LAKES

Michigan has assumed the name the Great Lake State because it borders on four and controls the area of much of the five large lakes that are collectively called the Great Lakes. The lake basins (Figure 4.2) were eroded during the great Ice Age more than 10,000 years ago, and taken together, they contain the largest volume of freshwater in the world. The waterways connecting them form part of the largest inland water transportation route, the St. Lawrence Seaway. Only one of the lakes, Lake Michigan, is completely within the United States; the others are shared with Canada. The state of Michigan controls parts of Lakes Superior, Michigan, Huron, and Erie.

Lake Superior, the largest of the Great Lakes, has a water surface area of 31,700 sq mi (82,103 sq km) and a maximum depth of 1,333 ft (406.3 m). The surface of Lake Superior is large enough to contain the land area of the states of Connecticut, Delaware, Hawaii, Maryland, and New Jersey combined. Lake Huron is the second in size with 23,050 sq mi (59,699.5 sq km); Lake Michigan, third, with 22,300 sq mi (57,757 sq km); and Lake Erie, fourth, with 9,910 sq mi (25,666.9 sq km). These lakes provide important water connections between the ports of Michigan, and between these ports and other ports of the United States as well as of the world. The four lakes represent a freshwater resource for domestic and industry use for many communities along the coast and those that can be reached by pipelines. The commercial fishery resources of the lakes are considerable but have been decreasing in recent years, especially since alewives have come in through the St. Lawrence Seaway from the Atlantic Ocean. These trash fish may now form as much as 90 percent of the total volume of fish in the lakes, but the introduction of salmon has begun to aid

in the control of this largely undesirable type of fish. Fishing for coho and chinook salmon, first introduced into the lakes in 1966 is now a major sports activity on the lakes and in the adjoining rivers. Commercial fishing is handicapped by the fact that there is too high a concentration of undesirable chemicals in a number of fish species, particularly the salmon and lake trout.

The beaches of the Great Lakes are some of the best in the world and add considerably to the recreational attraction of the state. Inland from the beaches, there are often beautiful windblown or dune grass and tree-covered sand dunes, a distinctive feature of the topography of Michigan, particularly along the eastern shore of Lake Michigan. Recently, a problem has developed in the level of the water in the western Great Lakes surrounding the state of Michigan. The level fluctuates from 4 to 6 ft (1.2 to 1.8 m) over a period of years because of the amount of precipitation and runoff received. In the 1970s, a near all-time high of nearly 4 ft (1.2 m) above the mean level was reached by Lakes Huron and Michigan, and considerable lakeshore damage occurred as a result.

Although individual owners as well as certain cities and villages along the shore are developing piers, breakwaters, groins, and seawalls of various kinds to protect the shore, high-water erosion and flood damage still threaten the shoreline. The erosive power of a fall or spring storm on Lake Michigan, Lake Superior, or Lake Huron is awesome. The Army Corps of Engineers is studying the problem of fluctuating lake levels, but there are no easy solutions. One possible remedy is to allow more water to go out through the southern end of Lake Michigan, via the Chicago River, and on into the Mississippi River. However, it is estimated that this action would have only a minor effect on the problem. Another suggestion has been made that the outlet near the St. Clair and Detroit rivers—and further, the Niagara River, which is the outlet of Lake Ontario—be

48

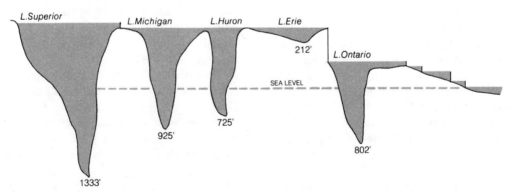

FIGURE 4.2. The Great Lakes drainage basin and Great Lakes profile. (Source: Adapted from Lawrence M. Sommers, ed., *Atlas of Michigan* [East Lansing: Michigan State University Press, 1977], pp. 42–43.)

Lake Michigan bluff erosion near Grand Haven just south of Muskegon. (Courtesy Michigan Department of Natural Resources)

Fences and groins erected to prevent water and wind erosion south of Little Point Sable and Ludington on Lake Michigan.

lowered so that the volume of water that can flow out through the St. Lawrence River would be increased. This may be a more effective solution, but it would take a great deal of coordination between the different states involved, as well as the cooperation of the government of Canada.

GROUNDWATER

Michigan is fortunate in that most parts of the state have sufficient supplies of water that can be reached by digging wells into the surface layers of glacial material or down into the rock layers that act as aquifers—water bearers. Water received in the form of rainfall or snowfall either flows off, evaporates, or seeps down into the surface soil and loose material and further into the bedrock below. Porous rock layers such as sandstone and limestone allow some water to collect in the spaces between the sand grains or particles that make up the rock layer, and this water may flow through these porous rock layers for a considerable distance. The sedimentary rock aquifers are good storage areas that can be drilled for domestic and industrial water supplies. Because the sandstone and porous limestone layers of Michigan are in a saucerlike basin, most of the Lower Peninsula does have the potential for springs and artesian, or naturally flowing, wells. As the demand on this water stored underneath the earth's surface increases because of population and industrial pressure, water's natural tendency to flow decreases, and the water must be pumped to the surface.

Most communities in the state get their municipal water from wells, and as the need increases, the wells often have to be dug deeper and larger to supply the greater amount of water. There is a problem of pollution as sewage and toxic, or poisonous, materials can get into the rock formations that supply freshwater, and another major problem is that the water supply can be depleted as a result of heavy withdrawals made by a city, industry, and wells dug by property owners. Such depletion is espe-cially troublesome during summer dry spells as an aquifer may actually go dry. This result is not too serious in the long run because the water will probably come back when the amount of surface water again is increased through rainfall or melting snow. Most urban communities in the state have a common source of water. The water is pumped into a storage tank 40 or 50 ft (12.2 or 15.2 m) above the ground, to provide pressure, and is distributed through pipes to homes throughout the community. The groundwater supply, especially that in the bedrock, is badly depleted along Lake Michigan between Muskegon and Petoskey and from the southern state line to the thumb area in southeastern Michigan. Portions of the Upper Peninsula have both quality and quantity problems, especially the igneous rock areas of the western Upper Peninsula. Salt layers in the rock also mean that salt can sometimes get into the water supply in certain regions like Detroit, Midland, and Montague-Whitehall just north of Muskegon.

Michigan is fortunate in that it generally has abundant underground water resources (Figure 4.3). Added to these sources is the tremendous supply that Lakes Superior, Michigan, Huron, and Erie represent. In the case of the Great Lakes, Michiganians are dependent upon their neighbors in other states, such as Illinois, Wisconsin, and Minnesota, as well as upon the people of Ontario to help maintain the quality of the water in the lakes for human use, for the fish and other life they contain, and for their beauty and recreational use.

Michigan has enough water to meet its yearly needs, but problems of distribution and quality must be solved. Water conservation and pollution control must get more attention from the people of Michigan in the 1980s and 1990s. Homeowners, industrialists, politicians, and citizens in general must be conscious of the importance of water as a resource and of ways of preserving it for the future. Michigan's water resources and related problems must be viewed locally as well as broadly because

51

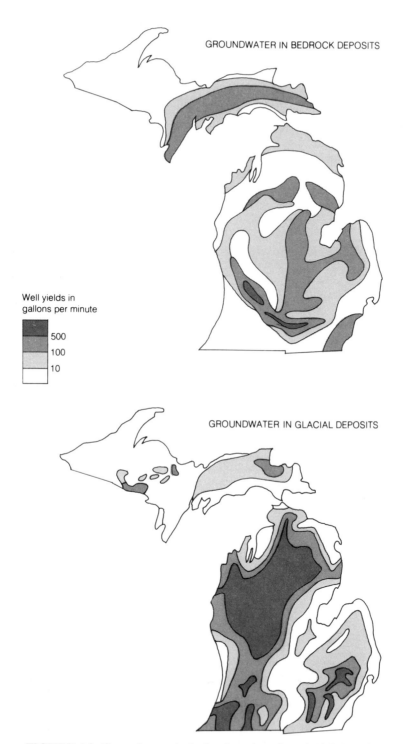

FIGURE 4.3. Groundwater in bedrock and surface glacial deposits. (Source: Adapted from Lawrence M. Sommers, ed., *Atlas of Michigan* [East Lansing: Michigan State University Press, 1977], p. 44.)

the use and control of water is an issue within the state, among states, and among nations.

LANDFORMS

Landforms—the mountains, hills, valleys, plains, and coastlines—are the foundation on which the modern state of Michigan was created. The landforms of most of the state are a result of radical changes brought about by continental glaciation—geologically, a relatively recent process. Glacial landforms dominate the surface of the whole state except the western half of the Upper Peninsula, where eroded remnants of some of the oldest mountains on earth are found. Thus, there is considerable diversity in Michigan—from the glacial lake plains near Detroit, to the sand dunes bordering Lake Michigan, to massive moraines in the northern Lower Peninsula, to

Eroded rock structure at Pictured Rocks National Lakeshore in Alger County along Lake Superior. (Courtesy Michigan Department of Natural Resources)

the roots of ancient mountains in the Upper Peninsula. The slope and soil variations associated with the diverse landforms are major factors in the agricultural and other differences in economic activity and population density in various parts of Michigan.

GEOLOGIC FOUNDATIONS

The underlying bedrock of Michigan is mostly hidden from view by a mantle of unconsolidated material deposited during the various stages of continental glaciation. However, there are a number of places in the Lower Peninsula where the bedrock can be seen, such as in rock quarries and in outcrops along rivers and lakes. In the western Upper Peninsula, a considerable amount of bedrock is visible.

Two major rock types are found in Michigan. The Lower Peninsula and the eastern parts of the Upper Peninsula are underlaid by a series of sedimentary rock layers that compose the Michigan Basin (Figure 4.4). These rock formations, consisting largely of shales, limestones, and sandstones, were deposited on the bottom of ancient seas that covered Michigan on and off for millions of years. The basin is estimated to be about 14,000 ft (4,267 m) thick, and its rocks rest on the top of a very old Precambrian (the oldest geologic period) surface. The various layers of sedimentary rock are piled up on top of one another like a series of saucers. The character of the rocks has been determined by geologists from surface exposures and information gained from numerous wells that have been drilled for oil and water.

The ancient igneous and metamorphic rocks that compose the Precambrian, or Canadian, Shield in the western part of the Upper Peninsula make up the second category of rocks and are estimated to be at least 3.5 billion years old. The igneous rocks are hard, crystalline, resistant to erosion, and are largely made up of granites and metamorphic rocks—rocks that have been changed through heat and pressure—composed mainly of gneisses and schists.

The higher areas in the Upper Peninsula are the remnants of ancient peaks that have been worn down over millions of years by the erosive action of wind, water, and moving ice. The Porcupine and Huron mountains in the western half of the Upper Peninsula have been greatly altered over their long geologic history through uplift and erosion and are now only remnants of once-high mountains.

Both major types of rocks found in Michigan are important to humans. The igneous type contains valuable minerals such as iron ore and copper, and the sedimentary rocks contain petroleum, natural gas, salt, gypsum, and limestone (used as a flux in the iron and steel industry).

EFFECTS OF GLACIATION

The nature of the surface landforms of Michigan is largely a result of the activities of the extensive glaciers of the Pleistocene period. There were several stages of ice advance during the periods of glaciation, and during the last major stage, four different ice sheets affected Michigan. In between each of these stages, the ice sheet receded, because of a warming of the climate of the Northern Hemisphere, but then returned again as the ice accumulated during colder periods in Canada and moved south in huge masses up to 10,000 ft (3,048 m) or more thick. The entire Pleistocene period covered about 2 million years, but it was the most recent ice advances during the Wisconsin stage that sculptured the current Michigan landscape. As the ice moved south, it leveled off the existing hills; filled in the valleys; blocked the drainage of the rivers; gouged out major basins, such as those now filled by the Great Lakes; and in general, changed the existing surface by grinding, eroding, leveling, and depositing.

As the ice receded, it stopped at various points and built up landform features known as moraines—ridges that vary in height and composition depending on the length of time the ice remained at a particular point and on the materials being eroded

54

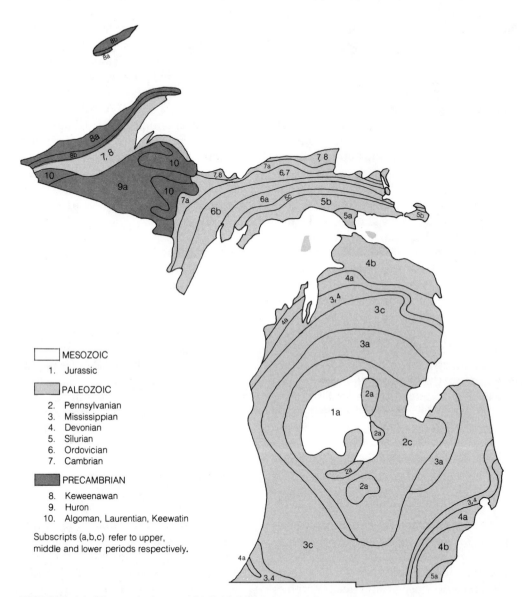

FIGURE 4.4. The geologic age of Michigan's bedrock. (Source: Adapted from Lawrence M. Sommers, ed., *Atlas of Michigan* [East Lansing: Michigan State University Press, 1977], p. 30.)

Silurian bedrock near Fayette State Park, Delta County. (Courtesy Michigan Department of Natural Resources)

Lake of the Clouds and Porcupine Mountains in Ontonagon County. (Courtesy Michigan Travel Bureau)

FIGURE 4.5. Glacial surface formations. (Source: Adapted from Lawrence M. Sommers, ed., *Atlas of Michigan* [East Lansing: Michigan State University Press, 1977], p. 32.)

(Figure 4.5). The large quantities of water that flowed from the melting ice also deposited various kinds of materials, the most important of which are called outwash plains. These are characteristically flat and consist of layers of sand and other fine sediments. Such plains with their sandy soils are often used for specialized kinds of agriculture, such as the potato production in Montcalm County. The impressive sand dunes along the eastern shore of Lake Michigan were created partly by glacial moraine

deposits and partly by the prevailing westerly winds blowing the sand deposited along the beaches into the dune formations.

Another major result of the glaciation was the disruption of previous river drainage systems and the creation of a large number of inland lakes, swamps, and wetlands. The more than 11,000 inland lakes are largely the result of water accumulating in depressions created by the glaciation, forming lakes of various sizes. A great deal of Michigan's farmland was originally

Blowout dune bordered by tree and dune grass vegetation, Warren Dunes State Park, Berrien County. (Courtesy Michigan Department of Natural Resources)

swampy and had to be artificially drained in order to make it useful for raising crops. Many depressions, lakes, and morainic ridges were formed where lobes, or southern extensions, of the vast ice sheet came together. These interlobate areas are characterized by highly varied and complex landform surfaces that contain numerous lakes and swamps and have a hilly topography. The Waterloo Recreation Area, in the vicinity of Ann Arbor, Brighton to the north, and extending south to the Irish Hills, is an example of such an interlobate region where the Lake Erie and the Saginaw Bay lobes of the ice sheet met and piled up irregular ridges between them.

The flattest areas of Michigan are plains that are the result of deposits on the bottom of glacial lakes; the area involved depends on the size of the original lake. Lake Erie and Saginaw Bay on Lake Huron were once much higher and extended inland, and what was once part of the bottom of those bodies of water now makes up the lacustrine plains near Saginaw and Monroe. In both of these cases, specialized crops now flourish—navy beans and sugar beets in the Saginaw Valley, and truck-gardening, soybeans, and intensive farming south of Detroit to the Ohio border. The till plains, or areas between moraines, are also gently rolling to flat and are generally good for agriculture.

The present-day lake basins of Lakes Superior, Michigan, Huron, and Erie were formed when large masses of ice gouged out the preglacial river valleys. The varying depths of the lakes are in part attributed to the differences in the thickness of the ice at the time of glaciation. The greatest depth of Lake Superior is 1,333 ft (406 m); of Lake Michigan, 925 ft (282 m); of Lake Huron, 725 ft (221 m); and of Lake Erie,

Wetlands coast along Lake Huron just north of Saginaw Bay. Marsh vegetation, forests, and shallow water dominate the area. (Courtesy Michigan Department of Natural Resources)

212 ft (65 m). Certain parts of the basins were depressed by the enormous weight of the 10,000-ft-thick (3,048 m) ice sheets; and when the ice receded, a rebound in elevation took place so that portions of these areas were brought out of the water. The Saginaw Bay lowland is an example of this interesting phenomenon.

Thus, the major characteristics of the current landscape of the various parts of Michigan are closely related to the continental glaciation process. Agriculture, recreation, forestry, and the difficulty of highway construction are examples of activities that are affected by the differences in glaciation to be found from place to place in Michigan. Contrasts in topography and soil, also the result of the glaciers, are found both on a large scale, such as the variations between the Upper and Lower Peninsulas, and on a small scale, within an individual field, farm, or township.

LANDFORM REGIONS

Michigan can be divided into many landform regions, but only the six major

ones will be discussed here: four in the Lower Peninsula and two in the Upper Peninsula (Figure 4.6). These regions are largely related to the character of glacial deposition and the nature and influence of the old crystalline bedrock in the western part of the Upper Peninsula. The chief characteristic of the topography of Michigan is that it is level compared to that of the mountain states. Nevertheless, certain parts of the state are quite hilly, and there is great variation from place to place—often within very short distances—as a result of the different kinds and amounts of material left behind by the glaciers.

Hilly Moraines

The first region dominates much of the interior part of the lower half of the Lower Peninsula and is largely made up of a series of slender moraines from 10 to 25 mi (16 to 40 km) apart. The moraines are low ridges, and the area between them is often much flatter and is generally composed of outwash plains or till plains. There are two interlobate moraine areas in this part of Michigan: One extends from the Indiana

FIGURE 4.6. Landform regions.

border north toward the thumb area of Michigan and includes the Waterloo Recreation Area; the other is found north of Kalamazoo and Battle Creek, and it extends east of Grand Rapids and north toward the city of Big Rapids in Mecosta County.

The region as a whole can be characterized as gently rolling to hilly with a considerable amount of relatively level topography and many lakes and poorly drained land. For agriculture and industry, this is one of the best developed parts of the state. On the northern edge of the region, a high sandy plain marks the dividing line between the densely populated portions of the Lower Peninsula and the more sparsely populated areas to the north (often called the tension zone because it marks the geographic limits of a number of species).

Beaches and Dunes

The beaches and dunes bordering Lake Michigan are among the most beautiful along the Great Lakes. They vary from being low and forest-covered to being high and bare sand, like the Sleeping Bear Dunes in the northwestern part of the Lower Peninsula. Many of the dunes are glacial ridges that have been added to by blowing sand from the beaches of Lake Michigan. The prevailing westerly winds have piled the sand up in mounds of various heights, and some of them, like the Sleeping Bear Dunes and Silver Lake Dunes, are still moving inland. But generally speaking, the

Sand dunes and Lake Michigan coastline, Benzie County.

forest or dune-grass cover means they are rather permanent in character. Because of the natural beauty and the quality of the sand, beaches, and water, this area is important for recreational development. The dune sand is also being mined as industrial sand in several places—a source of increasing worry for environmentalists and other concerned citizens.

Much of the Lake Michigan coast has been developed, in varying degrees, by owners of private cottages, the establishment of public parks, and commercial resort and recreation enterprises. The beaches are outstanding: The fine, white sand extends along virtually the entire Lake Michigan shore. The actual amount of beach varies from time to time depending upon the level of Lake Michigan and the kind of erosion or deposition that is taking place. When the lake is high or there are heavy storms, serious erosion takes place, and the waves eat away large quantities of sand. Erosion has been cyclical along the coast over the years, so the width of beach and dune area varies with a rising or falling lake level.

High Plains and Moraines

Most of the area north of the Muskegon–Saginaw Bay line is dominated by the region called the high sand plains. This glacial landscape differs from the areas to the south in that the concentrations of sand are much higher, the moraines are more massive, and the general elevation is higher. Many of these hills are well-developed meccas for winter ski enthusiasts, and for the summer tourist, a large number of inland lakes dot the landscape. The combination of varied topography, limited farmland, large areas of forest and lake country, and clear trout streams form the basis of a region that is highly utilized by the large urban population of southern Michigan for summer as well as for winter recreation. Some farming does take place, but other activities such as forestry and tourism are much more important than in the southern Lower Peninsula. Excellent highways have

Glacial moraine landscape in Emmet County. (Courtesy Michigan Department of Natural Resources)

made this area easily accessible to the urban south, and thus the increase in tourist and resort activity has been very rapid in recent decades. This was one of the fastest-growing population areas of Michigan during the 1970s, in percentage terms.

Eastern Lower Peninsula Lowlands

Very flat topography is found near the coast in the southeastern part of the state, and it extends north to the Saginaw Bay area and along Lake Huron to the tip of the Lower Peninsula. This land was lake bottom during the glacial period, and then as the land rose and the lakes lowered, the rather extensive, flat, fertile plains were brought into existence. Besides being important for specialized agriculture, part of this region contains the outstanding urban concentration in the state—metropolitan Detroit. The flatness of the topography has allowed this city to develop in a sprawling fashion as the only major obstacle to urbanization in this area has been the great amount of poorly drained land.

Eastern Upper Peninsula Lowlands

The eastern half of the Upper Peninsula is a relatively flat, largely lacustrine lowland. In places, the surface material is very thin; and on some of the eastern islands, such as Drummond Island, the sedimentary rocks are visible. Glacial hills are scattered throughout the areas, and the Niagara Escarpment (an outcropping of resistant Niagara limestone) is found along the southern flank. Large portions of this area are covered by state and national forests, wildlife refuges, lakes, ponds, and poorly drained land. Agricultural land is limited, but a few places—such as the Munising area—are quite well developed considering the northerly latitude and the relatively short growing season.

A large number of short streams flow south into Lake Michigan or north into Lake Superior—most are excellent trout streams—and the striking Tahquamenon Falls on the Tahquamenon River are a major tourist attraction. Along the Lake

Tahquamenon Falls, Luce County, in the Upper Peninsula. The upper falls, shown here, are 50 ft (15.2 m) high and 200 ft (61 m) wide and are the main feature of the state park. (Courtesy Michigan Travel Bureau)

Superior shore, there are two additional outstanding features: the Pictured Rocks National Lakeshore, with its beautifully sculptured sedimentary rocks in the vicinity of Munising, and the high sand dunes near Grand Marais to the east. St. Marys River, which forms the boundary between Canada and the United States in this area, has several rapids and falls that have been eliminated by a series of locks that allow vessels to go between Lake Huron and Lake Superior. Two cities, each called Sault Ste. Marie, have developed on both sides of the international border in the vicinity of these important locks.

The economic development of the eastern Upper Peninsula has been aided considerably by the building of the Mackinac Bridge, which connects the area with the Lower Peninsula. High-speed travel and excellent highways have opened the region up to tourists from the urban south.

Crystalline Uplands

The western Upper Peninsula is one of the most scenic regions in Michigan. Old resistant mountain cores, especially the Porcupine and Huron mountains, and other resistant, igneous rock areas are part of an old Precambrian Shield that extends north into Canada. The rocks were sculpted into various forms by the continental glaciation, and the soil is generally thin and infertile. Glacial materials often form ridges on top of the igneous rocks. The highest point in the state—Mount Krawood, 980 ft (299 m) above sea level—is found in the Porcupine Mountains near the shore of Lake Superior. The Gogebic Range extends into this part of Michigan, as do several other highlands that contain considerable iron ore.

Copper is mined on the Keweenaw Peninsula, and for a long time this mineral was an important resource base for many

Cambrian sandstone and Precambrian metamorphic unconformity at Presque Isle Point near Marquette. (Photo by John Plough)

of the urban developments there. When copper mining declined, settlements were abandoned as people moved on to areas where the economy was more reliable. Today, a few crumbling ghost towns remind one of the prosperous copper era. Copper mining has made a partial comeback in the recent years, however, as demand for this mineral has increased, and methods have been developed to process low-quality ore. Today, though, the extraction of iron ore is the most important mining activity in the area, and towns such as Ishpeming and Negaunee near Marquette largely owe their existence to this mineral. Other major cities in this area such as Marquette and Escanaba, are important because they are ports the iron ore is shipped from.

Forests, both national and state, cover much of the western Upper Peninsula, and forestry is a leading activity. The forested hilly land, often dotted with lakes, is attractive to tourists, so the recreation industry is growing in importance here as well. The hilly topography and the cold, snowy weather are also conducive to winter sports. A problem in the recreational use of this land is that the area is not close to the big cities of southern Michigan. Actually, the Upper Peninsula is more accessible by rail, highway, and air from Wisconsin and southeastern Minnesota than it is from much of southern Michigan. This fact has been utilized by people who want the Upper Peninsula, and especially this western portion, to become part of the state of Wisconsin. The bridge across the Straits of Mackinac has decreased the merits of this argument, however, as the bridge has helped tie the two peninsulas of Michigan more closely together.

Agriculture is relatively limited in the western Upper Peninsula because of topography, elevation, and the shortness of the growing season. Potatoes are a major crop in this landform region, and the rest of the agricultural activity centers largely around dairying. Forestry is important

Winter scene in the Upper Peninsula. Note the mixture of deciduous and coniferous trees. (Courtesy Michigan Travel Bureau)

throughout the area, and there is also some commercial fishing of white fish and lake trout along Lake Superior.

SUMMARY

The geology of Michigan is dominated by two rock formations: the sedimentary Michigan Basin, which covers the entire Lower Peninsula and the eastern half of the Upper Peninsula, and the old crystalline, igneous shield found in the western Upper Peninsula. These rocks are covered to various depths by material deposited during the Ice Age. The preglacial topography was much disturbed by the power of these vast ice sheets as they eroded and leveled certain areas and deposited materials in other sections of the state. The present surface is characterized by ridges of sand, gravel, and clay known as moraines, which were deposited as the ice advanced and retreated in the state.

This generalized landform analysis has divided Michigan into major landform regions, which are easily observable on the landscape. The dividing lines between these regions are shown as lines on maps, but they are most characteristically transitional areas of considerable width. An exception is the division between the high sand plains of the northern Lower Peninsula and southern Michigan, which is often a very sharp line. This line can be easily seen in Clare County as the landscape changes quickly from the southern, largely agricultural area to infertile, higher, sandy, forested land with little or no agriculture.

Within the major landform regions, the great variety of glacial features, each used somewhat differently by humans, results in a large number of smaller regions, some even microscopic in size. In a small area, such as a county, three or four or more local landform categories can be identified.

There are other dominant topographic

This region north of Clare marks the boundary (tension zone) between the northern, forested high sand plains and the southern agricultural plains. The boundary runs through the lower right-hand portion of the photograph. (Courtesy Michigan Department of Natural Resources)

features of Michigan. There are the large number of inland lakes and the great area of swampy or poorly drained land (wetlands). There is also the state's division into two peninsulas, and the fact that it is bordered by four of the five Great Lakes, with the longest freshwater coastline of any state. However, landforms are only one of the important physical characteristics of the state.

SOILS

The soils of Michigan vary widely with the diversity of landform, climatic, and water conditions, but the broad soil types are related to the landform regions discussed in the previous section. Soil is one of the major resources any region possesses, and in some parts of Michigan, it is the single most important resource.

Soil is the layer of weathered material, both organic (living) and inorganic (nonliving), on the crust of the earth. It is made up of air, water, minerals, and plant and animal materials. If any of these elements are missing, the soil is limited in its ability to produce plants and crops.

Soils are formed through a very complex process involving the nature of the parent bedrock, climate, animals, vegetation, slope of the landform, and length of time the soil has been in existence. Most of Michigan's soils were developed from material deposited during the Ice Age. As the huge ice sheets moved southward over Michigan, they picked up, eroded, and deposited rocks, sand, gravel, and silt. When the ice receded, the material collected in and underneath the ice sheets was left behind. Since then, the surface layers have been changed by the action of water, ice, wind, plants, animals, and people. Thus, there are a great variety of soils, and in Michigan, soil characteristics may differ dramatically from region to region, from field to field, or even within a single field.

SOIL CHARACTERISTICS

Soils are characterized by the differences in the various layers of a soil profile (Figure 4.7). The top layer of a soil is called the A horizon and contains the partially decomposed vegetable matter called humus, which helps to hold moisture and provide food for plants to grow. The A horizon is also the layer in which the mineral matter will normally be found in fertile soils. In Michigan, however, the mineral matter is often found in the B horizon because water causes the minerals to be dissolved and carried down out of the A horizon—a process called leaching.

The B horizon is usually made up of smaller, more tightly packed particles, clay grains, and minerals such as iron and lime. Water washes the small particles and minerals down through openings in the A horizon by a process called eluviation and these materials may form a clay barrier or "hard pan." The process of concentrating fine particles in a soil zone is called illuviation. Many of Michigan's soils are infertile because of the two processes of leaching and eluviation. The water that is in the ground is normally located in the B horizon and at the top of the C horizon. The C horizon is made up of the weathered or unaltered parent material. In Michigan, the parent material is mostly glacial debris, but parent bedrock is important in places like the western Upper Peninsula.

The soils of Michigan vary greatly. Sandy soils are dominant in the western and northern portions of the Lower Peninsula; clays and loams, in the southern Lower Peninsula. The size of particles, or texture, varies in different kinds of soil. Most loam soils are a combination of soil particle sizes determined by the predominant parent materials. There are sandy loams, silty loams, loamy sands, and clay loams.

Loam soils are best for plant growth because sand, silt, and clay together provide desirable characteristics. First, the different-sized particles leave spaces in the soil for

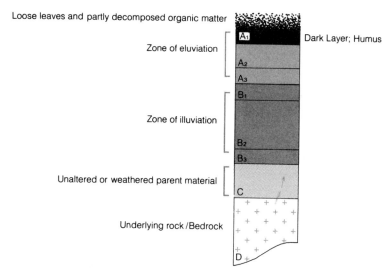

Loose leaves and partly decomposed organic matter

Dark Layer; Humus

Zone of eluviation

Zone of illuviation

Unaltered or weathered parent material

Underlying rock / Bedrock

FIGURE 4.7. Soil horizons.

air and water to flow and roots to penetrate. The roots feed on the minerals in the suspended water. Deep sands do not hold moisture well and are very infertile. Clays hold moisture better than sands and may be more fertile, but they tend to swell when they get wet, which may limit the movement of water and roots. Clays crack when they dry and the clods become very hard and do not furnish plants with nourishment. A desirable soil is a loam with enough sand to drain well yet with enough clay and silt to hold moisture. Silt—fine materials resulting from the erosion of sedimentary rocks—also contains nutrients and helps make a soil workable. Some soils contain a large amount of partially decayed vegetation (humus) and are called peat or muck. They are often used for growing vegetables because of their high fertility. Thus, the distribution of various kinds of soils in Michigan relates closely to the various types of crops grown and how productive the agriculture is.

SOIL DISTRIBUTION PATTERNS

Soils are classified on the basis of their properties according to a system adopted in the United States in 1965. Of the ten orders in this system, six are found in Michigan. They are (1) Spodosols—characterized by an accumulation of iron, aluminum, and humus in the B horizon; (2) Alfisols—with accumulations of clay in the B horizon; (3) Histosols—developed from organic materials; (4) Inceptisols—with weakly developed B horizons; (5) Entisols—showing little or no development in the B horizon; and (6) Mollisols—characterized by thick, dark-colored A horizons. These orders are further divided into suborders, great groups, subgroups, families, and soil series. Such detail will not be gone into here; instead, the emphasis will be on the relationship between a soil's major physical characteristics and its productivity or infertility.

Figure 4.8 is a generalized soil map of Michigan and shows the result of the relationship of soils, climate, vegetation, landforms, parent materials soils were formed from, and the length of the weathering process. The major factor that accounts for soil differences in the state is the tremendous variety of parent materials—a result of the type and number of glacial deposits often found within a small area. Thus, a very sandy soil and a heavy clay can be

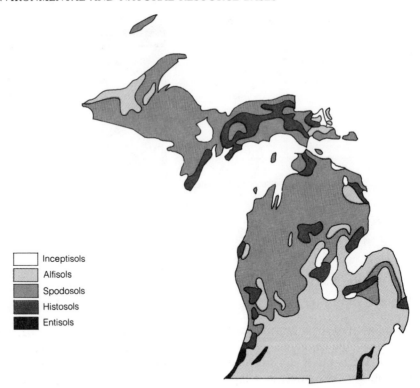

FIGURE 4.8. Major soil associations. (Source: Adapted from Lawrence M. Sommers, ed., *Atlas of Michigan* [East Lansing: Michigan State University Press, 1977], p. 36.)

found in the same field. The frequent differences in natural drainage conditions are also strongly reflected in the soil types. The nature of the original vegetation cover also influences the color of the soil, the amount of partially decayed material (humus) it contains, the mineral content, and thus, its general fertility. The types of natural vegetation are closely related to the climatic characteristics, so major changes in climate must also be considered in explaining the variety of soils.

Spodosols

Spodosols dominate the northern two-thirds of Michigan. A considerable amount of leaching has taken place in this area so humus and minerals, particularly iron and lime, have moved from the top, or A horizon, into the B horizon. The color of the soil is often gray, which indicates a lack

of humus because pine is the dominant natural vegetation for most of this region. Pine needles do not break down into humus easily and lie undecayed on the forest floor. The short growing season also slows the biological and physical breakdown of the pine needles and other vegetable matter. The exact nature of the soil found in any area will depend upon the variety of factors mentioned earlier.

The border between the Spodosols and the Alfisols in southern Michigan separates the dominant areas of agriculture to the south from the agriculturally poor areas to the north. Much of the northern area has a sandy soil that derives from materials laid down during the glacial period. Besides, there are many poorly drained soils with thick marsh vegetation. There are exceptions to this generalization because of some local conditions that give rise to greater fertility and special types of agricultural production. Examples are the important cherry areas in the vicinity of Grand Traverse Bay and further south in the Hart-Shelby area of Oceana County. These concentrated fruit belts are related to factors such as sandy loam soils and their nearness to Lake Michigan. The lake retards the first frost in the fall and also keeps the area cool in the spring until there is considerable assurance that frost will not recur.

Alfisols

In the southern part of the Lower Peninsula, the dominant soil color changes from gray to a gray-brown, because of a change in the dominant type of natural vegetation from a pine to a deciduous or broad-leaved forest—a combination of oak, beech, and hickory. This type of vegetation gives rise to more undecayed and partially decayed humus material in the A horizon of the soil, and thus the change in color from gray to gray-brown. The soil is characterized by heavy leaching and accumulations of clay in the B horizon, but the longer growing season and the deciduous vegetation results in a generally more productive soil than that in northern Michigan. Its greater fertility results from more humus, a higher mineral content, and the longer growing season, which results in a greater breakdown of the surface organic material as well as permitting a greater variety of crops.

The result is that the best general farming region of the state is in the area where the soils are classified as Alfisols. Certain crops, such as corn, can be grown for cash, partly because of the more suitable soil and partly because of the longer and warmer growing season. Dairying is also important in this part of the state, but overall, the area is characterized by mixed farming.

Mollisols

In southwestern Michigan, including parts of Newaygo County, a few small areas of Mollisols, or prairie soils, exist. The original vegetation was prairie grasses with a scattering of burr oak trees. The soils are dark brown in the A horizon, the result of a considerable amount of organic material that accumulated as a result of the decay of prairie grasses. The fibrous roots of the native grasses also added a considerable amount of organic material to the A and the upper part of the B horizons, so that the soil is a deeper brown or black than most other soils in Michigan except the true organic, or muck, soils. The Mollisols are normally very productive agriculturally.

Histosols

Histosols are scattered throughout both the Upper and the Lower Peninsula. They are found in marshy areas with a thick vegetation that does not decompose completely, and much of the soil consists of undecayed vegetable matter or peat. These soils are chiefly found in lacustrine areas that were covered with water or were drainage channels during the glacial period. In some places, depressions were filled with shallow lakes, and these have overgrown with vegetation and gradually changed from lake to swamp to organic soil.

This type of soil is generally very poorly drained and can be cultivated only if artificially drained by a system of clay tile pipes to take off the excess water. When a sandy peat is drained, the soil often becomes very light and is subject to erosion by the wind, so rows of willow trees or bushes are often planted in strategic places on the borders of these fields to act as windbreaks. Often, such soil must be irrigated to offset the rapid loss of moisture during the summer. Organic soils are heavy producers of vegetables and other specialized crops in Michigan.

Entisols

Entisols are soils with little or no evidence of B horizon development and are found in three areas in the southern part of the Lower Peninsula. They are alluvial, or water-deposited, soils associated with the beds of glacial streams or with the sands and gravels of glacial outwash. They tend to be low in humus and dry out quickly because of the high sand or gravel content and are of limited importance in Michigan.

Inceptisols

Inceptisols are soils with weakly developed B horizons. In Michigan, they are located primarily in the Saginaw Valley and two areas in the eastern half of the Upper Peninsula. Little eluviation or illuviation has taken place, and the soils are characterized by poor drainage and waterlogging. If artificially drained successfully, they can be productive—as in the navy-bean-producing areas of the Saginaw Valley.

SUMMARY

Michiganians have made good use of many of the areas of relatively infertile, sandy soil by employing technology. In some situations, farmers have scientifically improved the soil; in others, crops have adapted to soil types. By using the soils well, the people of Michigan have developed a valuable and varied agriculture.

The variety of landforms, soils, and drainage conditions has produced a diverse landscape, and this diversity also provides different habitats for wildlife and natural vegetation. These factors are interrelated and produce challenging conditions for the people and their activities.

CHAPTER 5

ENVIRONMENTAL SIGNIFICANCE OF A GREAT LAKES LOCATION

Jay R. Harman

Michigan's location in the middle of the North American continent and the fact that it is bordered by four of the Great Lakes have an important influence on the nature of the weather, climate, and natural vegetation patterns that characterize the state. The relationships between the climatic types and kinds of vegetation are strong. This chapter outlines the major characteristics of these important elements of the physical environment and explains the distributions of climate and forest vegetation.

CLIMATE

Climate is the long-term average of weather. Daily weather in Michigan can be much like that in Ontario, Iowa, or Missouri, but the climate in each of these areas is different because the patterns of day-to-day variability are different. For example, July is cooler in Michigan than in Missouri because periods of high temperature in Michigan are usually broken after a day or two by a passing weather disturbance whereas hot weather in Missouri is normally more prolonged.

The range and frequency of daily weather variations differ between places because of what are called climatic controls. These controls are relatively constant and therefore account for long-term geographic differences of weather and, hence, climate. Only the most important controls responsible for the climate of Michigan are described here, along with their effects on the resulting climate of the state.

CLIMATIC CONTROLS

The climates of the world differ because of many controls, but comparatively few are largely responsible for the climate of Michigan. These controls are discussed in decreasing order of importance.

Latitudinal Position

The state's location in the middle latitudes is the primary cause of its seasons. The inclination of the earth on its rotational axis and the revolution of the inclined earth about the sun produce great differences in the amount of heat received in the summer and in the winter. Long summer days, particularly in the Upper Peninsula, and the high angle of the sun above the horizon mean that the state receives much more solar energy during the summer than during the winter when short days and the very oblique angle of incoming solar radiation severely reduce the amount of heat received. Although the earth is about 3 million mi (4.8 million km) closer to the sun in January than in July, the distance between earth and sun is so great that this variation itself has little effect on the seasons. Radiation receipts are least in December and greatest in June, but mean temperatures do not reach their yearly extremes until at least a month later in each season because the earth is slow to respond to seasonal radiation trends.

Continental Location

The location of the state in North America affects both temperature and precipitation. Because Michigan is far from any oceanic influence, it has a "continental climate." Land masses retain much less heat than do large bodies of water, so they change temperature more quickly in response to variations in the amount of solar energy received. Consequently, continental climates are characterized by great ranges between summer and winter temperatures. If Michigan were located at the same latitude on the West Coast of North America, it would have less extreme seasons—summers would be cooler, and winters milder.

The state's position also helps account for the extremes of its daily weather. Differences in weather from day to day are due largely to the influence of the different air masses that flow across the Midwest. An air mass is a large, rather uniform body of air that has acquired some characteristics of the surface over which it was formed; many are so large that they may cover Michigan for two or more days at a time. Any one of three different air masses may invade the state, bringing with them their own characteristic conditions (Figure 5.1). Polar air originates over the Arctic reaches of Canada, or even Siberia, and enters the state from the northwest, north, or northeast, bringing cold (for the season) and generally dry weather (except near the Great Lakes in the winter). Pacific air enters the state from the west or northwest after it has been modified by its passage over the Rocky Mountains. By the time Pacific air reaches Michigan, it is mild for the season but dry. Tropical air originates over the Gulf of Mexico or the Caribbean and accordingly is warm and moist. It reaches the state from the southwest, south, or southeast and produces the hot, humid days of summer.

The fact that Michigan lies in the interior of North America also has an influence on the state's precipitation pattern. Rain or snow results from a combination of two factors: moist air and a source of air uplift that causes the moisture to condense into clouds that yield precipitation. Frequent uplift is provided by the numerous weather disturbances—air-mass fronts and cyclonic storms—that cross the state, but atmospheric water vapor adequate for precipitation is often missing. Of the air masses that affect Michigan, only those of tropical origin contain sufficient moisture to generate widespread, heavy precipitation; but of the three air masses, they are the least common in Michigan, in part because the state lies so far from the source region. Therefore, many weather disturbances cross the state without generating significant precipitation. Across Michigan and much of the eastern United States, the amount of moist tropical air that is available accounts for the general patterns in mean annual precipitation. Annual precipitation is higher in states south and east of Michigan where passing disturbances more often interact with tropical air, since they lie closer to the source. Precipitation is less to the west and the north of Michigan because tropical air reaches those areas even less frequently.

73

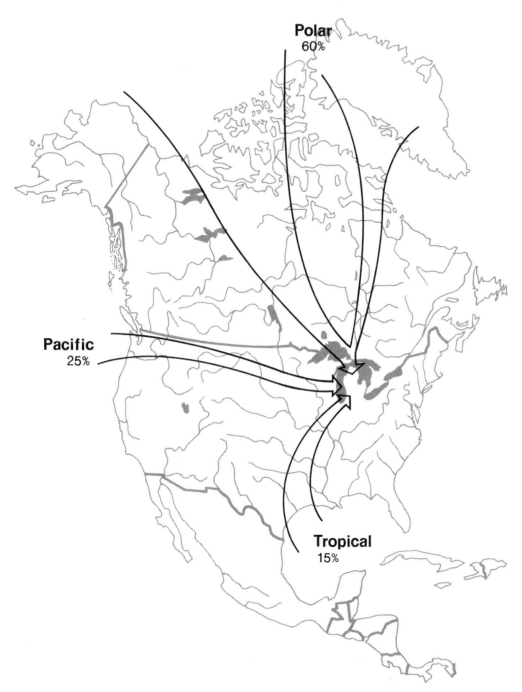

FIGURE 5.1. Average annual percentages of major North American air masses affecting Michigan.

Upper Atmospheric Circulation

Air masses and passing disturbances bring precipitation and changes of temperature, but the frequency of these disturbances and their paths depend upon the circulation of the middle and upper atmosphere. Surface weather is "steered" by air flow above 20,000 ft (6,906 m). Although this flow is generally from west to east (causing it to be termed "westerly" or "westerlies"), it is changeable and sometimes has a strong northerly or southerly component, and such deviations can continue for weeks or months. The fact that Michigan is located in the westerlies assures that it will have changeable weather, perhaps one of its most prominent climatic characteristics. Slight deviations in the direction taken by these upper-air westerlies lead to repeated invasions of air masses characteristic of the regions in which the weather originates: A northerly component brings Arctic or polar air south out of Canada; a southerly component imports mild Pacific or tropical air masses and excludes polar ones. Short-term weather trends result from deviations in the upper-atmospheric flow that favor one air mass over the others, but the state's long-term climate is tempered by an interplay of all three.

The core of strongest west-to-east winds in the upper atmosphere, the jet stream, changes latitudinal position as the seasons progress—shifting north in the summer and south again in the winter (Figure 5.2). As a result, the Upper Peninsula, which lies nearest the jet stream in summer, normally experiences the most changeable summer weather, and the southern Lower Peninsula may have more periods of prolonged, unchanging weather—particularly of heat and humidity, which are associated with slow-moving tropical air masses. But during the winter, the westerlies and the associated jet stream again shift south and bring changeable weather to all portions of the state.

The Great Lakes

No control on Michigan's climate probably receives more public attention, and is more misunderstood, than the Great Lakes. Although the lakes do have a limited impact

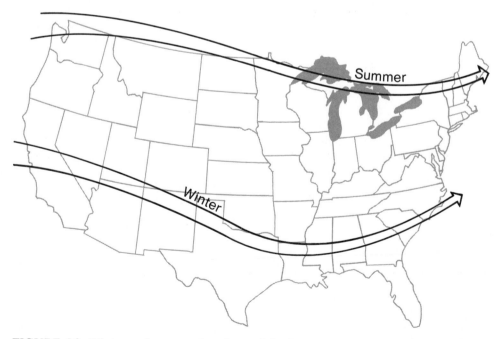

FIGURE 5.2. Winter and summer locations of the jet stream over the United States.

on general weather disturbances crossing the Midwest, they do not spawn these disturbances and are not the sources of the great changeability that is so much a feature of Michigan's weather. The majority of the state's population, living in the southeastern quarter of the Lower Peninsula, is far removed from most of the influence of the Great Lakes. Their effect is primarily local and is best developed on the lee-shore (eastern and southeastern shoreline) areas of each of the lakes. There this localized effect of the Great Lakes on the climate is of great importance to the state's agricultural economy.

The Great Lakes exert only a minor influence on the general weather patterns affecting the Midwest. During the season when they are generally colder than the air over them—April to August, but particularly in the spring—they extract heat from the overlying atmosphere. This chilling effect may strengthen the polar air masses entering the Midwest from northern areas and allow them to reach Michigan stronger and colder, and more persistent, than they might otherwise be. The Great Lakes alone do not generate these cool air masses but may prolong them over the Midwest, particularly during May and June when the lakes are colder in relation to the surrounding land than at any other time. The Great Lakes have a reverse, though minor, effect on passing cyclonic storms when the lakes are a source of heat, especially October through December. Certain winter cyclones that cross the Great Lakes probably gain strength or size because of the heat and moisture they acquire from the relatively warm water, but the path these storms take is largely determined by the upper-air circulation. So, we cannot blame the lakes for the frequency of winter storms in Michigan, but they may strengthen the storms that do occur, prolonging the associated cloudiness and inclement weather.

If the lakes exert only a minor influence on general Michigan weather, their influence on local weather is more varied and dramatic. During the winter months, when cold air crosses the relatively warm water, the air takes up heat and moisture from the lakes. As a result, the lower layers of the atmosphere are warmed, and upward-moving air currents develop. How much warming there is depends upon the length of time the air spends over the water and the temperature difference between the water surface and the overlying atmosphere. Contrasts in excess of 15° F (8° C) are common, and differences as great as 50° F (28° C) or more are possible. This low-level warming leads to the formation of cumulus clouds, since the ascending currents transport water vapor acquired with the heat from the water's surface. In general, the stronger the ascending air currents, the thicker the resulting cloud layer and the more likely it is to produce precipitation, usually as snow. The snow clouds then drift inland with the prevailing low-level winds, resulting in "lake-effect" snow showers within a 15–40-mi-wide-zone (24–64 km) starting on the lee shore of the lake. With a contrast of less than 15° F between the temperatures of the lake's surface and the lower atmosphere precipitation is unlikely, and with a contrast of less than about 6° F (3° C) clouds may not even develop.

Some lake-effect snowfalls can be spectacularly heavy; but such snowfalls require not only a great contrast between the temperatures of the water and of the air but also a comparatively long over-water trek to maximize low-level atmospheric heating and cloud formation. Because most extremely cold winter air masses in Michigan are accompanied by westerly or northwesterly surface winds, the air crosses the narrow axis of Lake Michigan or, in the case of the Keweenaw Peninsula, passes over only the western portion of Lake Superior. Consequently, the time the air spends over the water is much less than if the flow had been parallel to the lake, and the associated snowfalls seldom exceed 6 to 10 inches (15 to 25 cm). Still, because lake-effect snows are frequent in winter, their cumulative effect greatly augments the average annual snowfall in the lee-shore counties. Lake-effect shore snow seldom falls in significant amounts further inland than about 40 mi (64 km), but it is accentuated where inland-moving snow clouds cross higher terrain, as in Otsego County or on much of the Keweenaw Peninsula. Often, the lee-shore counties can be getting significant lake-effect snow while the sun is shining in eastern Michigan. Under exceptional conditions (severe cold and strong low-level westerly circulation), snow clouds from Lake Michigan may cover much of the Lower Peninsula far beyond the usual snow belt, though accumulation in the central and eastern counties is usually small.

A secondary consequence of lake-induced wintertime cloudiness is a moderation of severe cold immediately downwind from the shoreline. Not only do the lakes add heat to the lower atmosphere and hence prevent exceptionally low nighttime temperatures in lee-shore locations, but the resulting cloudiness slows nighttime reradiation, which helps retain heat. Thus, regions about 20 mi (32 km) downwind from Lake Michigan enjoy somewhat higher minimum temperatures than do locations farther inland.

Just as the Great Lakes are a source of heat in winter, they remove heat from the atmosphere in spring and summer, and this influence again is strongest over the peninsulas and downwind areas. Thus, maximum July daily temperatures, when there is strong, low-level southwesterly flow, may be 10°–18° F (6 – 10° C) lower along the Michigan shore of Lake Michigan than along the Wisconsin shore. But this effect seldom extends more than a few miles inland, and beyond about 20 mi (32 km) the influence is often hard to detect; it may very well be absent even along the shoreline if strong offshore winds prevail on a particular day.

Often, the cooling influence of any of the Great Lakes is developed in a rather sharp zone and coincides with what is called a "lake breeze." The lake breeze develops when there is a strong temperature contrast (more than 15° F [8° C]) between the cool

lake water and the warmer air over the nearby land surface—as is typical on almost any summer afternoon. Under these conditions, a shallow layer of lake-cooled air spreads inland in all directions. Since it is driven only by the slightly higher atmospheric pressure over the cooler lake surface, its circulation is weak and local, rarely penetrating more than a few miles inland (though tens of miles have been documented). The lake breeze advances inland like a small-scale cold front, bringing a wind shift and a quick drop in the temperature (10° F [6° C] or greater under extreme conditions). The breeze progresses farthest inland where it is not opposed by the regional surface wind, but it usually affects only shoreline areas and may not develop at all when the surface wind blows strongly offshore. The effect of the lake breeze is such that daily summertime maximum temperatures in areas near a shore average several degrees lower than in areas farther inland. For example, the east side and northeastern suburbs of Detroit are often cooler than the western suburbs, and Muskegon is often cooler than Grand Rapids during the heat of a summer day. When the lake breeze develops, it suppresses afternoon cumulus-cloud formation, and the sky is often clear. For this reason, coastal locations in Michigan are sunnier on the average during the summer than are inland locations.

Places along the shore do have fog more often, however—chiefly during spring and early summer when the Great Lakes are still cold. The surface layers of warm, moist air moving offshore are cooled by the water, and the moisture in the air may condense into visible droplets, fog. A slight shift in the direction of the wind then transports this fog inland. Although usually confined to the immediate shoreline, the fog may extend several miles inland under ideal conditions. The area that is foggy most frequently during the summer is the shoreline of Lake Superior because, of the five Great Lakes, Superior is the deepest, largest, and hence the coldest during this season.

Over the open lake, fog is even more prevalent than along the shoreline and has considerable significance for lake shipping.

Terrain and Elevation

In most areas of Michigan, the landforms are not a significant control on the local climate, since neither elevation nor relief (a term describing local extremes of elevation) is great. But in portions of the central-northern Lower Peninsula and the western Upper Peninsula, they may affect local weather. The elevation of some regions—Kalkaska, Antrim, and Otsego Counties in the Lower Peninsula and Ontonagon, Houghton, and Keweenaw Counties in the Upper Peninsula—may cause additional lifting of cold, moisture-laden clouds moving eastward from the Great Lakes in winter, and thus more snow falls than would otherwise be the case.

The hilly terrain in parts of the northern Lower Peninsula and the western Upper Peninsula also encourages the drainage of cold air and the formation of frost pockets in basins throughout these areas. On calm, clear nights, cold air, because it is denser than warm air, collects near the ground and flows down the slope and settles in depressions. Many of the settlements and much of the arable farmland in northern Michigan are located in such basins, which, unfortunately, experience later spring and earlier autumn frosts than the surrounding higher countryside does. Thus, many of the lower, better soils are not as well suited climatically for agriculture as the poorer but warmer sites on the surrounding hills.

CLIMATIC PATTERNS

Temperature

The annual mean temperature within the state ranges from a maximum of about 50° F (10° C) in the southern Lower Peninsula to a minimum of almost 40° F (4° C) in the Upper Peninsula (Figure 5.3). The lower average temperatures in northern Michigan result generally from the fact that

this area receives more frequent polar air masses and a lower annual amount of solar energy. Lying nearer the source region for the cold-air masses than the southern Lower Peninsula, these northern areas are under the influence of polar air a greater number of days during all seasons.

During the summer, the south-to-north decline in mean temperture is less evident (Figure 5.4). In the Lower Peninsula, temperatures are highest in the extreme southern counties, away from the moderating effects of Lake Michigan, and in the Upper Peninsula the highest are in the western counties. The southern Lower Peninsula is warmest because it lies comparatively near the source of warm air (which in the summer covers much of the southern Great Plains and Gulf coastal states) and farther from the polar-air source in northern Canada.

Average July temperatures are lowest in the eastern Upper Peninsula and the Keweenaw Peninsula, in part because these regions lie immediately downwind of Lake Superior and often experience lower afternoon temperatures because of the chilled air that moves off the water. But the lowering of the maximum temperatures by Lakes Superior and Michigan cannot entirely explain the pattern of lower summertime mean temperatures in the eastern Upper Peninsula. Further explanation lies in the normal evolution of daily weather patterns. Weather disturbances (cold fronts and cyclonic storms) cross the northern Great Lakes regularly during most summers and are preceded by a period of southwesterly surface winds lasting a day or longer. Air drawn northeastward in this flow originates over Iowa, Minnesota, the Dakotas, Nebraska, or from areas even more distant where, because of normal summer patterns, temperatures are higher. Since the warm air comes from the southwest before it is interrupted by a new southeastward-moving cold front, the western counties of the Upper Peninsula warm faster and have higher temperature extremes. For example, the absolute maximum temperatures at Wa-

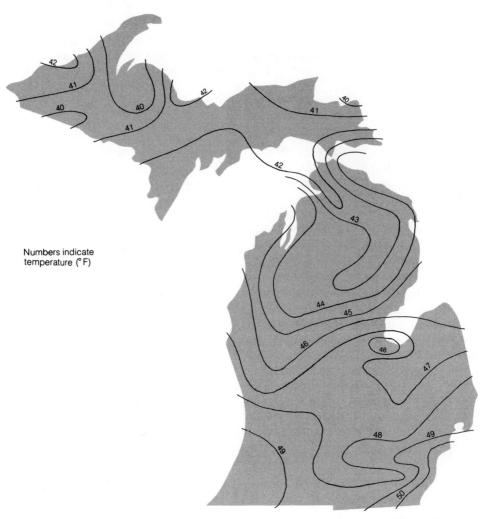

Numbers indicate
temperature (°F)

FIGURE 5.3. Annual mean temperatures. (Source: Adapted from Michigan Weather Service, *Supplement to the Climate of Michigan by Stations* [East Lansing: Michigan Department of Agriculture, 1982].)

tersmeet in eastern Gogebic County and Iron Mountain have been 100° F (38° C) and 102° F (39° C), respectively, but the absolute maximum temperatures of Sault Ste. Marie have been only 98° F (37° C) in August and 94° F (34° C) in July.

The pattern of average daily maximum temperatures in July clearly indicates the greater frequency of warm air masses in the southern Lower Peninsula and, to a lesser extent, the western Upper Peninsula (see Figure 5.4). Air capable of pushing afternoon temperatures above 90° F (32° C)

in the southern Lower Peninsula normally resides over the western and southern Great Plains and a good part of the states bordering on the Gulf of Mexico. Time is required to transport this air into Michigan, and the farther north and east it is to move, the longer a weather pattern that is favorable to a surface southwesterly flow must hold. Because weather disturbances sweep eastward across the northern Midwest every two to four days, there is seldom enough time between systems for the warmer air to reach into northern Michigan before it

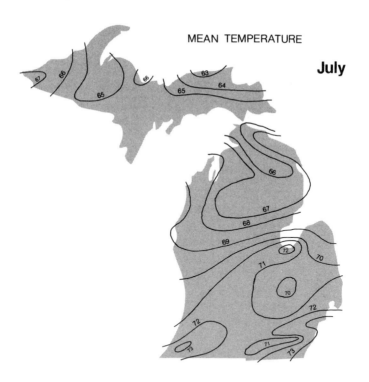

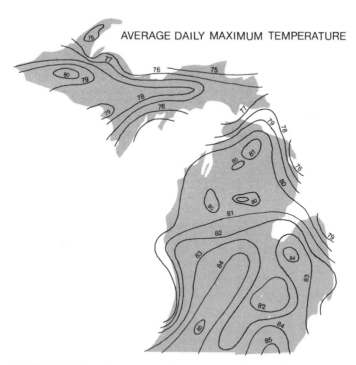

FIGURE 5.4. July mean and average daily maximum temperatures. (Source: Adapted from Michigan Weather Service, *Supplement to the Climate of Michigan by Stations* [East Lansing: Michigan Department of Agriculture, June 1976].)

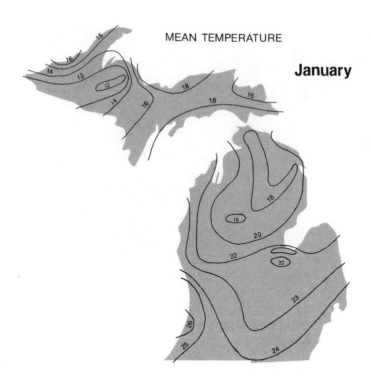

MEAN TEMPERATURE

January

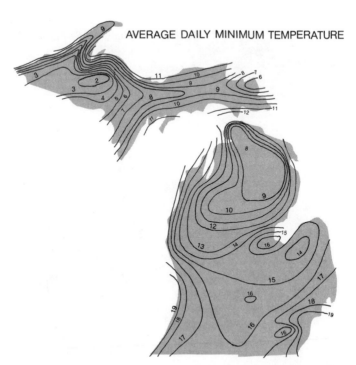

AVERAGE DAILY MINIMUM TEMPERATURE

FIGURE 5.5. January mean and average daily minimum temperatures. (Source: Adapted from Michigan Weather Service, *Supplement to the Climate of Michigan by Stations* [East Lansing: Michigan Department of Agriculture, August 1976].)

is displaced by a new cool-air mass from the northwest. The southern Lower Peninsula, lying closer to the warm air source, is more frequently affected by this air and also experiences weather changes less often, which means the southwesterly flow has more time to transport warm air into the region. Hence, the processes responsible for the higher average summer temperatures in both the southern Lower Peninsula and the western Upper Peninsula are similar.

The south-to-north decline of mean July temperatures is less than that observed in January (Figure 5.5). In summer, lower mean temperatures in the northern areas are primarily the result of the atmospheric circulation patterns that develop over the Midwest; they are not reinforced by the pattern of radiation receipts, since days are longer and the mean amount of solar radiation received in the Upper Peninsula is greater than in the southern Lower Peninsula. During winter, however, reduced solar radiation in northern Michigan reinforces the effects of the regional weather patterns since the day length, which is short in the state everywhere (less than nine hours), is shortest in the northern counties. Consequently, during the winter, the difference between the mean temperatures of the Upper Peninusla and the southern Lower Peninsula is greater.

Snow cover also contributes to lower winter temperatures in the north. Once established, snow promotes faster nighttime reradiation and colder overnight minimum temperatures than there would be otherwise, so the average daily minimum temperatures are lower. Since daytime heating must then start from lower minima and a greater percentage of incoming solar radiation is reflected from snow than from a darker, snow-free landscape, snow cover helps create lower maximum temperatures as well.

The weather patterns that maintain the lower mean winter temperatures in the north are similar to those that keep the northern areas cooler in the summer. Lying nearer the cold-air source areas, the Upper

and northern Lower Peninsulas are affected by polar air more often than the southern Lower Peninsula is. In addition, brief intrusions of milder southwesterly air produce occasional thaws in the southern Lower Peninsula; these normally prevent the snow cover from lingering continuously all winter. Without a deep snow cover, a quicker temperature recovery is possible during the intervals of a milder southwesterly flow, and nighttime minimum temperatures will be less extreme. In contrast, the combined effects of more polar air masses and deeper, more persistent snow cover—itself partly a result of a higher frequency of polar air—produce lower mean and extreme temperatures in the Upper and northern Lower Peninsulas during the winter. The liberation of heat and the generation of cloudiness by the Great Lakes both lead to less-extreme minimum temperatures in the shoreline areas than in the interior.

Precipitation

Annual mean precipitation ranges from a maximum of more than 36 inches (91 cm) in the southwestern Lower Peninsula to a minimum of fewer than 27 inches (69 cm) in the northeastern Lower Peninsula (Figure 5.6). These variations result primarily from statewide differences in the availability of moisture-laden air associated with passing disturbances. The number of such disturbances (fronts and cyclonic storms) is as great or greater in northern Michigan than in the southern Lower Peninsula; the lower precipitation amounts in the north reflect a northward decrease in the amount of water vapor present in the atmosphere that can interact with these disturbances.

Air masses acquire water vapor through transpiration by plants, evaporation from the soil, and most important, directly from bodies of water. Large amounts of moisture, however, can be acquired only from warm-water bodies such as tropical oceans. Thus the Great Lakes supply only a small percentage of the total water that falls as rain or snow in the state; most of it originates

Numbers indicate inches
of precipitation

FIGURE 5.6. Annual mean precipitation. (Source: Adapted from Michigan Weather Service, *Supplement to the Climate of Michigan by Stations* [East Lansing: Michigan Department of Agriculture, June 1974].)

in tropical air masses that move north from the Gulf of Mexico. Although tropical air may not always be detectable at the surface, its presence in the lower or middle atmosphere during the passage of a weather disturbance normally leads to general precipitation. Since these air masses originate in areas far south of Michigan, they most often reach only the southern Lower Peninsula before being driven out by a passing disturbance. Hence, average annual precipitation is highest in this area and decreases to the north.

Not all of the state's precipitation is in

the form of rain, of course, and of that which falls as snow, some of it that falls to the lee of the Great Lakes originates as water vapor acquired from the lake surfaces themselves. Only in these lake-effect snow areas is the contribution of moisture from the Great Lakes important, however; elsewhere, the primary source of moisture is the tropical air masses.

Local differences in annual mean precipitation are related to either the Great Lakes or to elevation. Cooler lake breezes advancing inland off the Great Lakes during warm summer afternoons may destroy or weaken some thundershowers in the coastal areas. Repeated often enough, this process results in a somewhat lower amount of summertime precipitation than in the inland areas, which are unaffected by normal lake-breeze patterns.

Local relief in Michigan is ordinarily insufficient to modify precipitation patterns resulting from large-scale weather disturbances. When the precipitation is local and mainly in the lower levels of the atmosphere, however, certain more-prominent terrain features may have an effect. For example, lake-effect snow usually falls from clouds with bases less than 5,000 ft (1,524 m) in height, and the greatest amounts from these storms consistently fall in the most-elevated portions of the lee-shore areas. This fact suggests that even the relatively subdued terrain features of Michigan can modify certain local precipitation.

Snowfall. On the Lower Peninsula, the average annual snowfall increases both west and north from the southeastern counties; on the Upper Peninsula, it increases toward Lake Superior (Figure 5.7). Snowfall results

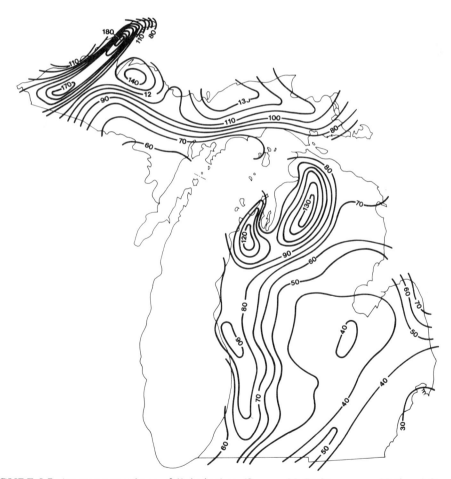

FIGURE 5.7. Average annual snowfall, in inches. (Source: N. D. Strommen, National Oceanic and Atmospheric Administration, climatologist and assistant professor, Agricultural Engineering Department, Michigan State University, November 1972.)

from both passing cyclonic storms and lake-effect clouds, but the snow that falls in most of the eastern half of the Lower Peninsula and the southern third of the Upper Peninsula is primarily cyclonic and indicates what would generally prevail across the state if there were no lake-effect. In other words, the relatively low annual snowfall of 50 to 60 inches (127 to 152 cm) in the northeastern Lower Peninsula and southern Upper Peninsula would be typical of all the northern areas if Lakes Superior and Michigan did not contribute to local snowfall. Thus, the annual total of 180 inches (457 cm) on the Keweenaw Peninsula, the highest average statewide and one of the greatest seasonal averages in the nonmountainous region in the eastern United States, may be as much as two-thirds lake-effect snow, and the snowfall in Otsego and Antrim Counties in the Lower Peninsula may be at least 50 percent lake-effect.

The greatest seasonal snowfall totals are found in northern lee-shore areas over higher terrain—the so-called snow-belt regions. The contribution of the lake-effect to total annual snowfall decreases southward through the western Lower Peninsula until it contributes less than half of the total in Berrien and Van Buren Counties. The annual snowfall decreases southward through all the Lower Peninsula because the percentage of winter precipitation that falls as rain is greater in the southern counties where the mean temperatures are higher. Lake-effect snow also falls less often in the snow belt of the southwestern Lower Peninsula than in the north because there are fewer days when the atmosphere is sufficiently colder than the water of Lake Michigan to generate the lake-effect.

FORESTS

Before it was settled by Europeans, the area that is now Michigan was predomi-

nantly a forested landscape (Figure 5.8). The composition of these forests varied considerably from place to place, however. Although most of the original stands have long since been lumbered out, second- and third-growth forests, which are particularly widespread in the Upper and northern Lower Peninsulas, provide useful information about the composition of the early forests—although they also have a diversity of their own. Much of the general pattern of original forest composition can be explained by the environmental characteristics that have already been discussed; in this section, we will review their specific importance.

ENVIRONMENTAL CONTROLS

Topography and Soils

Probably no environmental factors account for more differences in woodland composition than do soil texture and topographic position. Both of these factors strongly influence what amount of annual precipitation will actually be available for plant growth on a given site and thus put limits on which plants will be competitive there. Coarse, sandy soils are porous, have a low water-holding capacity, are often acidic, and usually support dry-site trees such as oaks and hickories—or in northern Michigan, jack and red pine with a shrub layer of blueberries. Soils of intermediate texture (loams) usually support a wide variety of species, but shade-tolerant hardwoods such as beech and sugar maple often dominate these sites. In the northern Lower Peninsula, hemlock and yellow birch may prevail along with beech and maple, and in the western Upper Peninsula, where there are no beeches, red oak and basswood are important also. Heavy, clay-rich soils with poor internal drainage may support communities of red or silver maple, ash, elm, and red oak.

The complex glacial history of the state left a jumbled array of sediments that became the soils, and since the soils influ-

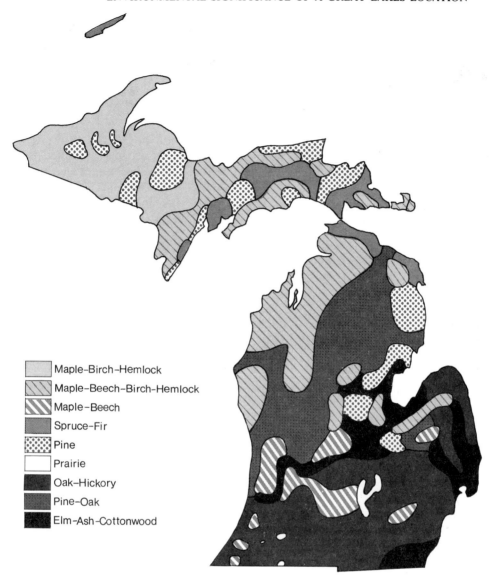

FIGURE 5.8. Presettlement forests. (Source: Adapted from Lawrence M. Sommers, ed., *Atlas of Michigan* [East Lansing: Michigan State University Press, 1977], p. 45.)

enced the composition of both the primeval and present forests, much of the patchwork of local forest patterns can be traced directly back to the state's glacial heritage. Topography influences forest composition in that it is one of the factors that determines how far below—or above—ground the water table will be. The woodlands that occupy low, boggy sites throughout the state are among the most striking examples of this control. (Bogs are technically differentiated

from swamps, which are less cold, less characterized by the presence of northern plants, and usually have better soil and surface water circulation so that the soils may be better developed.) Bog vegetation generally exists where the water table is at or slightly above the surface much of the year and where that water is poor in minerals. Cold, poorly aerated soils discourage a thorough breakdown of organic matter and therefore encourage the development

Eckerman Bog, a portion of a large bog area in the Tahquamenon River basin of the Upper Peninsula.

Hartwick Pines State Park in Crawford County. This stand of pines and hemlocks is similar to the forests that covered much of the northern portions of the state prior to the lumbering era. (Photo by John Plough.)

of acidic peat deposits. Such sites are heavily dominated by Canadian (boreal) elements throughout Michigan—spruce, fir, larch, leatherleaf, blueberry—as these are the only plants that can be competitive on acidic, cold sites.

The distribution of remnants of tall-grass prairie, found largely in southwestern lower Michigan, is also partly related to topography. Vestiges of an earlier prairie advanced into that part of the state from Illinois and Indiana during a postglacial period of warmer, drier climate, and these prairies and oak openings persisted on scattered patches of level or nearly level land of medium-or-better drainage until European settlement. Presumably, the low relief of these sites exposed them to a higher wind and fire risk. Once started by natural or human causes, fires could sweep across the flat terrain more easily than they could on the adjoining hillier landscape, resulting in damage to the invading woody vegetation and preserving the isolated prairie stands long after their former connection with the continuous prairie in Illinois and Indiana had been closed off by reinvading forests.

Past Disturbances

Following European settlement, the primeval forests of Michigan were quickly exploited, first for their pines and later for their hardwoods. Intense and extensive logging of the white and red pine stands in central and northern Lower Michigan, and later in the Upper Peninsula, had drawn to a close by 1900, leaving behind a legacy of impoverished, stump-filled wastelands. Although most of the pine was used for construction lumber, the hardwoods were used for such specific purposes as the manufacture of fine furniture. The large-scale commercial destruction of the pine stands and the local, less-organized cutting of the hardwood forests left very little primeval forest to enjoy today. Nearly every woodlot or forest stand on the present Michigan landscape has been disturbed; in many cases, this disturbance brought about several changes in the composition of the woodland, but in others, the stand may be made up much as the ancestral forest was. For example, we know that the impact was greatest on the drier (sandier) sites, which were subjected to the most severe exploitation—the pinelands. So, northern Lower Peninsula forests today are dominated by birch, aspen, oak, and jack pine and bear only a distant resemblance to their primeval state, whereas the composition of some other hardwood stands may be quite close to the original.

The fact that nearly all current Michigan forests are at least second-growth and have been subjected to repeated episodes of cutting or grazing means that the forest landscape today is certainly not the primeval forest that confronted the early settlers. However, the enclaves of uncut forest that do remain—such as Hartwick Pines, Estivant Pines, and the Sylvania tract—also contain evidence of prehistoric disturbances such as fires or storms. Thus, European settlement did not introduce disturbance into the forests, but it did usher in an era in which the extent and degree of forest alteration were greater than before, and extensive second-growth forests have been created that have no known prehistoric analogue.

Climate

The climate of all of Michigan is favorable to the development of forest vegetation, and much of the compositional variety evident in the contemporary forests is unrelated to climatic gradients within the state. However, certain patterns in the present composition of forests in the Lower Peninsula do appear to be responses to general climatic gradients. These extend both south to north and east to west across the state.

Moving south to north through the Lower Peninsula, one notices an increase in the number of evergreen species, particularly in the vicinity of Clare. These species (white spruce, balsam fir, jack pine) are boreal in distribution but extend south into northern Michigan on upland sites where they are usually only minor associates of other native hardwoods (though jack pine occurs extensively on sandy uplands). Apparently sensitive to warm, dry summers and neutral or basic soils, and unable to compete with more temperate-climate associates, they are limited primarily to the northern Lower Peninsula—north of a line from Bay City to Muskegon (the tension zone)—and to the Upper Peninsula, where cooler summers and lower evaporation are typical along with the acidic, sandy soils on which these trees are most competitive. Warmer summer weather with higher evaporation rates combined with less favorable soils seem to restrict their occurrence in southern Michigan.

A less conspicuous forest gradient exists from the central to the western portions of the Lower Peninsula. Woodland composition in the central Lower Peninsula is a mosaic of beech-maple mixed with some oak-hickory communities that results from the patchwork of different soils. Westward through the state, however, the more drought-sensitive beech–sugar maple forests become more common, and north of about Muskegon, they are mixed increasingly with yellow birch and hemlock. Close to Lake Michigan, these communities may be found even on sandy soils that in the interior could support only dry-site oak-hickory-pine forests. This westward increase of beech, sugar maple, and other drought-sensitive associates may be related to climatic modifications by Lake Michigan. Augmented winter snowfall (lake-effect) and, on the sand dune sites near the water itself, lower summer temperatures may combine to create a more generous amount of water and thus permit these species to compete near the lake on coarser soils than they could flourish on in the interior. This pattern is particularly evident near the shoreline in the central and northern Lower Peninsula, where dune soils consisting of more than 90 percent sand may support a mixture of mesic (moderately moist) forest species along with boreal elements (jack pine, balsam fir, white spruce).

GENERAL FOREST PATTERNS

In the Lower Peninsula, the tension zone separates two broad regions of different forest composition. The cause of the abruptness of this line has been the object of some study and is still being debated. The gradual increase of northern flora through the Lower Peninsula appears to be climatically controlled, but the peculiar sharpness of the tension zone may be related to the soils. Coarse, sandy soils are more widespread in the northern portion of the Peninsula, and their porosity leads to rapid weathering and increasing acidity through time. Thus, though the soils of the north are not chronologically older than those in the southern Lower Peninsula, they are more acid and older developmentally. The greater prevalence of these sandy soils in northern Michigan permits the more northern flora to be competitive on a greater number of sites, but south of the tension zone, the greater prevalence of the heavier glacial till soils, combined with a less favorable climate, restricts these species to rare, isolated sites.

Upland forests south of the tension zone are generally of either oak and hickory or beech and maple composition. The drier-site oak-hickory forests are most commonly found on porous, loose-textured soils (except near Lake Michigan) or locally on heavy clay soils with impaired internal drainage. The dominant species include black, red, white, and burr oaks; shagbark and pignut hickories; black cherry; black walnut; and red maple. Although these forests have an open canopy that admits considerable daylight to the forest floor, even during the summer, the variety of spring wildflowers is less in these woodlands than in some other types of forest.

Woodlands dominated by beech and sugar maple contain more plant species than do their dry-site counterparts. Most common on soils of heavier texture (loams) that are not excessively drained, these species are often found with red oak, basswood, white ash, tulip tree, black cherry, black walnut, and bitternut hickory. Although beech-maple stands share some dominants (black cherry, red oak, white oak) with oak-hickory stands, they have a more luxuriant aspect during the period of summer foliage; certain species such as spicebush, papaw, and musclewood (blue beech) are characteristic of beech-maple sites only.

Wetlands in the southern Lower Peninsula harbor a variety of species. The floodplains are often dominated by elm (although Dutch elm disease has decimated that species), green and black ash, and red and sugar maple. Upland wetlands (former lakebeds) frequently support ash, red maple, pin and swamp white oak, whereas acidic, boggy sites may contain the full complement of boreal flora that persist in this area as outliers (remnant populations dating back to Ice Age climates) of the Canadian forests. Black spruce, larch (tamarack), red maple, several evergreen shrubs, and locally rare herbaceous plants may grow on a mat of partially decomposed sphagnum moss.

In the northern Lower Peninsula, both of the upland forest types present in the southern region still occur but with modified composition. The deciduous members of the oak-hickory species become fewer, and upland pin oak may be the dominant species. Dry sites that have been heavily disturbed are dominated by red maple, bigtooth and quaking aspen, and some pines (both red and jack), but recurrent fires eradicated the pines on some sites. Extensive jack-pine plains characterize sandy sites that have been burned less often or those sites that are a bit less xeric (excessively dry). Beech and sugar maple are still present on the moister upland sites (which usually have heavier soils) but are associated in this region with Canadian hemlock and yellow birch, as well as with some of the associates that are characteristic farther south. Locally, balsam fir and white spruce are minor constituents. These communities, too, may have been heavily disturbed, leading to dominance by quaking aspen, red maple, white birch, and sugar

Heavily disturbed fir-birch-aspen community on sandy soil in the Upper Peninsula.

Poor quality, second growth pine and hardwoods on a sandy upland in the northern Lower Peninsula.

maple depending on site factors. Wetlands in the northern Lower Peninsula are more often dominated by bog vegetation than in the southern areas. Extensive black spruce–alder–northern white cedar stands may develop and in some local areas give a strongly boreal appearance to the landscape.

In the Upper Peninsula, upland forest communities are particularly widespread west of a line running from about Marquette to Escanaba. This line marks the general eastern extent of outcrops of Precambrian crystalline rocks; farther east, these rocks are either buried by glacial debris or are replaced by younger sedimentary types. Much of the topography in the western Upper Peninsula is therefore controlled by the bedrock; that is, the hills and valleys consist of rock rather than of loose glacial debris like most of the remainder of the state—particularly on the Keweenaw Peninsula. The associated upland forests are similar to the beech-maple stands discussed earlier except that beech is absent and its place in the canopy is taken by other associates, especially yellow birch. Scattered white and red pines are more common, as are the boreal elements, which assume a greater role on upland sites here than elsewhere in Michigan. Excellent examples of this type of forest can be seen in the Porcupine Mountains and Tahquamenon Falls State Parks. Heavy logging of these forests has led to extensive mixed

stands of maple, white birch, quaking aspen, and balsam fir; in some areas, this successional association is the most important community type.

Similar upland forests, with the addition of beech, are found in the eastern Upper Peninsula. Taken as a unit, however, this region differs from the western Upper Peninsula in that the wetlands cover a far greater proportion of the landscape. Large, flat tracts of glacial outwash or remnants of lake beds have permitted the development of extensive bogs, and these lend a remarkably boreal aspect to parts of the landscape—the Seney Wildlife Refuge in Schoolcraft County contains some splendid examples. Black spruce and jack pine, with varying amounts of larch, dominate the more acidic sites, and northern white cedar is found on wetlands that have slightly more-mineralized groundwater.

The flora of the best-developed, peaty black-spruce bogs in this area is indistinguishable from the vegetation that is typical of the poorly drained landscapes more than 1,000 mi (1,600 km) to the north. The survival of these boreal communities in a climate that is only marginally conducive to their growth can be attributed to the poorly drained sites where cold soils, deficient oxygen in the soil water, and high acidity compensate for the marginal climate and create local habitats on which other species from the nearby uplands are less able to compete. Thus, the bogs are dominated by plants that are most successful in this type of habitat only—geographically, they are the plants of high-latitude North America.

THE FORESTED LANDSCAPE TODAY

The proportion of Michigan's rural landscape that is forested today is lowest south of the tension zone. There, the agricultural potential, as well as land values, is relatively high, and much of the land that was originally cleared for agriculture is still being cultivated. The remaining woodlots, disturbed second-growth remnants of the primeval forest, have chiefly been left when they are on less-than-choice land thought too rocky, sloping, wet, or otherwise unsuited for agriculture. Few of these woodlots have remained uncut as nearly all have been subject to at least occasional firewood culling and many have been grazed, a practice that interrupts normal regeneration within the woods. The most extensive woodlands today are generally under state ownership (game areas) and were among the least attractive for agriculture because of various physical limitations.

North of the tension zone, the amount of woodland increases significantly, signaling a decline in agricultural potential because of the greater sandiness and acidity

Christmas tree farm in Benzie County, an increasingly common use of poor soils in northern Michigan.

of the soils combined with the cooler summers and a shorter growing season. Pockets of better soil have remained in cultivation since the general lumbering activity ceased, but the poorer soils have been left to forest regeneration after brief episodes of general farming. The proportion of forested landscape decreases westward toward Lake Michigan where dairying and fruit growing, particularly, become more economically attractive. In the Upper Peninsula, nonforest land is the exception, and, again, it corresponds to the patches of better soil or is located near urban markets where dairy produce is in some demand. In many areas across the entire state, farmland continues to be abandoned because of increasing farming costs, and fields that have not been cultivated for only ten to fifteen years are slowly reverting to a woody condition.

UNUSUAL HABITATS

Apart from the general patterns of plant geography, Michigan contains a number of unusual habitats. They may harbor species more typical of regions beyond Michigan's border or a combination of local species that are not normally found together. Such communities exist because Michigan, in a general sense, lies astride two major vegetation transition zones—one between the eastern forests and midwestern prairies and the other between broadleaved temperate

Regenerated jack pine stand along Stephan Bridge road near Grayling.

forests and the boreal forests of Canada. These transition zones shifted considerably because of apparent climatic changes during and after the close of the last Ice Age, but they left behind remnant populations on locally favored sites well out of the principal ranges of the plants. Such sites exist because of the state's environmental diversity, resulting from the variety of soils and glacial sediments as well as the varied topography and local climatic amelioration provided by the Great Lakes.

Some of these unusual habitats, such as the bog assemblages of Canadian plants and the prairie remnants in the southwestern Lower Peninsula, have already been described. Other unusual habitats are to be found in the sand dunes along the eastern shoreline of Lake Michigan, where a combination of coarse soils, diverse terrain, reduced summertime evaporation and daytime temperature, an extended growing season, and a moderation of severe winter cold because of the nearby water has permitted an extraordinarily rich mixture of plants to coexist. Within Berrien County, particularly, small areas of dune landscape contain a greater number of plants than is found in any other comparably sized area of the state. Here, northern shrubs (blueberries, bearberry) and trees (jack pine, balsam poplar) may mingle with Canadian hemlock, white pine, and eastern-temperate species like sour gum (tupelo) and tulip tree. Other dry-site communities nearby may be composed of a mixture of prairie grasses and forbs (broadleaved nonwoody plants) with prickly pear. Northward along the dunes, from about Muskegon, the vegetation becomes more boreal but remains

Lake Michigan sand dune vegetation. (Courtesy Michigan Department of Natural Resources)

complex and locally varied.

Other unusual or extreme habitats in Michigan include the "big prairie" area in Newaygo County, a region of loose, sandy soils and more xeric vegetation; the Seney Wildlife Refuge, an unusually large bog expanse in the Upper Peninsula; and the exposed mountain tops in portions of the Keweenaw Peninsula and Huron Mountains. In one way or another, these habitats are examples of the way local environmental factors may cause a vegetation assemblage that is considerably different from the regional pattern.

CHAPTER 6

MINERAL RESOURCES

The geologic formations of Michigan span more than 3.5 billion years, from some of the oldest Precambrian rocks to loose, unconsolidated drift left behind by the continental ice sheets of the Pleistocene period. Surface rock outcrops are rather rare as most of the rock surfaces are covered with glacial drift, some as much as 800 ft (244 m) deep. The deepest glacial deposits are in the central and western portions of the northern half of the Lower Peninsula; the shallowest coverings—some extremely so—are chiefly found in the western and extreme eastern portions of the Upper Peninsula.

There is a marked contrast between the old resistant Precambrian and Cambrian rocks of the western half of the Upper Peninsula and the sedimentary rocks of the rest of Michigan. The limestones, sandstones, and shales, which dominate the Michigan Basin, are approximately 500 million years old, some perhaps less. The sediments that form these sedimentary rocks were deposited on the bottoms of ancient seas, and the rock layers are piled on top of each other like saucers. The edges of the sedimentary rocks appear at or near the surface in northern Michigan—for example, near the Straits of Mackinac. In the center of the basin, they are about 14,000 ft (4,267 m) thick.

These geologic diversities in the state have a direct relationship to the mineral occurrences. The iron and copper minerals are found in the igneous (granitic and volcanic) and metamorphic (changed through heat and pressure) Precambrian rocks of the western Upper Peninsula. Petroleum, natural gas, coal, gypsum, and salt are found in the sedimentary rocks of the Michigan Basin. Sand and gravel are obtained from the loose, unconsolidated surface deposits, largely those left behind by the Pleistocene continental glaciers. Building stones have been quarried from various rock layers found near the surface and have been obtained as well from glacial boulders found in the glacial drift. Glass sand is obtained from Devonian Sylvania sandstone, and foundry sand from Lake Michigan dune sand.

COPPER AND IRON ORE

Michigan produced 5,385,849 short tons (4,884,965 t) of copper between the beginning of commercial operations in 1845 and 1969 when several companies ended operations because of labor troubles. Since 1969, several new efforts have been initiated, and 65 tons (59 t) were shipped from a new concentrating plant in 1975. The White Pine deposit in Ontonagon County is the current major producer of copper; in 1979, it mined 87,469,886 lbs (39,711,328 kg) valued at $79,195,000.

The state's copper deposits extend in a narrow band from the Michigan-Wisconsin border to the tip of the Keweenaw Peninsula and out into Lake Superior (Figure 6.1). The copper-bearing rocks are late Precambrian and mostly volcanic (basaltic lava

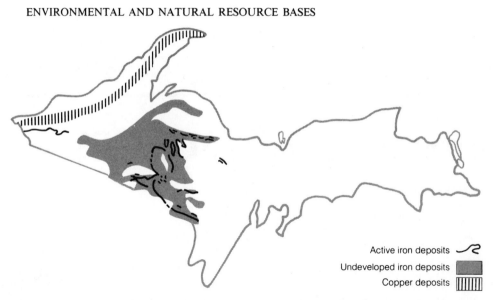

Active iron deposits
Undeveloped iron deposits
Copper deposits

FIGURE 6.1. Iron ore and copper formations. (Source: Adapted from Lawrence M. Sommers, ed., *Atlas of Michigan* [East Lansing: Michigan State University Press, 1977], p. 123.)

flows) and sedimentary in origin. The mineral occurs in fissures, or veins and lodes, in these rocks. The largest amount has been obtained from lodes in which the copper minerals are found as layers in the rock. The White Pine deposit, also Precambrian, is a sulfide copper rather than a native copper. The rocks are fine-grained, and the copper is only one of the minerals that compose the rock.

Michigan has three iron-ore ranges—the Gogebic, Marquette, and Menominee—which are the roots of middle Precambrian mountains. The natural ores produced most of the iron until 1955; since that time, most of the ore has been obtained from beneficiation (concentration) of low-grade iron-ore deposits. The iron-ore formations are found in the southern half of the western Upper Peninsula Precambrian rock area. There were five active mines in 1979 in the Marquette and Menominee ranges, but one of these five—the Mather mine—closed in July 1979. In 1979, 17,351,000 long tons (17,628,616 t) of iron ore, valued at $607,200,000, were shipped. This figure represents about one-fifth of the iron ore produced in the United States and means that Michigan ranks second in its production among the fifty states.

Rocks with about 50 percent or more iron constitute natural iron ore, but as this ore became depleted, methods were developed to profitably mine lower-grade iron formations, called taconites, which have 25 to 30 percent iron content. The taconite is crushed and the iron separated out through gravity and flotation processes. The fine iron particles are agglomerated through heat and molding before being shipped. This is an expensive process, but it brings the product up to about 65 percent iron and makes it profitable to transport. Competition with foreign producers of high-grade iron ore continues to be a cost problem.

The first Michigan iron ores to be mined were soft ones (hematites), and they were mined near the surface. These ores were soon exhausted, and mines were developed that were 3,000 to 4,000 ft (914 to 1,219 m) deep. With beneficiation, the hard ores (magnetites)—low-quality iron ores that were passed by earlier—are being mined in open pit or shallow mines.

The decline of copper and iron-ore mining was a serious economic setback for the

Webster Iron Mine south of Marquette. (Courtesy Michigan State Archives)

Upper Peninsula, but with the development of new mining and processing methods, this mining industry has recovered somewhat. The employment high in iron-ore mining was 6,972 in 1952, and the low point was 2,226 in 1972; this figure rose to 3,083 in 1979. Mining industries wax and wane with the general economic health of the U.S. economy, but in general, the future for both the iron-ore and copper industries is brighter than a decade ago.

FOSSIL FUELS

Petroleum and Natural Gas

Petroleum and natural gas are trapped in various ways in sedimentary rock layers. The 14,000 ft (4267 m) of sedimentary rocks found on top of the Precambrian formations in Michigan represent a potential for the accumulation of oil and gas. However, rocks of the Mesozoic and Cenozoic eras are largely absent from the Michigan geologic column, and those are the

rocks that produce much of the petroleum and natural gas in other parts of the United States and the world. Thus, liquid fossil fuels in Michigan must come dominantly from the sandstones, limestones, and shales of the Paleozoic era.

In 1979, fifty-five of the eighty-three counties in Michigan were producers of petroleum—all in the Lower Peninsula (Figure 6.2). In fact, only thirteen of the

Oil well and storage tanks, Kalkaska County.

FIGURE 6.2. Oil and gas fields, 1979. (Source: Michigan Department of Natural Resources, Geological Survey Division,
Michigan's Oil and Gas Fields, 1979 [Lansing, 1980].)

Lower Peninsula counties produced no oil,
and six counties produced over 1 million
barrels (140,845 t):[1] Manistee, 8,460,019
(1,191,552 t); Otsego, 6,278,046 (884,232
t); Grand Traverse, 4,525,299 (637,366 t);
Kalkaska, 3,882,057 (546,769 t); Crawford,
1,542,332 (217,230 t); and Ingham, 1,233,150
(173,683 t). All of these counties are part
of the Niagaran-Silurian Reefs, which have
been exploited since the late 1960s because
improved technology and higher prices made
greater profits possible despite the considerable risk involved. Five of the six
counties are in the northern Niagaran Reefs
area—currently the most active oil and gas
region in Michigan—where production began in 1969. Considerable amounts of oil
and gas were sealed in the Niagaran Reefs,
which formed along the edges of a salt sea
that covered Michigan during the Silurian
period. The small pinnacle reefs were coral
formations that have changed to porous
carbonate rock. They are isolated from one

another and average from 100 to 200 acres
(40.5 to 81 ha) in size: thus the search for
them has resulted in a number of dry holes.
Of the total number of wells drilled in
Michigan from 1925 through 1979, 16,109
were dry, 12,359 produced oil, 2,274 produced gas, and 2,057 were classified as
service wells. The success rate has improved
in recent years with better exploration and
seismic testing methods. Improved pipe
technology in the holes has also contributed
to the increased success rate.

The production trends can change rapidly within the state (Figure 6.3), as has
been the case because of recent developments in the northern Niagaran Reefs that
have made them the leading producing area
in Michigan. The recent deep well find by
the Dart Oil Company in Missaukee County
may shift the center of production in the
state again. Significant levels of petroleum
and natural gas were discovered at a depth
of more than 10,000 ft (3,048 m). This find

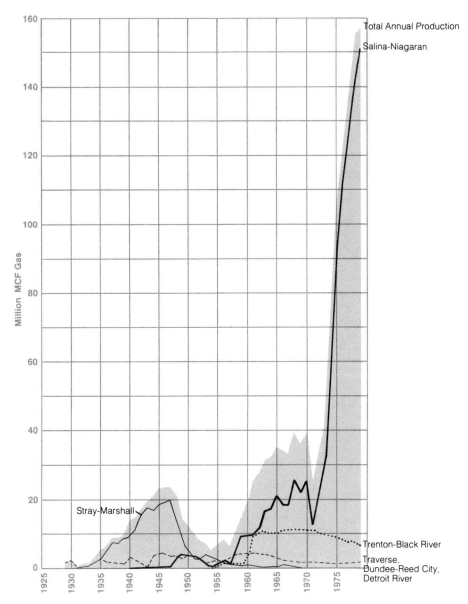

FIGURE 6.3. Trends in Michigan's production of natural gas from the geologic formations indicated. (Source: Michigan Department of Natural Resources, Geological Survey Division, *Michigan's Oil and Gas Fields, 1979* [Lansing, 1980].)

has set off a boom in that area, and exploration rights for land have increased considerably. The deep find has opened up the potential of a whole new era of oil and gas exploration in Michigan—one that is attracting major oil companies as well as some of the larger independents. Smaller companies will be largely excluded because

the drilling costs are over a million dollars per well.

The annual oil production in Michigan has varied considerably since exploration began in 1920, and which formations have contributed to the total has varied as well—in 1979, the Silurian-Niagaran Reef (Figure 6.4) accounted for 29 million barrels

98

Petroleum field near Central Lake in Antrim County. The light spots are oil exploitation sites. (Courtesy Michigan Department of Natural Resources)

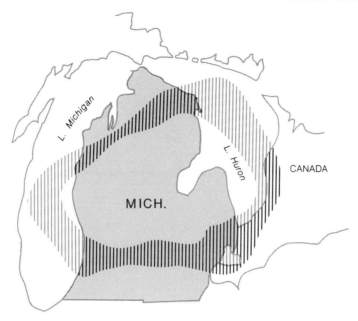

FIGURE 6.4. Probable extent of the Salina-Niagaran Reef. (Source: Michigan Department of Natural Resources, *Energy Facility Siting in Michigan* [Lansing, 1981], p. 35.)

(4,084,507 t) of the 35 million barrels (4,929,577 t) produced. Gas production trends show similar fluctuations in the total produced and from which formations.

Michigan's production of both represents only a small percentage of the state's oil and gas needs, but there is considerable potential for further production in existing and new fields. Drilling is only beginning under controlled conditions in state forests—permission was granted in 1980 for drilling in the Pigeon River Forest near Gaylord—and Michigan has many acres of state and national forests in the Lower Peninsula with possible oil potential. Oil is known to lie under extensive areas of Lake Michigan, but there is little likelihood of drilling in the lake in the near future. Michigan ranked twelfth among the oil-producing states in 1980, and the maintenance or bettering of this position depends on exploration and production developments within and outside the state, the price of oil per barrel, national and international production trends, the suc-

cessful development of deep-oil potential, and technological improvements.

Coal

Coal from the Pennsylvanian age lies under a large part (11,600 sq mi [30,044 sq km]) of the central part of the Lower Peninsula (Figure 6.5). It lies near the surface in Ingham and Jackson Counties, and the thin overburden of glacial drift means that it can be mined by open pit methods. In the center of the coal-bearing area, coal is found at depths of about 800 ft (244 m) in Midland County. The seams vary in thickness, but the major coal-producing strata are 3 ft (approximately 1 m) thick. The largest deposits found and the most coal mined in the past were in counties of the Saginaw Valley. The height of production was 2 million tons (1.8 million t) in 1907, but most mining operations had stopped by 1920 except for some small-scale, open pit mining near Williamston just east of Lansing, which ended in 1952. The major problems are

Depth to possible
coal-bearing rocks

Over 500'

Under 500'

FIGURE 6.5. Potential coal resources. (Source: U.S. Department of the Interior, *Coal Resources of Michigan*, Circular 77 [Washington, D.C., June 1950].)

the low quality of the coal, including a weak structure that makes the coal break down into powder when transported; thin seams; a limited extent of productive seams; and large amounts of glacial drift, which handicaps the utilization of open pit methods. It is estimated that the coal reserves of Michigan total 220 million tons (199.5 million t), of which half could be mined with the present technology.

NONFUEL MINERALS

Michigan ranks first in the United States in the production of calcium chloride (salt) and gypsum, ranks fourth in cement and sand and gravel, and is a large producer of crushed stone for a variety of purposes. These minerals are found in the sedimentary rocks of the Michigan Basin or in the extensive glacial deposits. Salt is obtained from a bed of rock salt (the Salina Formation) over 1,100 ft (335 m) below the

surface in Detroit and from natural and artificial brines of dissolved salt that are pumped to the surface in Midland, Manistee, Muskegon, Wayne, and St. Clair Counties. The salt layers were laid down as evaporite deposits in the seas of the middle Paleozoic era—in the Mississippian, Devonian, and Silurian periods. Gypsum is another such evaporite deposit, and it is produced commercially from open pit quarries near Tawas City and Alabaster in Iosco County and from underground mines near Grand Rapids. The salt and related evaporite deposits form much of the basis of the Dow Chemical Company in Midland and of other chemical companies in and around Detroit and Muskegon. Michigan has seven active cement plants, five of which use raw material from nearby limestone quarries.

Michigan is fortunate in having an abundance of sand and gravel well distributed throughout the state. Sand and gravel are

Gypsum production facilities at Alabaster.

obtained from eskers, kames, moraines, deltaic deposits, outwash plains, and old lake beds and shorelines—all Pleistocene Ice Age deposits that have concentrated these materials in commercial quantities. Huge amounts have been used in the construction industries of the cities and in the state's extensive highway building program. Thus, as one would expect, the leading counties in the production of sand and gravel are those with a large city in or very near the county because these bulky commodities normally cannot economically stand the costs of long-distance transportation. The leading sand and gravel counties in 1979 were Oakland, Wayne, Macomb, and Livingston (Detroit and its suburbs); Kent, Allegan, and Ottawa (within or near Grand Rapids); Washtenaw (Ann Arbor); and Clinton (near Lansing)—all with over 1 billion

Cement factory, Manistee.

short tons (0.9 billion t) of sand and gravel sold. Sand and gravel contributed over $100 million ($116,597,000) to the economy of Michigan in 1979.

Most of the industrial sand (molding, core, and glass sand) is obtained from fifteen deposits mined by eleven companies from the sand dunes along the east shore of Lake Michigan, dunes that have been formed by glacial, wave, and wind action. All of the sand dune operations except one (Mackinac County) are in the Lower Peninsula, from Mason County to the Indiana border. These operations are now monitored under the Sand Dune Protection and Management Act, and of the seventeen permits sought as of July 1983, thirteen have been approved, one has been denied, one is in litigation, and two are pending. This legislation is intended to protect the environmental value of the dunes from uncontrolled sand mining. In 1976, 5,461,398 short tons (4,953,488 t) of sand were sold at a value of $20,198,262—including, however, sand from inland deposits and industrial sand from the Sylvania sandstone deposit found in Wayne County.

Looking at the mineral industry of the state as a whole, the petroleum, natural gas, and iron-ore sectors dominate in terms of total value of production. These industries are followed by the cement, natural saline, and sand and gravel segments. The leading mineral-producing counties are Marquette (iron ore), Manistee (oil and gas), Grand Traverse (oil and gas), Wayne (salt, industrial and glass sand, and sand and gravel), Otsego (oil and gas), Alpena (cement and limestone), Mason (salt, lime, and sand and gravel), Dickinson (iron ore), and Kalkaska (oil and gas). Sand and gravel are widespread resources that give almost every county some mineral production, and the future success of the deep oil and gas finds may considerably alter the leading mineral areas in terms of value. The diversity of Michigan's geology has resulted in marked contrasts among the type, value, and distributional patterns of the minerals produced and has helped considerably in the diversification of the economy of the state. The potential for some increases in the liquid fossil fuel production looks bright in the near term, and the potential for most of the other metallic and nonmetallic minerals appears stable.

NOTES

1. The average weight of a barrel of oil is 310 pounds, which means 7.1 barrels equals 1 metric ton (A. I. Levorsen, *Geology of Petroleum*, 2d. ed. [San Francisco, W. H. Freeman and Company, 1954], p. 175).

PATTERNS OF
HUMAN ACTIVITY

Michigan's human activities are based on the diverse natural resources found within the state as well as on the large amounts of raw materials and fabricated goods that are imported. Agriculture, forestry, fishing, and mining are important primary-type activities. Most of the people of the state are employed, however, in the secondary and tertiary sectors of industry that are heavily related to motor vehicle manufacturing. Service and professional activities have been growing rapidly, and it has been suggested that Michigan is entering a postindustrial period in which the economy will be less industrial based and more service oriented in terms of sources of personal income and employment. The growing recreation and tourism activities are good examples of service-related employment.

Michigan's economy is greatly affected by recession and boom cycles because of the state's heavy dependence upon the automotive and related parts industries. The state is very influential in automobile manufacturing as the headquarters of the four major automotive companies are found in the Detroit area and many automotive assembly and parts companies are located in Michigan. This overdependence upon one industry and the likelihood that it will not again reach its past levels of production and employment are major problems facing the future economy of the state.

The next three chapters analyze the historical evolution of economic activity in Michigan and the major bases and character of the current activity. Emphasis is upon the three major economic pillars—manufacturing, agriculture, and recreation and tourism.

CHAPTER 7

ECONOMIC DEVELOPMENT

Laurie K. Sommers

An understanding of Michigan's past economic development is an important framework for looking at the current nature of the state's economy. The years of pioneer settlement, the timber and mineral exploitation, and the advent of the automobile all helped create the base for the present economy. Four key industries have played major roles in Michigan's history and economic development—agriculture, lumbering, mining, and automobile manufacturing. By looking first at this historical backdrop, we can better comprehend the complexities and challenges of the present.

AGRICULTURE— A RURAL REVOLUTION

Agriculture has always played an important role in the economy of Michigan, but the nature of its role has changed greatly since the early period of pioneer settlement. The state's indigenous peoples—its first true farmers—supported themselves through a combination of hunting and gathering and simple agricultural techniques. Their modest plots produced corn, beans, peas, squash, and pumpkins. However, the Indians used only a portion of their holdings for crops and so caused few lasting changes in the countryside.

Thus, the French explorers in the seventeenth century found the land virtually untouched. French farming, too, was limited in scale, because from the beginning, the crown's New World interests centered more on the lucrative lumber and fur trades than on agriculture. One notable exception was in the cultivation of fruit trees, especially pear and apple, and the French developed three new apple varieties in and around Detroit.

As the fur trade declined and trapping operations moved westward, farming grew more important. Its early development, however, was deterred by a number of factors: The continuing presence of hostile fur traders, the prospect of British rule, and a series of unfavorable land survey reports kept many prospective farmers from coming into the territory. For example, the 1816 Tiffin survey described Michigan as a land of unhealthful swamps and a sandy waste that was wholly unsuitable for agriculture. Such misleading reports were widely circulated and did little to encourage the sale of land.

In the following decade, however, several key events opened the door for pioneer settlement. The 1825 completion of the Erie Canal opened a new and easy route to the territory via the Great Lakes and Detroit, and by 1833, federal Indian policies had removed most Native Americans to the west of the Mississippi, which paved the way for government land surveys and,

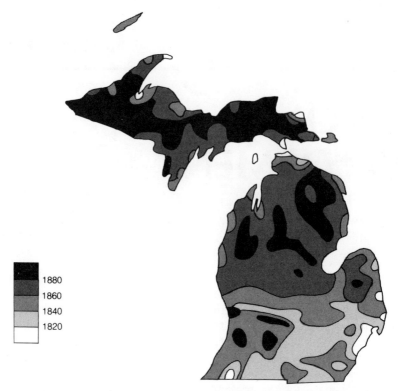

FIGURE 7.1. Progression of settlements. (Source: Adapted from Lawrence M. Sommers, ed., *Atlas of Michigan* [East Lansing: Michigan State University Press, 1977], p. 113.)

thus, for increased agricultural settlement. It was these government surveys that divided the land into sections and townships, designations that are still applied, and greatly influenced the size and location of early farms.

The southern third of the state was settled first (Figure 7.1). It was the first portion surveyed and included some of the best farmland in the state. In addition, the Chicago Road, the Monroe Pike, and other transportation arteries provided easy access from principal entry points such as Detroit. A majority of the early pioneers were New Englanders who brought with them Puritan ethics and staunch antislavery sentiments that caused the state to be filled with "underground railroad" stations during the Civil War. These settlers found that the small prairies and oak openings of southern Michigan were well adapted for wheat, and

wheat and wool eventually became the state's principal cash agricultural products. People arrived in such numbers that between 1820 and 1834, the population increased tenfold. By the time Michigan was about to become a state, Michigan Territory had become the most popular destination of people moving west.

The Upper Peninsula's more limited agricultural potential was not tapped until the mid-1800s. As that area's fledgling lumbering and mining industries drew more and more people to the region, agriculture was introduced to provide food for the new arrivals. It was found that many crops, particularly hay and potatoes, did well in the rigorous northern climate.

During the late 1800s, European immigrants began pouring into Michigan, mixing their cultural traditions with those of the state's previous settlers. Although

Early homesteading log cabin in Ingham County. (Courtesy Michigan State Archives)

most immigrants were subsistence farmers, some were highly skilled; and the efforts of these people helped to diversify the crop base of the state. Of the many ethnic groups that populated and farmed Michigan, only a few will be mentioned here (Figure 7.2). The Germans settled predominantly in southeastern Michigan and in Saginaw and Berrien Counties, areas that proved to have excellent farmland and even today are top agricultural producers. Besides farming skills, the Germans also introduced the Prussian system of education, which became the model for Michigan's educational program. The Danes were another group of skilled farmers, and they specialized in growing potatoes in the area northeast of Muskegon. The Dutch arrived in 1846 and introduced the raising of celery; even today, the area around Grand Rapids remains a Dutch stronghold, and celery and other truck crops are still grown there. Some groups, such as the Finns, were brought to Michigan in the 1870s to work in mines of the Upper Peninsula; their real interest,

however, lay in farming, and settling on the eastern edge of the mining district, they worked long and hard to raise money to buy farms.

Agriculture continued to be the principal source of livelihood for Michigan residents throughout the 1800s, but by the turn of the century, the Industrial Revolution was transforming agriculture from a small, self-sufficient family art to a large, mechanized, scientific industry. The tractor, the telephone, and the automobile revolutionized cultivation, communication, and transportation, and rural isolation was broken. Although farm conditions improved, people left the farms in droves and resettled in the cities. Rural depopulation became so severe during the 1920s that many farmers and growers had to import migrant labor.

The transformations in the life of the farmer brought changes in crop production as well. Before 1900, the state was the nation's largest producer of winter wheat, but an increase in the amount of wheat grown in states farther west and compe-

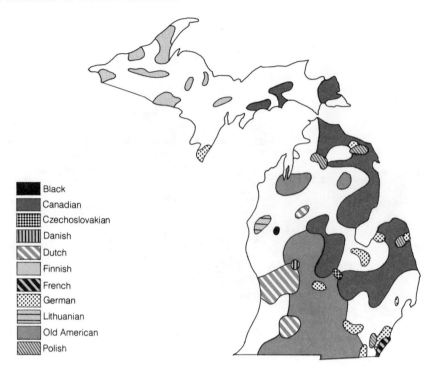

Black
Canadian
Czechoslovakian
Danish
Dutch
Finnish
French
German
Lithuanian
Old American
Polish

FIGURE 7.2. Rural ethnic stocks. (Source: Adapted from Lawrence M. Sommers, ed., *Atlas of Michigan* [East Lansing: Michigan State University Press, 1977], p. 78.)

tition from the prairie provinces of Canada caused Michigan to drop in rank. The state's wool production, once of primary importance, now ranks twenty-third in the country. Michigan now leads the nation in the production of cherries and navy beans, and other major agricultural products in the state include dairy products, grains, and livestock.

The key to Michigan's agriculture in the twentieth century has been specialization that utilizes the state's great diversity of soil, topography, and climate. Potatoes in selected sandy soils of the north, navy beans in the Saginaw Valley, sugar beets in the thumb area, fruit along the Lake Michigan shore, peppermint and spearmint in the midlands, soybeans in the Monroe area, and vegetables in the muck soils of the south have supplemented much of the general agriculture of an earlier era. Because of increased specialization, however, farmers are now less self-sufficient, and scientific techniques have resulted in fewer and larger

farms, bigger yields, and a greater use of fertilizer and mechanization. Michigan State University, a pioneer land-grant college in the country, supports outreach and research programs to develop better farm practices and improve crop varieties.

Thus, although agriculture is still a leading industry in Michigan, its role is relatively less important than in the past. The following statistics indicate the scope of the change. In 1860, 85 percent of the population depended upon agriculture for its livelihood; in 1960, only 26.6 percent of the people lived in the country, and even fewer actually supported themselves through farming. Rural Michigan has indeed been revolutionized.

LUMBERING— REIGN OF THE WHITE PINE

The introduction of the sawmill into Michigan marked the beginning of the state's transformation from an agricultural to an industrial economy. The pioneer settlers of the 1820s found a land covered by dense stands of virgin timber; scarcely fifty years later, Michigan was the leading lumber producer in the nation. The clear-cutting was so extensive that by 1910, the once-abundant forests had almost completely vanished. Yet for the brief time that lumber was king, Michigan prospered and grew.

Timber was utilized early in Michigan's history. The hardwoods, although found throughout the state, were most prevalent in the Lower Peninsula; the softwoods, chiefly pine, were found in the northern Lower Peninsula and in the Upper Peninsula. The British and French built ships, forts, and other structures from local hardwoods, and each town had a sawmill to take care of its own needs. Commercial lumbering did not begin in earnest until the 1830s, however, when the rich pine forests of the Saginaw Valley became the backbone of the emerging industry.

Initial cutting satisfied local demand, but subsequent changes in communication, urbanization, and transportation—particularly shipping on the Great Lakes—soon caused rapid growth and expansion of markets in the Midwest. Throughout the 1840s, the market shifted east to such places as Albany and west to Chicago and the prairie states, until most of the settled United States was receiving lumber from Michigan. While the Saginaw region prospered in the eastern Lower Peninsula, the founding of Muskegon in 1837 marked the west coast's entrance into the lumber business. At one time, the Muskegon River floated more pine logs than any other stream in the world.

The early lumbering centers were mainly situated at the mouths of rivers, which made harvesting the nearby timber a relatively easy and efficient task. Communities such as Muskegon (1837), Traverse City (1850), and Menominee (1865) owe their existence to the logging boom. As the coastal supplies were depleted, cutting operations moved upstream and inland, and interior mill towns like Cadillac, Roscommon, and Grayling were founded.

Early lumbering scene. (Courtesy Information Services, Michigan State University)

By 1860, lumbering was second only to agriculture as the state's principal means of livelihood, and the industry created new towns, new railroads, new jobs, and new profits. The excellent reputation of Michigan pine initially attracted thousands of lumbermen from the cutover forests of Maine and elsewhere in the East, but later, Scandinavians, French Canadians, and Irishmen all flocked to Michigan with dreams of wealth and riches. Unfortunately, of the countless numbers who tried, few people really made their fortunes from

Beginning of a log drive. (Courtesy Michigan State Archives)

The harvesting of pine during the heyday of lumbering. (Courtesy Michigan State Archives)

Michigan timber, and those few were often eastern lumber barons whose interests lay more in personal gain than in public economic development. Huge and elaborate mansions in fashionable towns such as Petoskey and Cheboygan stand as testaments

to the opulence of the timber boom, but staggering profits were the exception, not the rule. Most of the small operators struggled to survive recessions, panics, and a devastating Civil War; bankruptcies were common. Lumber workers, too, suffered disillusionment. Unhappy with their pay, they made unsuccessful attempts to strike and to unionize. With no alternative employment options available, these attempts were doomed to failure.

From 1870 to 1890, Michigan was the nation's leading timber producer, and its sawmills were among the most efficient in the world (Figure 7.3). Logging had become a large-scale industry that utilized the latest technologies like steam-powered sawmills and circular saws. The spread of the railroad, accelerated by the development of narrow-gauge moveable track, made the more remote forest areas accessible. Production peaked in 1888 at 4,292,000,000 board feet (1 board foot is a length of lumber 12 inches [30.048 cm] long, 12 inches wide, and 1 inch [2.54 cm] thick).

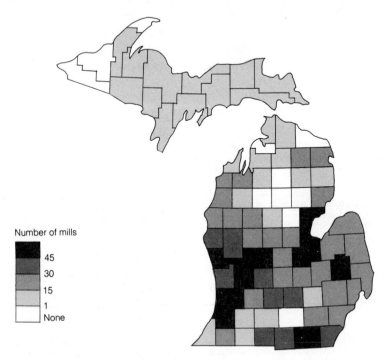

Number of mills
- 45
- 30
- 15
- 1
- None

FIGURE 7.3. Distribution of sawmills, by county, 1880. (Source: Adapted from Lawrence M. Sommers, ed., *Atlas of Michigan* [East Lansing: Michigan State University Press, 1977], p. 124.)

Narrow-gauge railway utilized during the lumbering era. (Courtesy Michigan State Archives)

Economic prosperity, however, was breeding ecological disaster. Timber waste, forest fires, and a total lack of interest in conservation practices all contributed to the devastation. A great fire in 1871, for example, damaged the entire Lake Michigan shoreline, destroyed the cities of Holland and Manistee, and spread across to Port Huron. By 1900, the lands of the northern Lower Peninsula and the eastern Upper Peninsula were stripped of pine, and scores of lumber towns were dying. Today, ghost towns such as Singapore, at the mouth of the Kalamazoo River, are silent reminders of the bygone era.

The railroads saddled with miles of different widths or gauges of track, found themselves with neither product nor market. In desperation, owners tried to lure settlers north again by promoting agriculture and tourism. Rail companies financed huge resort hotels, including the famed Grand Hotel on Mackinac Island just east of St. Ignace, in the hope of reviving their profits through the tourist trade. Despite these attempts, mergers and bankruptcies proved inevitable, and the railroads never fully recouped their losses.

However, the twentieth century brought new life to the lumber industry. Reforestation began in the 1920s, initiating the slow process of rejuvenation. Trees planted in 1920 were sawtimber size in 1966, and

Wind erosion in a cutover area in Clare County. (Courtesy Michigan State Archives)

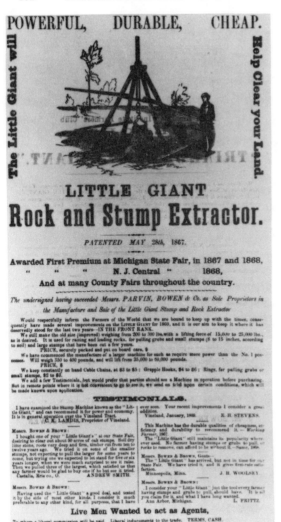

Advertisement for a rock and stump extractor that was used extensively in clearing land for agriculture after lumbering operations were completed. (Courtesy Michigan State Archives)

Michigan once again took the lead in timber production in the Great Lakes area. Today, the forest industry is partially recovered, but its focus has changed considerably as the center of the state's economy has shifted elsewhere. Michigan is currently a leading world supplier of bird's-eye maple and Christmas trees. The Grand Rapids furniture industry, begun in 1836, survived by importing hardwoods when native species grew more scarce, and the city is still a major furniture center. But of the once vast expanse of white pine, only a few trees remain; those preserved in Hartwick Pines State Park serve as reminders of the boom years a century past.

MINING—TREASURE CHEST OF THE NORTH

As reports of mineral riches flowed back from the Upper Peninsula during the 1840s, people who had taken a dim view of the 1837 exchange of that area for the area around Toledo that had been contested with Ohio began to have second thoughts. From 1860 to World War I, copper and iron mining brought millions of dollars to the state, and the rich mineral deposits were the chief motivation for the settlement of the Upper Peninsula.

Copper

Michigan's copper deposits were remarkable for their quality and purity. Bands of native copper were contained in outcrops 2 to 8 mi (3.2 to 12.9 km) wide and of varying depth. The surface deposits first attracted the notice of Native Americans who dug out the easily accessible chunks and fashioned copper tools and adornments from them. The British and French saw the indigenous pieces but did little to exploit the resource. The first copper mine opened in 1771, and its owner, Alexander Henry, sent the massive Ontonagon Boulder—of pure copper—to Detroit as evidence of the region's richness. But speculative activity did not begin in earnest until 1841, hastened by the favorable reports of the first state geologist, Douglas Houghton. These reports, combined with publicity given the Ontonagon Boulder, sparked the first mineral rush in the nation, predating by several years the more famous California gold rush. Between 1843 and 1846, thousands of prospectors arrived from the East with the hope of "striking it rich."

From 1847 to 1887, Michigan was the nation's largest producer of copper, and as copper production grew, the population of the Upper Peninsula, particularly the Keweenaw Peninsula, grew with it. The towns of Houghton, Hecla, and Calumet, among others, were all copper towns peopled by workers employed in the mines. The Cornish, in particular, left Cornwall in droves during the 1840s and brought their ethnic traditions and deep-mining techniques to the mines on the Keweenaw Peninsula.

By 1860, three major copper-producing regions had been developed, all on the Keweenaw, all utilizing shaft mines, and almost all financed by Boston capitalists. Of these areas, only the Portage Lake area near Houghton was still active by the 1880s. It was here that the world-famous Calumet and Hecla mines were located; here too, the 1916 war boom sparked a production peak worth an estimated $76 million.

Rising prices and increased competition forced the smaller companies to close or to consolidate, but by 1936, even the two remaining giants, Calumet and Hecla Consolidated and the Copper Range Company, could no longer compete with the newer and cheaper western copper. The economic success of Michigan mines had been based on an inexpensive extraction of high-grade ores. As sources were depleted and quality ore became harder and harder to obtain, these copper mines lost their national prominence. Today, some copper is mined on a

Deserted eight-gable mine operations building of the Quincy Copper Mine near Hancock on the Keweenaw Peninsula. (Courtesy Michigan State Archives)

limited scale, and there is talk of reopening some mines if it becomes profitable to extract low-grade ore.

Iron

In 1844, William Hurt, an associate of Douglas Houghton, noticed a strange movement of his compass needle while surveying near where the present town of Ishpeming is located. His observation led to the important discovery of iron in the area. About the same time, iron was also discovered by another Michiganian, Philo Everett, founder of Michigan's first mining operation, the Jackson Mining Company. Everett's company, like most Michigan mining concerns, was controlled and financed by wealthy eastern bankers.

Before the Civil War, the major iron-producing region was the Marquette Range, but the postwar discovery of iron in the Menominee and Gogebic ranges greatly expanded Michigan's production capacity. With the 1855 completion of the Soo Locks, the early lakeside mines were able to easily transport the bulky ore to smelting sites and markets, but as operations moved inland, the need for reliable, efficient, internal improvements became apparent. Railroads seemed to provide the solution. Construction began in the late 1850s, and the first interpeninsular line was completed in 1881.

Throughout the early phase of production, the ore was smelted on the mine site, using charcoal from local hardwoods, and then shipped via the Great Lakes. The needs of the smelting operation, combined with the activity of the lumbermen, succeeded in stripping the Upper Peninsula of most of its timber. It was perhaps fortunate, then, that during the 1870s, the center of the iron and steel industry moved to the markets, smelters, and coalfields of the Ohio Valley. Shipping patterns changed, and local smelting plants closed down, but Michigan's iron ore still remained a significant component of the growing steel industry, and iron shipped from port cities such as Marquette and Escanaba was still the major cargo of Great Lakes freighters.

Underground iron crew and equipment, Barnes-Hecker Mine near Ishpeming, in Marquette County. (Courtesy Michigan State Archives)

Like copper mining, iron mining brought many ethnic peoples to the Upper Peninsula, among them Irish, Welsh, Cornish, Italians, Swedes, Danes, Norwegians, Finns, and French Canadians. So many immigrants flocked to the region that the mining counties had the largest foreign population in the Upper Peninsula in the late 1800s: 12,000 in Houghton County, 10,000 in Marquette County, and 8,000 in Gogebic County.

With the eclipse of mining interests in Michigan at the turn of the century, the wealthy financiers moved west to the iron fields of Minnesota, but the immigrants stayed on in the peninsular society largely created by their presence. Thus, iron towns like Negaunee, Ishpeming, Marquette, and Escanaba continued to exist despite the number of dying towns and rusting blast furnaces (Figure 7.4).

Yet even though national dominance has been lost, iron extraction still provides regional employment in portions of the Upper Peninsula, and ghost towns, abandoned mines, and increased competition notwithstanding, Michigan's iron ore is still important to the state and the nation. And as with copper, the industry's importance could grow significantly if it becomes more profitable to mine low-grade ore.

Remnants of a boom town in Delta County—now part of Fayette State Park. Fayette was an iron-ore-smelting town in the 1860s; also a company town. (Courtesy Michigan Travel Bureau)

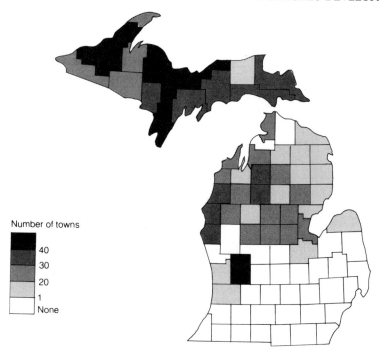

Number of towns

40
30
20
1
None

FIGURE 7.4. Distribution of boom towns, by county. (Source: Adapted from Lawrence M. Sommers, ed., *Atlas of Michigan* [East Lansing: Michigan State University Press, 1977], p. 125.)

Open pit mining in a Wakefield iron-ore body; electric shovel in foreground, steam shovel in background, October 26, 1934. (Courtesy Michigan State Archives)

AUTO MANUFACTURING— WHEELS OF THE WORLD

Although nineteenth-century lumbering and mining activities somewhat altered the state's rural character, the automobile in the twentieth century was the chief catalyst in the transformation of Michigan from an agricultural to an industrial economy. The importance of car making is due in large part to Detroit's early emergence as the nation's automobile capital. The city had long been the site of a wagon-and-buggy industry, and this heritage, combined with an advantageous location in relation to key raw materials, set the stage for Detroit's automobile production.

In the late 1890s, Ransom E. Olds organized Michigan's first operating automobile company, the Olds Motor Vehicle Company, and Olds proved to be a shrewd assessor of popular taste. The sluggish market for high-priced cars prompted him to

J. Allen Gray carriage and light wagon company in Detroit in the 1890s. Many of these companies provided skills and technology for the auto industry that followed. (Courtesy Michigan State Archives)

design the first relatively cheap car, "the merry Oldsmobile," and by 1904, gasoline-powered vehicles like the Oldsmobile had surpassed steam-and electric-powered competitors and had become the most dependable and fashionable method of conveyance on the market. With this rise in status came an increased demand for heavier, higher-priced models. Olds's desire to enter this newer market led him to reverse his earlier inclination toward manufacturing more moderately priced cars, and in 1904, he reorganized his enterprise as the Reo Motor Car Company, moved to Lansing, and created a heavier, more expensive touring car.

Twelve years after the introduction of the first Oldsmobile, the major companies of Packard, Cadillac, and Buick, as well as hundreds of smaller establishments, like Oldsmobile, were struggling to compete for a select, affluent clientele. The average price per car was $2,000, well above most family budgets, but then Henry Ford introduced the Model T, a move that catapulted his company into prominence. The Model T was designed for utility rather than beauty and with the hope of providing a product that would be within the reach of the common man's pocketbook. The strategy paid off. For nine years, the Model T was the nation's most popular car, and despite a price as low as $360 in 1916, it proved a tremendously lucrative venture. Ford undercut his competitors by standardizing parts and using assembly-line techniques to produce a vehicle that was durable, cheap, and easily repaired. During the car's inaugural year of 1908, Ford Motor Company sold 10,000 Model Ts.

Henry Ford's career was a curious mixture of innovation and intransigence. In 1914, when the usual daily wage averaged from two to three dollars, he introduced the five-dollar day, thereby drawing thousands of workers to Detroit. Yet his refusal to accept yearly model changes and installment payments permanently cost him part of the market. When sales dropped to a crisis level in 1926, Ford finally introduced a new model, the Model A. This car proved successful as well, but Ford never regained his earlier dominance in the industry.

The Ford Motor Company's influence extended far beyond Detroit and its environs. From the 1920s to the 1950s, the company was the largest private employer in the Upper Peninsula because the company had devised a master plan to control all phases of auto production. Logging camps, hydroelectric dams, chemical and auto plants, iron mines, airports, hotels, and company towns were all built and controlled by Ford. Today, this Upper Peninsula empire has mostly vanished, the victim of distance and changing management, but in his time, Ford's impact on that area's economy was considerable.

With his personal control, integrated operation, and low-priced product, Ford retained and expanded his holdings throughout the teens and twenties, a period in which many companies specializing in medium-to-high-priced cars were absorbed through mergers. The merger king was William C. Durant, founder of General Motors. Beginning with the purchase of Buick in 1905, he gradually constructed a vast corporation of auto, truck, parts, and body factories that included Chevrolet, Cadillac, Pontiac, Oakland, Oldsmobile, Buick, and Fisher Body. Although Durant engineered the original mergers, his direction eventually resulted in severe financial difficulties. He resigned in 1921, later to go bankrupt, and General Motors was reorganized into a stable corporate structure.

As the size and profits of individual auto companies grew, so too grew the entire industry. Grand Rapids, Flint, Lansing, Pontiac, Kalamazoo, and Grand Haven all had auto plants, but Detroit was still the hub of the industry, producing over half the world's cars. The lure of employment and Henry Ford's five-dollar day drew thousands of unskilled workers from Michigan, the rest of the United States, and the world.

Model A Ford assembly line, Detroit, 1928. (Courtesy Michigan State Archives)

Ford's profit-sharing plan and the resultant raise in minimum wages were major steps forward in the auto industry in 1914. (Courtesy Michigan State Archives)

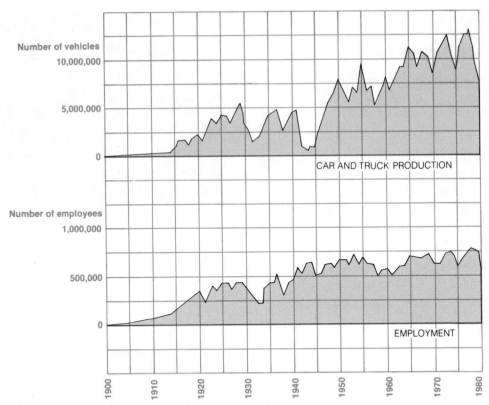

FIGURE 7.5. Car and truck production and employment in the United States, 1900–1980. (Sources: Adapted from Lawrence M. Sommers, ed., *Atlas of Michigan* [East Lansing: Michigan State University Press, 1977], p. 163, and *World Motor Vehicle Data* [Detroit, 1981].)

Rural blacks migrated north to Flint and Detroit after World War I, along with immigrants including Syrians, employed by Olds in Lansing; Poles, who settled in Hamtramck and worked mainly for Dodge; and Russians, Austrians, Czechs, and Lithuanians.

The first big boom was in the 1920s (Figure 7.5). Auto sales climbed steadily, and associated industries—such as road building, bus systems, petroleum and rubber manufacture, and tourism—flourished as well. Detroit exhibited all the characteristics of a boom town—pollution, sprawl, and rapid growth. A 1920 letter aptly described the city: "Its single characteristic is the smell of gasoline. Imagine this: A cluster of new skyscrapers thrusting gawkily

up out of a welter of nondescript old buildings."[1]

The twenties also witnessed the emergence of the Big Three Automakers: Ford, a vast single company; the reorganized General Motors Corporation; and Walter P. Chrysler's Company, founded in 1925. Through recessions, strikes, times of peace, and times of war, the three companies have continued to exercise tremendous influence over Michigan's economy. One of the most critical periods was the Great Depression of the 1930s; production in 1932 was less than half that of the 1929 peak, but it then gained steadily again throughout the remainder of the decade.

Although sheer size enabled the Big Three to survive the financial crunch, that same size exacerbated the workers' growing dissatisfaction with management. Unionization, not the Depression, proved the most problematic issue of the 1930s. The formation of the United Automobile Workers (UAW), and the Congress of Industrial Organizations (CIO) as well as the famous sit-down strike at Flint Fisher Body Plant No. 1 forced most firms to accept union demands. Only Ford held out. In 1941, however, a Supreme Court order demanded that the company stop discouraging union membership, and shortly afterward, 70 percent of Ford's River Rouge plant workers voted to join the CIO.

During World War II, the auto industry ceased civilian production and turned to making articles of war. Michigan provided more military transport than any other state, supplying the nation with 30 percent of its aircraft and parts, 30 percent of its military vehicles and parts, and 13 percent of its tanks. The loss of labor because of wartime enlistment opened up jobs to many women, blacks, and rural southerners. When peacetime production resumed, the pent-up demand for civilian vehicles spurred a fifteen-year-long postwar boom, and the state's population swelled to fill the growing labor demand.

By the late 1950s, however, the boom had slowed, and despite the renewed military production resulting from Cold War tensions, Michigan's leaders began to see the dangers of a one-industry economy. Automation, lags in research, and cuts in defense contracts all damaged the industry. Detroit lost its position as the world's major auto-manufacturing center, and as other national and international production cut into sales, the need for economic diversification became obvious.

In recent years, a fluctuating market has forced the automobile industry to be more responsive to government, consumer, and environmental pressures. Pollution control, safety devices, and a concern with gas mileage and efficiency have resulted, and an influx of small foreign cars has induced a slow trend toward more compact models. Recessions, fuel crises, profit losses, and the layoffs of the 1970s profoundly affected Michigan and the nation, resounding proof that the economy of Michigan has not yet been sufficiently diversified.

The automobile has shaped the way of life of the state and the nation. In Michigan, the industry turned a primarily agricultural region into an industrial one, breaking down rural isolation and linking markets. It gave jobs to immigrants and prompted a population shift from farms to cities. The high wages paid to auto workers have kept industries that rely heavily upon cheap labor from coming to Michigan, but industries that are complementary to auto production have been drawn there. Ready access to automobiles spurred the development of a massive highway system and increased tourist activity in the northern part of the state. The key to all this economic activity remains the automobile. Although the auto industry has expanded both nationally and worldwide, Michigan remains a vital component, and the economic well-being of the state and the nation still depends to a large extent on the success or failure of Michigan's auto industry.

NOTES

1. Webb Waldron, "Boom Days in Detroit," in Robert Warner and C. Warren Vanderhill, eds., *A Michigan Reader: 1865 to the Present* (Grand Rapids, Mich.: W. B. Eerdmans Publishing Co., 1974), p. 134.

CHAPTER **8**

THE ECONOMY TODAY

Michigan's current economy rests primarily on a three-pronged base of manufacturing, agriculture (including agribusiness), and recreation and tourism. The overdependence in manufacturing on the automotive industry has caused problems during recession years; the result was a 15.5 percent unemployment rate in Michigan in 1982 compared to the national average of 9.7 percent.

As the postindustrial period evolves the role of the automotive industry in employment and its proportion of value of production will decrease, and the relative importance of other kinds of manufacturing and particularly the service sector will increase. In 1982, 55 percent of the workers in Michigan were employed in basic, or the primary and secondary, industries such as manufacturing, construction, mining, agriculture, forestry, and fishing, and the other 45 percent were employed in the nonbasic, or tertiary service industries such as transportation, communication, utilities, wholesale and retail trade, and finance. The trend toward more and more dependence on service-related activities is destined to increase during the rest of this century.

MANUFACTURING

Significant changes have taken place in the nature and importance of various man-

ufacturing activities in Michigan since the early emphasis on the processing of agricultural and forest products. Since 1900, Michigan has been a major industrial state. It has had numerous advantages in the development of manufacturing: a central location on four of the Great Lakes and in the heavily populated Midwest; a variety of natural resources, including iron ore, petroleum, natural gas, forests, diverse soil types for agricultural production, and abundant water; a heterogeneous population with a wide variety of skills, which provides an excellent labor supply; managerial and professional talents of various kinds, which developed with the evolving industry and/ or were trained in the state's higher education system; efficient land, water, and air transportation facilities; and the availability of a good supply of capital for research and development of new and expanded industries as the state grew in population and the complexity of its manufacturing industries increased.

Michigan accounted for $99.3 billion of the $2,405.6 billion total U.S. income in 1981.[1] Manufacturing contributes a major share of Michigan's income, accounting for $24.6 billion, or 6.4 percent of the earnings of manufacturing establishments in the United States in 1981. The overwhelming importance of the automotive industry is indicated by the fact that motor vehicles and equipment accounted for 39.7 percent of the manufacturing earnings in Michigan in 1981 (Table 8.1). The second category

TABLE 8.1. Manufacturing in Michigan, 1976–1981 (in thousands of dollars)

Industry Group	1976[a]	1981[a]
Food & kindred products	672,696	931,795
Textile mill products	43,620	41,561
Apparel & other fabricated		
textile products	308,885	386,183
Paper & allied products	336,521	424,520
Printing, publishing, &		
allied products	391,469	576,868
Chemicals & allied products	764,086	1,083,682
Petroleum refining &		
related industries	46,250	67,557
Rubber & miscellaneous		
plastic products	314,196	570,804
Leather and leather products	35,731	50,941
Total nondurable goods	2,913,520	4,133,919
Lumber & wood products		
excl. furniture	123,558	180,484
Furniture & fixtures	251,047	460,157
Primary metal industries	1,532,076	1,888,294
Fabricated metal products	1,893,110	2,522,034
Machinery, except electrical	2,176,103	3,798,992
Electrical machinery	525,126	709,455
Transportation equipment		
excl. motor vehicles	176,431	377,934
Motor vehicles & equipment	7,305,611	9,778,613
Stone, glass, and clay	303,041	409,904
Instruments	128,489	239,944
Miscellaneous manufacturing	101,532	127,383
Total durable goods	14,516,124	20,493,194
Total manufacturing Michigan	17,429,644	24,627,113
U.S.	237,423,000	385,143,000

[a]Estimates based on 1972 Standard Industrial Classification.
Estimates have been revised to reflect the 1980 Comprehensive NIPA R
Revisions.

Source: David I. Verway, ed., Michigan Statistical Abstract, 1982–83
(Detroit: Wayne State University, 1983), p. 454.

Ford's River Rouge plant in Detroit. (Courtesy Michigan Department of Natural Resources)

of importance in manufacturing, machinery (except electrical), accounted for 15.4 percent of the manufacturing earnings. The Ford Motor Company's River Rouge plant is an example of integrated manufacturing as it encompasses all processes, from converting iron ore to basic iron and steel products to the assembly of the finished automobile. A wide variety of machines are produced, and a large number of them are utilized by the auto industry. Most of the automobile and related parts manufacturing is located in the southern third of the state.

Two other categories of manufacturing are important in Michigan, namely, chemical and allied products, 4.4 percent of the manufacturing earnings in 1981, and food and kindred products, 3.7 percent. In some parts of Michigan, specialized industries stand out such as logging and wood products processing in the northern two-thirds of the state, furniture manufacturing in Grand Rapids, and pulp and paper manufacturing in Kalamazoo County.

THE AUTOMOTIVE INDUSTRY

Michigan has been the capital of the U.S. automobile industry since its beginning. In 1982, Michigan accounted for 36 percent of the cars and 30 percent of the trucks and buses produced in the United States, and most of them were assembled in metropolitan Detroit, Flint, Lansing, Pontiac, Ypsilanti, and Kalamazoo (Figure 8.1). The assembly plants are supplied by a large number of small parts manufacturers, and these are concentrated near the assembly plants in the southeastern part of the state.

The importance of the automotive industry to Michigan is illustrated by the number of employees, amount of earnings,

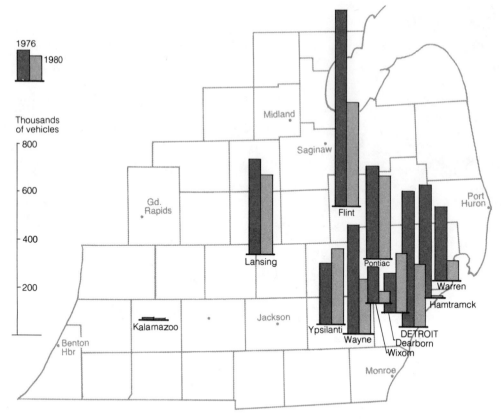

FIGURE 8.1. Production of motor vehicles, by city, 1976 and 1980. (Source: David I. Verway, ed., *Michigan Statistical Abstract* [Detroit: Wayne State University, 1981], p. 577.)

Assembly line of a Detroit automobile manufacturing plant. (Courtesy Michigan Travel Bureau)

number of local suppliers, and value of local purchases in seven cities where General Motors has plants (Table 8.2). Such concentration is a definite asset to the economy of these cities but results in severe unemployment problems in times of economic difficulty. Flint, for instance, had one of the highest national unemployment rates in the 1981–1982 recession. Of the Big Three, Ford and Chrysler have assembly plants only in Detroit and vicinity, and General Motors has plants in a number of Michigan cities. The Checker Taxi Cab Company had an assembly plant in Kalamazoo until it ceased manufacturing in 1982.

In the period of 1980–1982, there was a severe reduction in the number of automobiles produced and sold in Michigan as well as in the rest of the country. Total

TABLE 8.2. General Motors' activity in seven Michigan cities, 1981

	Employees[a]	Earnings in $000	No. of Local Suppliers	Local Purchases in $000
Bay City	2,581	$ 74,400	381[b]	$ 11,300[b]
Flint	65,738	800,000	7,548[c]	859,600[c]
Grand Rapids	143	222,000	1,200[b]	43,000[b]
Kalamazoo	2,763	103,000	300[b]	5,300[b]
Lansing	22,793	682,000	1,500[b]	202,900[b]
Saginaw	20,755	617,000	2,100[b]	146,000[b]
Three Rivers	1,840	52,000	68[b]	1,400[b]

[a]Average annual totals of monthly statistics.

[b]1980 figures.

[c]1979 figures.

Source: David I. Verway, ed., Michigan Statistical Abstract (Detroit: Wayne State University, 1981), pp. 583–585.

employment in the auto industry and employment by the parts suppliers have both been greatly affected by the down-sizing of the large cars and the rapid growth of the demand for small cars (many supplied by foreign producers, principally Japan and West Germany). Foreign auto companies accounted for 30.5 percent of all car sales in 1982, up from 14.9 percent in 1972, and it is unlikely that the U.S. auto industry will attain its former employment and income levels again. In fact, the 1980s are expected to show a 20 percent decline in auto-related jobs from the high point in the 1970s, which would mean a drop of about 250,000 jobs nationwide—a good portion of them in Michigan.

PATTERNS OF MANUFACTURING

The pattern of distribution of value added by manufacturing in Michigan shows an overwhelming concentration in the southern one-third of the state, especially in the southeast (Figure 8.2).[2] In 1977 the latest manufacturing census available, about 47 percent of the Michigan total was in the three counties of Wayne, Oakland, and Macomb, which correlates closely with the fact that 43.7 percent of the total population of the state lives in these three counties. As expected, the sparsely populated sections of the northern Lower Peninsula have small amounts of value added by manufacturing compared to the southeast. Clusters of manufacturing activity are centered around Grand Rapids, Muskegon, Holland, Kalamazoo, and Battle Creek in the western portion of southern Michigan; Lansing, Jackson, and Ann Arbor in the central portion; and Midland, Bay City, Saginaw, and Flint in the eastern portion.

MANUFACTURING ISSUES

The overdependence upon automobile and related parts manufacturing is the main issue in Michigan's manufacturing and results in severe effects during periods of recession. The unionization of the auto industry brought about high wage rates, and Michigan has some of the highest workman's compensation and unemploy-

Ford Motor Company complex, Dearborn, Michigan. The Fairlane shopping center and the University of Michigan, Dearborn, are located in the upper left. (Courtesy Michigan Department of Natural Resources)

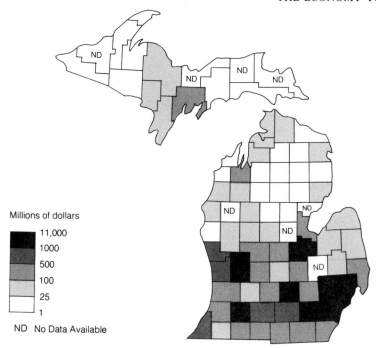

Millions of dollars

- 11,000
- 1000
- 500
- 100
- 25
- 1

ND No Data Available

FIGURE 8.2. Distribution of value added by manufacturing, by county, 1977. (Source: U.S. Bureau of the Census, *1977 Census of Manufactures, Geographic Area Series*, MC 77-A-23 [Washington, D.C., 1979], Table 2.)

ment-payment rates in the United States. These factors contribute to high production costs and as a result, some industries have left the state for the Sun Belt, where taxes and labor rates are lower and other significant incentives are provided to attract industry. The cost of producing automobiles in the United States makes it difficult to compete with foreign automakers, and the closing of some factories and the reduction of the number of employees in others have led to a migration of skilled and unskilled laborers from the state in search of employment elsewhere.

Michigan is attempting to diversify its manufacturing sector as well as to change the conditions that caused the problems, such as the level of the workman's compensation rate. There have been attempts to develop the high-technology industry in the vicinity of major universities such as Ann Arbor and East Lansing, but the head start that areas such as California, Mas-

sachusetts, and the industrial triangle of North Carolina have has made the development of any high-technology industry elsewhere difficult. Diversification is badly needed in Michigan's economy. Agriculture and recreation and tourism continue to remain strong even in difficult economic times, so the broadening of the manufacturing base is the most important challenge for Michigan's economy.

The manufacturing industry in Michigan is both labor and capital intensive. Michigan ranks fourth in the nation in the use of electricity and fossil fuels, and the following industries account for three-quarters of the commercial fuels used: automobile, basic steel, metal stamping, foundry, paper and paperboard, organic and inorganic chemicals, plastics, and cement. Of these, only the chemical industry showed a positive growth in the ten-year period from 1968 to 1978. The rising costs of energy in relation to labor will be a major deter-

minant in the future nature of manufacturing development, the direction of technological innovation, and the success of
attempts to diversify industry in Michigan.

AGRICULTURE

The relative significance of agriculture
declined steadily during the first three-
quarters of this century, but it is still a
major economic activity in most Michigan
counties. The total land in farms was
19,033,000 acres (7,708,365 ha) in 1920 and
40 percent less in 1981, 11,400,000 acres
(4,617,000 ha). There were indications in
the early 1980s that the decline in the
number of farm acres had stopped and that
slight increases were occurring. The 65,000
farms in Michigan produced crops worth
$1,987,657,000 in 1980, and the value added
by farming, and the processing, wholesal-
ing, and retailing of farm products, totals
about 10 percent of the state's gross product,
or about $2 billion per year. These activities
employ about 10 percent of the labor force
(450,000).

Approximately 40 percent of the land is
in farms, and of this amount, 80 percent
is located south of the Muskegon–Bay City
line. But it is also southern Michigan that
has been losing the greatest amount of
farmland due to the tremendous pressure
from urban sprawl. Whether this trend will
continue depends on the rate and extent
of recovery of the depressed automobile
industry, the continued net loss of population by many southern counties, a continued decrease in the rate of urban population increase, and the impact of rising
energy prices.

Michigan has a more diversified agriculture than its neighboring states. This
fact is largely related to the varied climatic
and soil conditions and some highly specialized agriculture such as the navy bean
production in the Saginaw Valley and the
intensive fruit growing near Lake Michigan.

Apple trees in blossom in the fruit belt of
southwestern Michigan near Benton Harbor.
(Courtesy Michigan Travel Bureau)

Michigan ranks first in the nation in the
production of blueberries, tart cherries,
processing cucumbers, dry beans, and navy
beans. It was in the top five in the production of nineteen other agricultural commodities in 1980 and ranked eighteenth in
the nation in terms of value of farm production.

RECENT TRENDS

An analysis of major agricultural trends
in Michigan indicates that significant
changes have been taking place since 1950.
The average size of the farm has been
steadily rising along with increasing mechanization, the loss of farm labor, and a
growing necessity for significant capital out-
lays in the average farm operation. The
average farm contained 111 acres (45 ha)
in 1950, but that figure had increased by
1978 to 158 acres (64 ha). In 1981, the
average size was 175 acres (71 ha) according
to the new definition of farms.[3] With the
changing trends in population growth, the
rising energy costs, and the questionable
overall economic development, it is difficult
to predict the future trends in farm size.

The range in farm size per county is
great (Figure 8.3). The highest averages are
in the Upper Peninsula and the northern
Lower Peninsula where the soils are gen-

Mechanical cherry harvesting near Traverse City. (Courtesy Michigan Travel Bureau)

erally poor, the growing season shorter and more unreliable, and the farms often contain large amounts of nonarable land such as forested and wetland areas. The average for many of the Upper Peninsula counties is over 200 acres (81 ha), and a high of 256 acres (104 ha) was reached in Luce County in 1978. The counties of the south-

ern half of the Lower Peninsula have the lowest averages, particularly in the highly urban counties such as Wayne (85 acres [34 ha]), Macomb (102 acres [41 ha]), Berrien (100 acres [41 ha]), and Ottawa (108 acres [44 ha]). In fact, the area south of the Muskegon–Bay City line has the largest number of farms of all sizes from a 10-acre (4 ha) plot to those over 1,000 acres (405 ha).

Of the total farmland, about 61 percent was in harvested cropland in 1978 as compared to 48 percent in 1959. The cropland acreage, however, decreased from 10 million acres (4 million ha) in 1959 to 8.4 million acres (3.4 million ha) in 1978. A marked increase in the amount of irrigated land took place, as is indicated by the fact that 226,000 acres (91,530 ha) were irrigated in 1978 compared to 97,000 acres (39,285 ha) in 1974.

There has been a general trend toward larger family farms as well as toward more

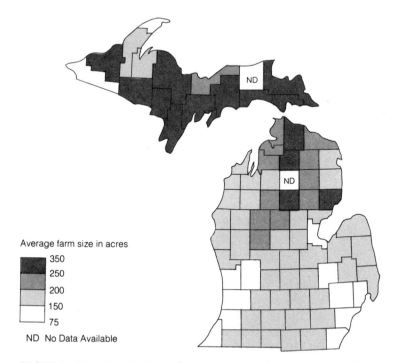

Average farm size in acres

350
250
200
150
75

ND No Data Available

FIGURE 8.3. Distribution of average farm size, by county, 1981. (Source: Karl T. Wright, "A Decade of Changes in Michigan Agriculture," Extension Service AM-31 [East Lansing: Michigan State University, 1983].)

Automated grape harvesting near Paw Paw in Van Buren County. (Courtesy Michigan Travel Bureau)

part-time, small farms;[4] the middle-sized farms have decreased rather rapidly in number. Improved mechanization, more productive varieties of crops, increased and more effective fertilization and herbicide methods, and greater marketing efficiency have facilitated more production from fewer acres on the family farm. The small and part-time farms are near cities where off-farm employment is available and there is a market for some of the farm produce. The area with the largest percentage of farmers whose principal occupation is farming is the southern half of the Lower Peninsula, and the same area also has the greatest percentage of part-time farmers. Other major trends in Michigan agriculture are (1) a marked increase in the amount of fertilizer used; (2) a rapid decrease in the number of hired farm workers, other than family members; (3) a corresponding increase in the use of machinery; (4) sharp increases in corn and soybean acreage and production; (5) a decrease in the number

of animals raised, especially dairy cattle; and (6) marked decreases in hay, wheat, and oats production.

MAJOR SOURCES OF INCOME

Of the total income from the marketing of major products in 1980, 58 percent was derived from crops and 42 percent from livestock and livestock products. Corn, fruits, soybeans, vegetables, dry beans, and wheat—in that order—were the principal contributors to crop value, and dairy products, cattle and calves, hogs, and eggs were the main producers in the livestock and products category. The counties in the southern half of the Lower Peninsula contribute the largest shares to the value of agricultural products sold (Figure 8.4). Huron is the leading county in terms of value of products sold followed by Allegan, Lenawee, Tuscola, and Sanilac. These are all specialized agricultural counties—soybeans and dry beans in the Saginaw Valley and

Dairy farm showing feed storage facilities and Holstein Frisian cattle. (Courtesy Michigan Travel Bureau)

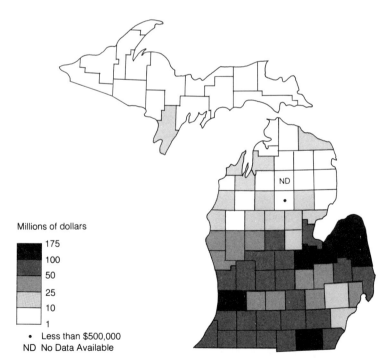

Millions of dollars

175
100
50
25
10
1
• Less than $500,000
ND No Data Available

FIGURE 8.4. Cash receipts from agricultural marketing, by county, 1979. (Source: David I. Verway, ed., *Michigan Statistical Abstract* [Detroit: Wayne State University, 1981], p. 441.)

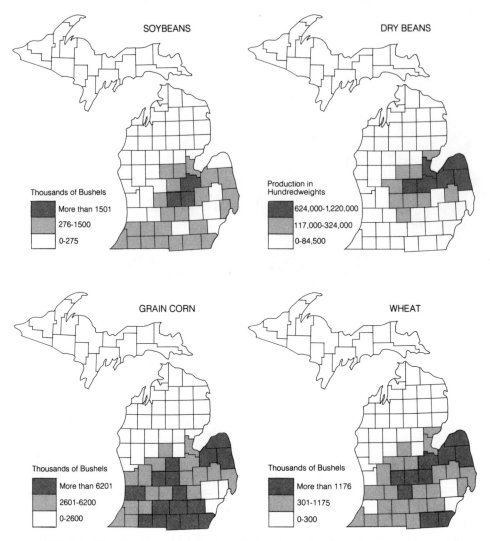

FIGURE 8.5. Distribution of selected agricultural production. (Source: Adapted from Michigan Department of Agriculture, *Michigan Agriculture Statistics 1981* [Lansing, 1981], pp. 23, 24, 25, 35, 51, 55.)

Grain and bean storage in Gratiot County near Breckenridge.

fruit and chickens in southwestern Michigan (Figure 8.5). The southern Lower Peninsula has some of the best soils, topography, and climate for agriculture in the state, a large nearby urban market, and good transportation—both to local markets and to the markets of neighboring states and foreign countries.

MAJOR AGRICULTURAL REGIONS

The regional patterns of Michigan's agriculture are not as consistent as those in

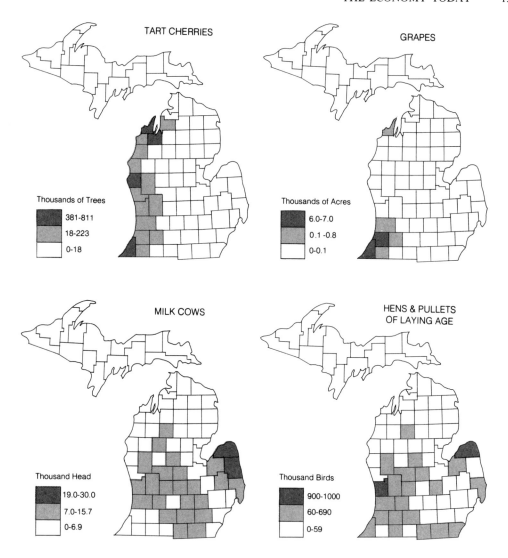

TART CHERRIES

Thousands of Trees

- 381-811
- 18-223
- 0-18

GRAPES

Thousands of Acres

- 6.0-7.0
- 0.1 -0.8
- 0-0.1

MILK COWS

Thousand Head

- 19.0-30.0
- 7.0-15.7
- 0-6.9

HENS & PULLETS
OF LAYING AGE

Thousand Birds

- 900-1000
- 60-690
- 0-59

the midwestern, corn-belt, prairie states, primarily because of more heterogeneous soils, topography (slope), drainage, and climatic characteristics and the state's location on the leeward side of Lake Michigan and, to some extent, Lake Superior. The state divides into two general regions, namely, (1) the southern half of the Lower Peninsula, which has the most farms, the largest amount of land in crops, the highest yields per acre, and the greatest volume and value of crops, animals, and animal products, and (2) the remainder of the state which has poorer agricultural conditions and much less volume and value of farm production.

In terms of emphasis in production, the following generalized regions can be identified on the basis of major farm products sold: (1) dairying in the southern and central parts of the Lower Peninsula and scattered throughout the rest of the state; (2) beans, soy and dry, in the Saginaw Valley and cash grain, mostly corn and wheat, in many of the central and southern counties of the southern Lower Peninsula; (3) the fruit-growing counties along Lake Michigan in the Lower Peninsula; and (4) nurseries and greenhouses in the three metropolitan Detroit counties—Wayne, Oakland, and Macomb. Small areas of specialization also occur, such as hogs and pigs in Cass County, poultry and poultry products in Ottawa, and field seeds in Roscommon.

PROBLEMS AND
FUTURE POTENTIAL

The great variety of farm production is an important characteristic of Michigan's agriculture, and as energy costs and the total costs of production continue to increase, this diversity should be an advantage. It is likely that the length of the food chain will have to be reduced in the coming decades, along with greater food self-sufficiency in smaller areas or regions, and the balance between animal and crop production in Michigan is important in reaching that objective. Also, having a large urban market near the major agricultural districts tends to ease the marketing process as well as to reduce the transportation costs. Complete self-sufficiency is unlikely, and is not recommended by agricultural experts, but there are many opportunities to increase the local production of needed food. Michigan has more marginal land than most nearby states, and this land could be devoted to agriculture and forests to fulfill more of the local basic energy, housing, and food needs.

Still, there are a number of continuing problems in the future growth of Michigan's agriculture. Much of the state is characterized by a climate that provides a short growing season and a minimum number of hours of sunlight for plant growth. There are large areas of wetlands, sandy soils, and hilly topography, which make profitable crop agriculture difficult, and large areas of the best farmland have been taken up by the growing urban areas. The cash grain emphasis means that less manure or organic material is being returned to the soil. Large numbers of part-time farmers are located in the urban south, and they occupy a large number of acres but have only limited agricultural production. Much vacant or idle land, held largely for price speculation, is located near many of the urban areas,

especially in the Lower Peninsula. Added to these problems is the PBB contamination that resulted from the accidental mixing of a fire retardant in animal feed that was distributed in the early 1970s. This contamination is now widely found in both animals and humans, and studies are still being conducted on the nature and significance of its current and long-term effects.

Thus, Michigan has advantages and disadvantages for additional agricultural development. There seems little doubt, however, that agriculture will continue to be one of the major bases of future economic development in the state.

TOURISM AND RECREATION

Tourism and recreation compose the second most important industry in Michigan. Estimates indicate that tourism accounts for about $5 billion annually, with another $4 billion generated by related industries. Nationally, Michigan ranks first in the number of registered watercraft and snowmobiles and second in total hunting and fishing license sales. About 48 percent of Michigan's tourists are nonresidents—it has been estimated that about 10 percent of the nation's population lives within a two-and-one-half-hour drive of Michigan and that 30 percent lives within a day's drive. Of the tourist expenditures in the state, about 36 percent is for food; 27 percent, for transportation; 10 percent, for lodging; and 27 percent, for other expenses. There are over 7,000 motels, hotels, and cottage developments, and more than 350,000 jobs are directly related to tourism; many more are indirectly related to the whole recreation industry. Recreation is a strongly established basic need of human beings and is engaged in even during times of recession and heavy unemployment—during the recessions of the 1970s and 1981–1982, the state's recreation and tourism industry actually increased. The effect of tight money

Golfing on Mackinac Island. (Courtesy Michigan Travel Bureau)

Charles Mears State Park and Lake Michigan shoreline in northern Oceana County. (Courtesy Michigan Department of Natural Resources)

Sailing, a popular sport in both Great Lakes and inland waters. (Courtesy Michigan Travel Bureau)

Boyne Highlands downhill skiing and golf complex. The ski area is based on massive glacial moraines. (Courtesy Michigan Department of Natural Resources)

Cross-country skiing, an increasingly popular winter sport. (Courtesy Michigan Department of Natural Resources)

seems to be that people do not travel as far for their recreation and they engage in more-economical activities such as camping.

The total character of the recreation and tourist industry is difficult to accurately define. It is usually described as all of the economic activities that do business with anyone engaged in recreation, and a tourist is defined as anyone traveling away from home to engage in recreational activity. The activities connected with recreation would include service stations, entertainment places, restaurants, personal services, hotels and motels, boat sales and service, camping facilities, and many other enter-

Camping in Wilderness State Park in the northern portion of the Lower Peninsula. (Courtesy Michigan Travel Bureau)

prises. Most of these businesses also serve the nontourist, which makes it difficult to assess the total economic impact of recreation and tourism.

Recreation is generally associated with outdoor activities and natural attractions. There are, however, a great many urban-related recreational activities such as bowling, golf, and tennis, and many people spend large amounts of money on these sports. It is difficult to obtain reliable statistics on urban-related recreational activities, so this section will largely discuss outdoor, nonurban recreational activities engaged in by both residents and nonresidents.

PHYSICAL RESOURCES

The recreation opportunities presented by the Great Lakes and the more than 11,000 inland lakes are probably Michigan's single greatest recreational asset. There are over 3,200 mi (5,100 km) of shoreline, more than in any other state, and this shoreline has excellent beaches, which are often backed by attractive dune and forested landscapes. Other attractions are offered by the 977 mi (1,572 km) of island shoreline and the thousands of miles of rivers and streams. The water resources provide fishing, boating, and swimming opportunities for the

Deer hunting results in an annual kill of approximately 160,000 animals. (Courtesy Michigan Department of Natural Resources)

tourist. Many streams in the northern Lower Peninsula and the Upper Peninsula are famous for trout fishing, and the introduction of coho and other salmon varieties has provided a sensational fishing atraction, both when the salmon are spawning in the streams as well as in the Great Lakes where they live for much of their life. The salmon are also helping to solve the overabundance of alewives—a small, largely undesirable fish that gained access to the Great Lakes from the Atlantic Ocean via the St. Lawrence Seaway. Alewives often die in early summer and float onshore to pollute the beaches, particularly along Lake Michigan. It is estimated that alewives account for approximately 90 percent of the quantity of fish life in the Great Lakes, but their numbers have been substantially reduced since the successful introduction of various species of salmon.

Abundant varieties of wild game provide the basis for another major recreational activity, hunting. Bears and deer; smaller animals like rabbits, squirrels, and raccoons; and wild fowl including pheasants, ducks, and geese are the major objectives for hunters. More than 7 million acres (2,835,000 ha) of state and federally owned land are open to hunting for specified periods for each type of game, and a great deal of private land is also made available for hunting under conditions established by the owners. Certain areas have become specialized hunting areas, such as the thumb area for pheasants and the northern parts of the state for deer.

The variety of landforms in Michigan is another major recreational asset. Even though the state lacks major mountainous topography, there are some remnants of old eroded mountains, such as the Huron and Porcupine mountains in the Upper Peninsula. Ice Age moraines also provide moderate topographic relief, and the abundance of lakes, streams, and forests adds to the landscape variety. Certain areas are unique and have been preserved as national

Sleeping Bear Dunes, part of Sleeping Bear Dunes National Lakeshore. (Courtesy Michigan Travel Bureau)

Colorful rocks rising 200 ft (61 m) above Lake Superior form the basis of Pictured Rocks National Lakeshore. (Courtesy Michigan Travel Bureau)

parks and lakeshores. These include Pictured Rocks National Lakeshore on the south shore of Lake Superior, the Sleeping Bear Dunes National Lakeshore in the northwestern portion of the Lower Peninsula, and Isle Royale National Park in Lake Superior some 50 mi (80 km) northwest of the Keweenaw Peninsula.

The combination of climate, topography, and lakes provides a winter recreation potential that is increasing in importance. Winter snow and ice, once considered a liability, is now a major asset. There are seventy downhill, or Alpine, ski facilities in Michigan with some 400 lifts and 700 ski runs. The majority of these facilities are in the northern Lower Peninsula and Upper Peninsula where the snow is more reliable, the terrain more rugged, and the slopes longer. The making of artificial snow offsets the whims of Michigan's winters and makes it possible to ski more regularly—especially in the somewhat warmer, densely populated southern one-third of the state. Snowmobiling, cross-country skiing, and ice fishing add to the winter recreation activities.

CULTURAL RESOURCES

The population of Michigan includes a large variety of ethnic groups, and some of their traditions are maintained through cultural events held in parts of Michigan where the various groups have settled. These ethnic festivals have become major tourist attractions and are increasing in number and importance as ethnic groups new to the state and more of the well-established groups are attempting to reestablish their "roots" in the form of traditional festivals and other cultural events. The Dutch-oriented tulip festival held in Holland, Michigan, is one of the oldest and most famous and attracts hundreds of thousands of visitors each year. Detroit is capitalizing on its diverse ethnic makeup through a series of twenty weekly festivals during the summer that feature the Greek, Polish, Ru-

Tulip festival at Holland. (Courtesy Michigan Travel Bureau)

manian, Italian, Chinese, and other cultural heritages that compose the city's fifty nationalities. In one recent summer, these Detroit festivals attracted a total of over 3 million visitors. A very successful Scottish Highland games festival has been organized in Alma in Gratiot County; a Bavarian festival is held each year in Frankenmuth; a Danish one in Greenville, Montcalm County; and a Polish one at Posen and Metz in Presque Isle County. Still other festivals are based on features or events, such as trout fishing in Kalkaska; coho salmon in Honor, Benzie County; the St. Lawrence Seaway in Muskegon; cherry production in Traverse City; and asparagus growing in Oceana County.

Other major tourist attractions are the Soo Locks and the Mackinac Bridge, and many places combine constructed, historical, and natural assets—for example, Mackinac Island, which has unique geologic formations, a fort dating from 1780, and summer sports facilities, all of which make the island a major summer resort. The Interlochen Music Camp just south of Traverse City, operated by the University of Michigan, is an example of a summer

Mackinac Bridge linking Michigan's two peninsulas. (Courtesy Michigan Travel Bureau)

educational facility that draws thousands of visitors to its outstanding musical events held in a beautiful natural setting.

The historical record of Michigan, as it is preserved on the landscape, provides the base for yet another type of tourist attraction. Greenfield Village in Dearborn is an outstanding example of a collection of historical homes and exhibits that depict the past. The life and work of Thomas A. Edison are featured in the village, along with exhibits depicting the life and achievements of such individuals as Henry Ford, Noah Webster, the Wright brothers, and Robert Frost. Greenfield Village attempts to re-create aspects of the life and activities of the 1800s, and nearby, the Henry Ford Museum complements Greenfield's exhibits. These two attractions draw thousands of visitors from the state, the nation, and the world. Other examples of historical attractions are the many beautiful homes that remain from the lumbering era such as those in Marshall near Battle Creek and the Bayview area near Petoskey. The capitol building in Lansing is also a major year-round attraction. Most cities and counties have museums that feature the historical past of the area and are recreational as well as educational assets to the community. Some communities have art museums, musical events, and legitimate theaters that serve to attract tourists and bolster income.

Still another type of tourist attraction features the industries, past and present, of Michigan. There are tours of major manufacturing facilities such as automobile plants, iron and steel mills, and cereal companies. Iron and copper mines in the Upper Peninsula, the salt mines under Detroit, and the huge limestone quarry at Rogers City in Presque Isle County are other tourist assets.

In total, the cultural resources add materially to the tourist and recreation resource base in Michigan. Most of these resources occur or are open all year, so they complement the more seasonal activities.

OWNERSHIP PATTERNS OF RECREATION RESOURCES

As the population increases and urban influences penetrate more and more into the rural and little-developed areas, access to recreation resources is critical. There are a large variety of ownership patterns of recreation land—both private and public—that affect the accessibility potential.

The federal government, a major owner of land, is responsible for a great deal of land that is used for recreation. The Forest Service, part of the Department of Agriculture, administers three national forests in the state totaling 2.7 million acres (1.09 million ha). The Huron-Manistee National Forest is located in the northern Lower Peninsula; the Hiawatha, in the eastern half of the Upper Peninsula; and the Ottawa,

Snowmobiling near St. Ignace with Mackinac Bridge in the background. (Courtesy Michigan Travel Bureau)

in the northwestern portion of the Upper Peninsula. Over 20 percent of the total land of seven counties in the Upper Peninsula and five counties in the northern Lower Peninsula is owned by the Forest Service (Figure 8.6). This land provides many recreation possibilities by means of public campgrounds; hunting and fishing sites; and snowmobiling, skiing, and hiking facilities.

The National Park Service, part of the Department of Interior, controls the wilderness area of Isle Royale National Park (210 sq mi [544 sq km]) and two national lakeshores—Pictured Rocks and Sleeping Bear—that preserve unique natural phenomena for public enjoyment (Figure 8.7). The Fish and Wildlife Service, also part of the Department of Interior, manages 111,400 acres (45,117 ha) of land, mostly in the form of wildlife refuges such as the wetlands of the Seney National Wildlife Refuge in the Upper Peninsula and the Shiawassee National Wildlife Refuge in southeastern Michigan.

State and local governments administer other lands that are significant for recreation. The Michigan Department of Natural

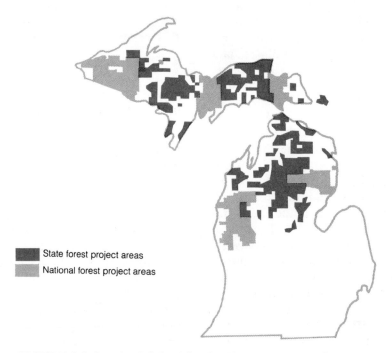

State forest project areas
National forest project areas

FIGURE 8.6. State and federal forests. (Source: Adapted from Lawrence M. Sommers, ed., *Atlas of Michigan* [East Lansing: Michigan State University Press, 1977], pp. 182–183.)

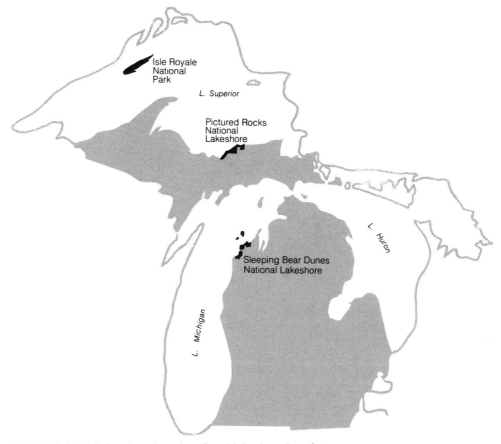

FIGURE 8.7. National park and national lakeshore locations.

Resources controls 4.25 million acres (1.7 million ha) in the form of state forests, state parks, and wildlife areas. The state has ninety-two heavily used parks and recreation areas, many of which are in the highly urbanized southern one-third of the state and thus are easily accessible to large numbers of people (Figure 8.8). Added to the federal and state public lands are a number of county, township, and city facilities that also provide a wide range of recreation opportunities. Privately owned land also enters into the recreation picture as owners, often as commercial ventures, may permit hunting, cross-country skiing, snowmobiling, and other leisure-time activities on their land.

IMPACT OF SALMON PLANTING— A CASE STUDY

In 1965, the first coho salmon were planted in the Platte River near Honor in Benzie County. From this start, a sports fishing activity has grown that attracts thousands of people each year to Lakes Michigan, Huron, and Superior as well as to the many rivers that serve as spawning grounds for the salmon. The varieties have been widened to include chinook, king, and Atlantic salmon. The fishing season extends from early spring to late fall and can be engaged in by individuals with simple tackle on the banks of rivers or by people who charter boats with sophisticated equipment

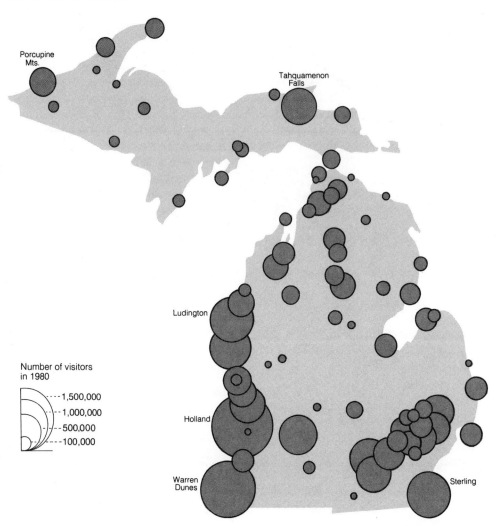

FIGURE 8.8. Usage of state parks, 1980. (Source: Adapted from David I. Verway, ed., *Michigan Statistical Abstract* [Detroit: Wayne State University, 1981], pp. 399–401.)

to fish on Lakes Michigan or Huron.

Salmon fishing has become a major stimulus to tourist and resort development wherever ports, marinas, or boat landings give access to fishing areas in the Great Lakes and along the many spawning rivers in the fall. Motel space must be reserved well in advance in Manistee, Ludington, Muskegon, and other ports along the Lake Michigan coast during the fall spawning runs, and, fishermen may line some of the streams where salmon are running.

The exact economic impact of the Great Lakes salmon fishing is hard to measure as it overlaps with other fishing and recreational activities. Without question, however, it has been a major stimulus to the economic life of coastal communities along Lake Michigan, and it has added greatly to the state's sports fishery potential. This development was initiated by Dr. Howard Tanner, Michigan Department of Natural Resources, who successfully implemented his idea for transplanting freshwater salmon to Michigan waters. His plans have borne fruit far beyond his dreams, and salmon sports fishing has enjoyed a miraculous increase in Michigan. A major by-product

Salmon fishing in Lake Michigan. (Courtesy Michigan Travel Bureau)

Sign as you enter Paradise, a village that caters to tourists, near the entrance to Tahquamenon Falls State Park, Upper Peninsula. (Michigan also has a town called Hell in the Lower Peninsula.)

has been the apparent control of the number of alewives as they are a major source of food for the salmon.

Not all is positive, however. In their feeding habits, the salmon consume a variety of smaller aquatic life that have accumulated amounts of the pesticide DDT and the chemical PCB in their bodies. These undesirable elements are, in turn, transferred to the salmon, and their amounts have been determined to be too large for the fish to be sold commercially. This pollution-caused contamination does not seem to deter the sports fisherman, but a commerical salmon-fishing enterprise had to cease operation shortly after it got started.

REGIONALIZATION OF TOURISM AND RECREATION

The distribution of tourists is related to the pull of various natural and cultural attractions, the access via various transportation routes (principally highways), and the location of potential users in the dense urban concentrations in both southern Michigan and nearby states. The Interstate Highway System has greatly facilitated automobile travel to the lake, forest, and stream areas of northern Michigan. Much of the state is now accessible in four or five hours' driving time from Detroit, which has made possible weekend travel to camp-

grounds, motels, and cottages in all the Lower Peninsula and the eastern portions of the Upper Peninsula. The same travel time will enable Michiganians to reach most of the Lower Peninsula's ski and snowmobile areas. U.S. Highways 31 and 131 make the western parts of the state accessible to the greater Chicago area, and Interstates 75 and 69 make travel to Michigan vacation country easy for Indiana and Ohio residents. Interstate 75 leads the tourist to Mackinac Bridge and the Soo Locks and is a major reason why Chippewa County is the leading tourist county in the Upper Peninsula and third in the entire state. Illinois, Wisconsin, and Minnesota residents have rather easy access to the western Upper Peninsula.

Marina at Leland in northern Leelanau County.

The major users of recreation facilities in Michigan are concentrated heavily in the southeast portion of the state, as is indicated by the fact that 28 percent of the boat registrations in 1979 were located in the three counties of Wayne, Oakland, and Macomb, but marinas are common in communities along all the Great Lakes as well as larger inland lakes. The following major recreation regions stand out in terms of the number of users (Figure 8.9). First, there is the southeast, which contains the urban attractions of greater Detroit and numerous glacial lakes and hills that provide recreational opportunities of many kinds during both winter and summer. Second is the northern half of the Lower Peninsula with its many inland lakes, abundant state and national forest land, and hilly terrain for skiing and snowmobiling. The eastern coast of Lake Michigan is a third area, and it has salmon and other fishing in Lake Michigan, the fruit belt, water, and sand dunes—including Sleeping Bear Dunes National Lakeshore—as its major attractions. Fourth is the Upper Peninsula and its Soo Locks, Mackinac Bridge, Mackinac Island, Tahquamenon Falls, the Keweenaw Peninsula, Porcupine and Huron mountains, the shore areas of Lake Superior, Isle Royale National Park, Pictured Rocks National Lakeshore, and numerous inland lakes and rivers. Fifth, there is the Grand River Valley and the Kalamazoo–Grand Rapids interlobate moraine

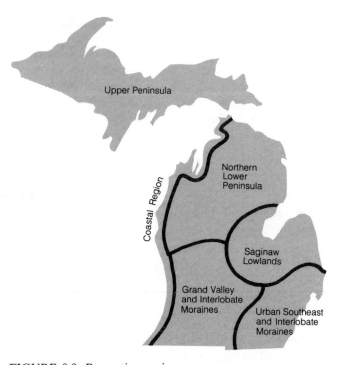

FIGURE 8.9. Recreation regions.

area, which has abundant lakes and an attractive, hilly terrain. Sixth is the Saginaw Valley, focusing on Saginaw Bay, which has fishing and boating, pheasant hunting, and the urban attractions of the cities in the area.

SUMMARY

The growing urban population of Michigan and nearby areas is placing increasing pressure upon the recreational assets of the state. In 1979, 51,128 vehicles containing campers and 38,227 day-user vehicles had to be turned away from state parks because of overcrowding. The private sector has been rapidly buying property that has potential and actual recreational value, and at the same time, federal, state, and local authorities have been trying to preserve more forest and park lands for the public. This conflict between private demands and the public good is far from settled. Heated controversy develops over the establishment of any new park, such as the Sleeping Bear National Lakeshore, but much of the desirable dune and beach areas of the Lake Michigan shore is in private hands, and lakeshore land values have gone up in the last twenty-five years from a few dollars to $200 or more per front foot. Such prices mean that the bulk of people will be able to enjoy this first-class recreational asset only through public parks or public access points. Michigan is fortunate in that a great deal of land is already publicly owned, but most of this land is in the northern part of the state. As higher energy prices and other rising costs change recreation habits, this area needs to be better served by mass public transportation.

Another issue is the pollution of recreation assets, particularly the water resources. Waste from the increasing population, urbanization, and industrialization has decreased the quality of inland rivers and lakes, as well as of the Great Lakes. Lake Erie is slowly recovering from an advanced state of pollution, but the southern portions of Lakes Michigan and Huron have been deteriorating in water quality, and even Lake Superior has had problems—such as the dumping of iron mining waste in the western part of the lake. Progress is being made in identifying the severity of the pollution problems, and steps are being taken by government, industry, and private individuals to lessen and control the rate, but more research and greater expenditures of money will be necessary to assure that these water and land resources are preserved for future generations.

Natural conditions have also presented problems, such as the rapid increase of the alewives and the lamprey eel in the Great Lakes, both of which gained access via the St. Lawrence Seaway. The lamprey eel almost eliminated the lake trout and whitefish fisheries in the Great Lakes, but an effective state and federal program has brought it under nearly complete control. As indicated previously, the introduction of salmon may be partially, at least, solving the alewife problem.

Whether the natural resources can be maintained to meet the increasing recreational demands of the people is a major question, as the time and money available to citizens for recreation place great pressure upon the available facilities. When the four-day workweek becomes a reality, the demand for weekend recreation possibilities will increase still further. Fortunately, there are over 7 million acres (2.8 million ha) of federal- and state-owned land in the state, and both public and private sectors are increasingly sensitive to the need to provide continuing quality recreation resources and facilities. Michigan has recreation opportunities during all seasons, and the total recreation system will continue to serve the diverse leisure-time needs of the people and provide significant economic opportunities and income to the state.

Future recreation and tourist levels will be greatly influenced by the availability and cost of energy as well as by the economic problems of Michigan and nearby states.

148

TABLE 8.3. Employment in motor-vehicle-related industries, March 1979 and March 1980

Industry	Present Relationship to Motor Vehicle Industry	Total Employment March 1979	March 1980
Automotive stampings	100.0%	58,800	45,225
Coated fabrics, not rubberized	100.0	*	*
Motor-vehicle & passenger-car bodies	100.0	238,400	209,750
Motor-vehicle parts & accessories	100.0	173,575	135,325
Storage batteries	100.0	*	*
Tires & inner tubes	100.0	*	*
Truck & bus bodies	100.0	1,225	1,875
Truck trailers	100.0	*	*
Woven carpets & rugs	100.0	*	*
Automotive trimmings	99.9	18,025	12,750
Malleable iron foundries	94.0	6,150	4,325
Fabricated textile products, NEC	93.7	*	*
Flat glass	92.3	*	*
Blast furnaces, steel works, & rolling mills	91.2	24,300	21,400
Gray iron foundries	87.3	27,725	19,500
Internal-combustion engines	86.2	*	*
Elec. equip. for internal-combustion engines	86.1	12,825	9,200
Bolts, nuts, screws, rivets, & washers	83.2	4,550	4,225
Rubber, plastic hose, & belting	78.2	850	250
Steel springs, except wire	76.9	1,950	1,300
Carburetors, pistons, piston rings, & valves	74.4	6,450	5,575
Special tools & dies	72.6	27,450	26,275
Hardware, NEC	69.9	16,400	14,475
Misc. plastic products	66.7	27,500	25,900
Iron & steel forgings	65.7	6,025	4,775
Paints, varnishes, & allied products	63.9	3,675	3,200
Gaskets, packing, & sealing devices	60.0	1,600	1,350
Screw machine products	48.3	6,750	6,075
Drawing & insulating of nonferrous wire	46.9	1,400	1,875
Aluminum foundries	45.4	4,400	3,900
Glass products	42.9	4,175	3,900
Public building & related furniture	29.7	2,650	3,125
Steel foundries, NEC	28.8	1,850	1,850
Radio & television receiving sets	16.0	1,400	1,175
Total		707,475	592,925

*Included in totals but not detailed in order to avoid disclosure of confidential information.

NEC = Not elsewhere classified.

Source: Michigan Employment Security Commission, Bureau of Research and Statistics, Motor Vehicle and Related Industries in Michigan (Lansing, 1981).

Nationally, one-third of all automobile travel is related to recreation and tourism. Thus, if the total number of miles driven is reduced because of conservation pressure, traveling on vacations becomes less frequent, there is increasing resistance to a recreation-oriented use of vehicles, or politicians attempt to downgrade the importance of recreation industries and activities in times of crisis such as during shortages of fuel, the character and total importance of recreation and tourism to Michigan will be greatly affected.

THE CHANGING ECONOMY

Michigan's heavy dependence upon manufacturing, especially of automobiles and trucks, was rapidly changing in the early years of the 1980s, and all predictions indicate the auto industry is unlikely to again reach the levels of employment and total sales value of the 1976–1979 period. The down-sizing of automobiles; the increased use of robots; the decreased use of automobiles because of the cost and shortages of liquid fossil fuel; and the changing conservation, journey-to-work, and leisure-time habits of the average U.S. family are having a marked impact on the demand for all motor vehicles as well as for those with high fuel efficiency and smaller size. Automobile and truck production in Michigan dropped from 3,944,126 units in 1976 to 1,981,703 in 1980, a 49.8 percent decrease. Average employment in the three major automobile companies decreased from 452,914 in the fourth quarter of 1976 to 397,485 in the fourth quarter of 1980, a 12 percent decrease.[5]

These changes in numbers, employment, and value seriously affect the viability of a number of the parts and other motor-vehicle-related industries. Table 8.3 indicates the variety and extent of the industries that have been affected by the automotive declines. Some of these establishments may

be able to shift their emphasis, market, or type of product, but others will be forced to close.

Considerable effort is being made by government officials as well as private individuals to diversify Michigan's economy. One type of industry being seriously considered is high-technology manufacturing, such as robotics, to take advantage of the expertise available in the institutions of higher education in Michigan as well as of the high skill levels of many employees in the existing industries. New technology in the agricultural, forestry, and biotechnology industries may also foster significant employment and income.

Michigan's major resource for a strong and viable economy in the future is its highly skilled labor force on both the blue collar and the managerial levels. Some loss of population to the Sun Belt is occurring, but the over 9 million people represent abilities of diverse character and ingenuity that will continue to assure Michigan of an important place in the economy of the United States. The abundant supplies of freshwater may also prove to be a most critical resource in the decades ahead.

NOTES

1. David I. Verway, ed., *Michigan Statistical Abstract, 1982–83* (Detroit: Wayne State University, 1983), p. 199.
2. Value added by manufacturing is obtained by subtracting from the value of shipments (including resales) the cost of materials, parts, components, supplies, fuels, goods purchased for resale, and contract work and adjusting for the net change in finished and unfinished product inventories during the year.
3. In 1979, the Bureau of the Census decided that the amount of annual sales of agricultural products must be $1,000 or more in order for a farm to be classified as such.
4. Part-time is defined as farms with less than $2,250 in sales, farmer's age is under 65, and the farmer works off the farm 100 days or more a year.
5. Verway, *Michigan Statistical Abstract*, pp. 577–582.

CHAPTER 9

TRANSPORTATION AND TRADE PATTERNS

Michigan's location and the character of its economic development have been major factors in the nature of its transportation and trade patterns. The Industrial Revolution brought railroad and water transportation to the manufacturing areas of southern Michigan, and the lumber industry did much to bring the railroads, often temporarily, into much of the northern Lower Peninsula and the Upper Peninsula. Water traffic has continually been important because of the navigable Great Lakes waters found on all sides of Michigan but the south, and water transportation became even more important when the locks of the St. Lawrence River and the Welland Canal, which bypasses Niagara Falls in Canada, opened up the Great Lakes to ocean traffic through the St. Lawrence Seaway. The density of federal and state highway development correlates well with the urban-industrial counties found south of the Muskegon–Bay City line.

WATER TRAFFIC

Despite its midcontinent location, Michigan has thirty ports that can handle lake carriers and oceangoing vessels of considerable size (Figure 9.1). The water transportation system is especially well adapted for handling bulky, low-value-per-unit-weight materials from northern to southern

Great Lakes ports and vice versa. Most of the iron ore from Michigan and Minnesota is carried southward by large lake carrier vessels, and coal is a major commodity transported northward. The annual tonnages are greatly affected by the health of the economy, especially the auto industry (Table 9.1). The tonnages carried clearly show the recessions of 1971–1972 and 1977, and in the midst of the 1981–1982 recession, the number of lake carriers in use and the total tonnage carried were also greatly reduced. Also, the methods of concentrating low-grade iron ore in Michigan and Minnesota have reduced the volume to be carried by ship, and the volume of coal carried is being affected by the greater demand for low-sulfur western coal.

Three major developments have facilitated the movement of traffic on the Great Lakes. First was the completion in 1855 of locks to allow negotiation of the falls on the St. Marys River located between Lake Superior and Lake Huron. The actual tonnage passing through the locks at Sault Ste. Marie varies from year to year, but the 1978 total was 88,634,900 tons (80,391,854 t) or 20 percent of the total freight tonnage carried on the principal Michigan waterways.

A second factor was the completion of the Welland Canal in 1932 and the building of locks on the St. Lawrence River to open

FIGURE 9.1. Michigan ports.

Large lake vessels carry iron ore from the Upper Peninsula to the iron and steel centers in southern Great Lakes ports. (Courtesy Michigan Travel Bureau)

the Great Lakes to ocean traffic. Between 1954 and 1959, Canada and the United States deepened canals and built and enlarged locks on the St. Lawrence River to permit oceangoing vessels to reach the Great Lakes. A gauge of the amount of this kind of traffic is the Detroit River where Canadian and overseas freight totaled 915,403,000 ton mi (830,270,520 t mi) in 1978.

The third major development was the building of facilities in Michigan's lake ports to handle lake carriers as well as oceangoing vessels. This meant deepening harbors and entrance channels, providing docking space and loading and unloading equipment, and developing space and storage facilities for very bulky materials such as coal and iron ore.

Most waterborne freight traffic in Michigan is handled by the Port of Detroit and ports loading heavy materials like limestone, iron ore, coal, and gypsum (Table 9.2). Detroit is also the major entry port

153

TABLE 9.1. Total freight on Lake Michigan, 1968–1980[a]

Year	Ton-miles (in 000s)
1968	19,761,932
1969	20,367,369
1970	20,044,778
1971	18,941,670
1972	19,550,013
1973	21,049,862
1974	20,031,082
1975	18,098,715
1976	19,358,885
1977	16,155,272
1978	20,647,576
1979	20,520,860
1980	15,943,761

[a]Includes the port of Chicago.

Sources: U.S. Department of the Army, Corps of Engineers, Waterborne Commerce of the United States, Pt. 3, "Waterways and Harbors–Great Lakes" (Vicksburg, Miss.); reproduced in David I. Verway, ed., Michigan Statistical Abstract (Detroit: Wayne State University, 1981), p. 634, and U.S. Department of the Army, Corps of Engineers, Waterborne Commerce of the United States, Pt. 5, "National Summaries Calendar Year 1979 (Ft. Belvoir, Va., 1980).

U.S. and Canadian locks at Sault Ste. Marie. (Courtesy Michigan Department of Natural Resources)

Dredged channel with the exit protected by piers extending into Lake Michigan at Muskegon. Muskegon State Park is in upper right of photograph. (Courtesy Michigan Department of Natural Resources)

World's largest limestone quarry and loading facilities at Calcite on Lake Huron. Limestone is a major item carried on the Great Lakes. (Courtesy Michigan Travel Bureau)

TABLE 9.2. Freight traffic of selected Michigan ports, 1979

Port	Tonnage in 000s	Principal Commodity
Port of Detroit	24,996.0	Miscellaneous
Escanaba	13,452.7	Iron Ore
Calcite	10,319.6	Limestone
Stoneport	9,357.6	Limestone
Presque Isle Harbor	8,121.7	Limestone
Port Dolomite	3,834.7	Limestone
Port Inland	3,893.0	Limestone
St. Clair	3,286.4	Miscellaneous
Saginaw	3,173.6[a]	Grain (Dry & Navy Beans)
Alpena Harbor	2,942.1	Limestone
De Tour	2,578.4[a]	Limestone
Ludington	2,764.9	Miscellaneous
Monroe	2,662.8	Coal
Muskegon	1,906.7	Miscellaneous

[a]1978 figure.

Source: U.S. Department of the Army, Corps of Engineers, Waterborne Commerce of the United States, Pt. 3, "Waterways and Harbors–Great Lakes" (Vicksburg, Miss.); reproduced in David I. Verway, ed., Michigan Statistical Abstract, 1982–83 (Detroit: Wayne State University, 1983).

for material being imported by water from foreign countries. Ludington and Frankfort car-ferry ports, with connections across Lake Michigan to Wisconsin, are being threatened with closure by the Ann Arbor and Chesapeake and Ohio Railroad Companies because of high costs and the decreasing volume of traffic. Some general cargo is entering various Michigan ports other than Detroit via the St. Lawrence Seaway, but the water traffic continues to be dominated by bulky commodities that originate and are consumed in the Great Lakes area.

RAILROAD PATTERNS

The first railroad line was chartered in Michigan in 1830, and since that time, the network has grown to serve most of the populated areas. The main east-west trunk lines connecting New York and Chicago lie to the south, but Michigan is a major railroad gateway of the United States to the Province of Ontario, Canada. A number of rail lines have been abandoned due to lack of profitable traffic in recent years, and the threatened car-ferry connections across Lake Michigan have already been severely reduced. Amtrak has the only passenger service connecting Detroit and Port Huron with Canada and Chicago via Michigan cities along these routes.

The densest part of the railway network is closely correlated to the urban-industrial portion of Michigan located south of the Muskegon–Bay City line (Figure 9.2). The automobile and related parts industries provide a significant share of the cargo carried by the railway companies. The trucking industry has provided strong competition in recent decades, but with the increasing cost of gasoline and diesel products, the place of the railroad should increase in Michigan as it is an effective, efficient means of bulk transportation. The role of com-

Junction of Interstates 75 and 675 north of Saginaw. The Zilwaukee Bridge across the Shiawassee River is shown in the lower right. (Courtesy Michigan Department of Natural Resources)

muter passenger trains may also increase in the heavily populated Detroit metropolitan area if plans for a light-rail system or a people mover can be completed.

HIGHWAY PATTERNS

The highway network is a major way of moving people and freight in Michigan (Figure 9.3). It is estimated that nearly 90 percent of the movement of people between cities is by means of vehicles on the well-developed interstate, U.S., state, county, and township highway system. Limited-access interstate and U.S. highways (94, 96, 75, 69, and 31) connect the major population centers of the state, and I-75 extends from Detroit to Sault Ste. Marie in the Upper Peninsula. The heaviest traffic flows are generated in southern Michigan, especially

FIGURE 9.2. Major rail lines, 1982.

FIGURE 9.3. Network of interstate, U.S., and state highways, 1982.

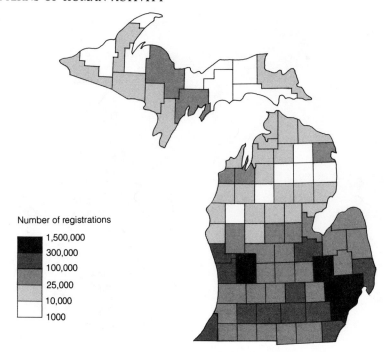

Number of registrations

- 1,500,000
- 300,000
- 100,000
- 25,000
- 10,000
- 1000

FIGURE 9.4. Motor vehicle registrations, by county, 1981. (Source: Adapted from David I. Verway, ed., *Michigan Statistical Abstract* [Detroit: Wayne State University, 1981], pp. 506–510.)

by Detroit and other major population concentrations. The state had a total of 7,331,268 motor vehicle registrations in 1980, of which 2,766,405, 38 percent, were in the three counties of Wayne, Oakland, and Macomb in the metropolitan Detroit area (Figure 9.4). The heaviest amount of vehicle traffic is on Interstate Highways 75, 94, and 96 and the freeway systems connecting the Detroit, Grand Rapids, Lansing, and Flint urban areas.

AIR TRANSPORTATION PATTERNS

The volume of both passenger and freight air traffic is dominated by Detroit Metropolitan Airport. In 1979, this airport accounted for 96 percent of the enplaned freight, 77 percent of the enplaned passengers, and 61 percent of the aircraft departures from airports in the state (Figure 9.5). Grand Rapids, Lansing, and Saginaw–Bay City–Midland airports accounted

for 12.5 percent of the enplaned passengers, and the remainder are accounted for by smaller southern airports and a few scattered airports in the northern Lower Peninsula and Upper Peninsula. Marquette is the most active airport in the Upper Peninsula as is Traverse City in the northern Lower Peninsula.

FOREIGN TRADE

Surprisingly, Michigan ranked third among the fifty states in value of manufactured shipments in 1977, accounting for 7.7 percent of the value of export and export-related shipments by manufacturing plants in the United States (Table 9.3). Transportation equipment provided 59 percent of the total manufactured-product export value, followed by nonelectrical machinery with 14 percent, fabricated metal products with 7 percent, and chemical products with 6 percent.

Detroit dominates the import and export

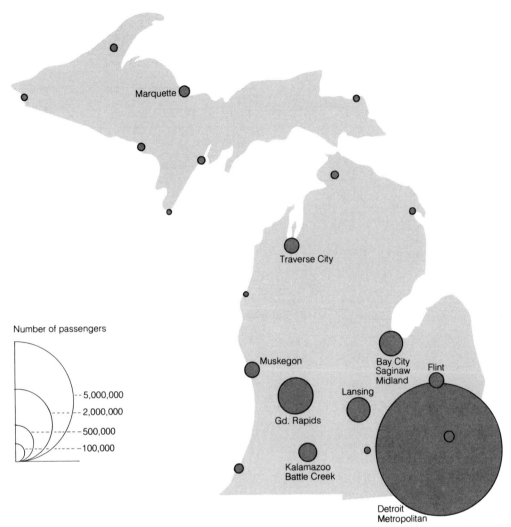

FIGURE 9.5. Commercial aircraft enplaned passengers, by airport, 1979. (Source: U.S. Federal Aviation Administration, *Airport Activity Statistics of Certified Route Air Carriers, 12 Months Ended 31 December 1979* [Washington, D.C., 1981], Tables 6 and 7.)

trade of Michigan as it is the principal U.S. Customs District Port of Entry. The value of exports and imports passing through the Detroit Customs District totaled $27.4 billion, or 5.9 percent of the U.S. total, in 1980. Detroit accounted for 75 percent of the waterborne imports by weight in 1979, but the exports were divided among a number of ports.

The export tonnage from Detroit consists largely of automobiles and automobile parts; limestone heading for the Canadian iron and steel industry dominates the tonnage

from Port Huron, Calcite, De Tour, Presque Isle, and Alpena; navy beans and soybeans, from Saginaw–Bay City; and iron ore, from Escanaba. The value and volume of foreign trade fluctuates considerably with the health of the world economy.

CONCLUSION

The transportation and trade patterns of Michigan developed in response to the productivity of a large urban-industrialized

TABLE 9.3. Value of manufactured shipments and exports, by state, 1977

| | Rank Based on Value of Shipments | | Value of Shipments, 1977 | | |
State	1977	1972	Total[a] (million dollars)	Total Export Related[b] (million dollars)	Total Export Related as Percent of Total Shipments
Alabama	22	28	21,010.1	2,061.4	9.8
Alaska	49	42	1,250.3	393.4	31.4
Arizona	35	30	7,022.4	1,049.8	14.9
Arkansas	31	24	12,276.1	1,085.8	8.8
California	1	4	120,895.8	13,319.4	11.0
Colorado	32	32	10,018.0	976.5	9.7
Connecticut	24	13	19,842.2	2,686.8	13.5
Delaware	37	36	5,208.7	345.8	6.6
District of Columbia	50	45	984.4	21.0	2.1
Florida	23	21	20,980.6	2,294.1	10.9
Georgia	13	19	32,856.4	2,723.2	8.3
Hawaii	45	43	1,974.0	65.8	3.5
Idaho	41	44	3,657.7	380.9	10.4
Illinois	4	3	93,081.3	10,216.2	11.0
Indiana	8	9	52,172.2	5,784.5	11.1
Iowa	18	18	23,514.9	2,228.5	9.5
Kansas	26	29	15,987.3	1,157.6	7.2
Kentucky	20	23	22,874.7	2,367.0	10.3
Louisiana	15	22	29,493.3	2,734.0	9.3
Maine	38	40	5,144.6	424.9	8.3
Maryland	27	25	15,930.4	1,326.7	8.3
Massachusetts	14	11	30,144.2	3,497.5	11.6
Michigan	3	1	93,757.1	10,975.3	11.7
Minnesota	19	17	23,021.2	2,298.0	10.0
Mississippi	29	34	12,765.8	1,111.0	8.7
Missouri	12	20	33,162.5	2,833.5	8.5
Montana	42	48	2,669.9	181.5	6.8
Nebraska	33	35	8,713.4	576.2	6.6
Nevada	51	49	942.0	70.4	7.4
New Hampshire	40	39	4,032.3	454.6	11.3
New Jersey	9	10	51,279.4	4,879.5	9.5
New Mexico	44	46	2,009.2	109.0	5.4
New York	6	5	86,216.4	8,893.5	10.3
North Carolina	10	15	40,912.2	3,883.3	9.5
North Dakota	48	47	1,312.9	98.0	7.5
Ohio	2	2	95,234.7	11,046.7	11.6
Oklahoma	30	31	12,564.5	1,044.2	8.3
Oregon	28	33	14,370.0	1,498.4	10.4
Pennsylvania	7	6	79,884.8	8,955.0	11.2
Rhode Island	36	38	5,364.6	540.3	10.1
South Carolina	25	26	18,882.4	2,117.2	11.2
South Dakota	46	50	1,793.7	130.5	7.3
Tennessee	16	16	28,752.0	2,716.1	9.4
Texas	5	7	92,735.7	9,195.8	9.9
Utah	39	37	5,092.8	415.5	8.2

TABLE 9.3 (continued)

State	Rank Based on Value of Shipments 1977	1972	Total[a] (million dollars)	Total Export Related[b] (million dollars)	Total Export Related as Percent of Total Shipments
			Value of Shipments, 1977		
Vermont	43	41	2,189.3	286.7	13.1
Virginia	17	14	23,988.6	2,480.3	10.3
Washington	21	8	21,746.9	3,716.1	17.1
West Virginia	34	27	8,705.9	1,108.1	12.7
Wisconsin	11	12	38,725.3	3,606.7	9.3
Wyoming	47	51	1,287.8	42.7	3.3
Total			1,358,397.3	142,403.6	10.4

[a]Includes total domestic and export shipments for all manufacturing establishments.

[b]Total export related is the sum of direct exports (value of manufactured products exported by the producing plants) and supporting exports (shipments of components, parts, supplies, etc., used by plants producing the export product).

Source: U.S. Bureau of the Census, 1977 Census of Manufacturing, Vol. 1 (Washington, D.C.: Government Printing Office, September 1981), Table 3.

population. Changes in these patterns reflect the nature of the domestic and world economy, domestic and world competition (for automobiles, for example), and a decreased emphasis upon manufacturing in the postindustrial period. The future success of the state depends greatly upon the ability of the population to adjust the transportation and trade patterns to meet these changing conditions.

PART 5

REGIONAL PATTERNS

The region is a major concept in geographic literature that simplifies and generalizes landscape complexity for the purpose of understanding the important patterns. There are two major types of regions—a homogeneous region and a nodal region. A homogeneous region is one that shows similarity over a given area based on one or more criteria, like a soils region or an industrial region. The degree of economic intensity based on the degree and type of population is an effective way to define homogeneous regions that summarize the diverse physical and human environments of Michigan.[1] A nodal region is defined by the dominating influence of a point or node, like the central business district of a city, which organizes the nature of space for some distance out from the center. Detroit is an example of an organizing node for the nodal region of southeast Michigan.

Michigan can be divided into two regions by the much-used Muskegon–Bay City line. This line separates the more intensely developed agricultural, manufacturing, and urban counties of southern Michigan from the raw-material-producing, sparsely populated, and small-scale manufacturing counties of the northern half of the Lower Peninsula and the entire Upper Peninsula. Manufacturing and construction are the dominant categories of employment income in all counties of the southern one-third of the state; north of the Muskegon–Bay City line, manufacturing is still the dominant source of income in a large number of counties but is followed closely by government (Figure V.1).

By using the criteria of population density and manufacturing intensity, the three counties of Wayne, Oakland, and Macomb dominate the economic development of Michigan, accounting for nearly half of the state's population as well as the value added by manufacturing (Figure V.2). The economic intensity decreases westward and northward from these three counties. The greater-Detroit area is the major economic core region of Michigan based on the concentrations of manufacturing, wholesale and retail trade, transportation, and government and service activities. The region contains the headquarters of the major automobile companies, and much of the economic activity of the region is closely tied to this dominant industry. The fact that the major centers of the banking and other industries, the port functions, arts and music facilities, and national-level professional sports teams are all located in Detroit also contributes to the significance of the city.

Secondary economic-intensity regions can be identified as follows:

1. Grand Rapids–Muskegon–Holland,
2. Kalamazoo–Battle Creek,
3. Lansing–Jackson–Flint,
4. Bay City–Midland–Saginaw.

Mackinac Island, an example of the regional character of northern Michigan. Note the developed southern tip, the air strip, and forested areas. (Courtesy Michigan Department of Natural Resources)

165

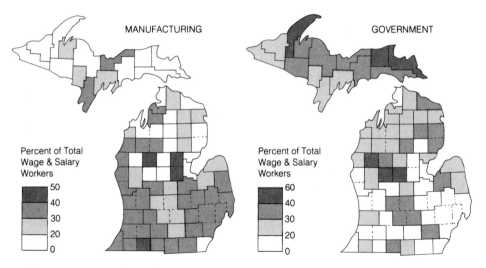

FIGURE V.1. Dominant income by employment and by county or groups of counties, 1980. (Source: David I. Verway, ed., *Michigan Statistical Abstract* [Detroit: Wayne State University, 1981], pp. 160–176.)

FIGURE V.2. Economic-intensity regions.

Each of these nodes has economic activities of major importance such as furniture and printing in Grand Rapids; paper, drugs, and cereals in Kalamazoo and Battle Creek; automobiles, government, and a major university in Lansing; automobiles in Flint; and chemicals in Midland. Much of the remainder of southern Michigan has enough small-scale manufacturing and intensive agriculture and fruit cultivation to make the average income levels per county greater than those north of the Muskegon–Bay City line.

The northern two-thirds of Michigan falls into the category of a minor economic-intensity region. Scattered manufacturing establishments are supplemented by tourism and recreation facilities, iron mining activities, petroleum and natural gas exploitation, and some specialized agriculture like the fruit-growing areas around Traverse City and along Lake Michigan. Forests provide raw materials for wood-processing industries.

This book, in total, deals with the regional nature of various geographic aspects of Michigan as regionalization is utilized to summarize a variable being discussed such as landforms, the economy, and recreation and tourism.[2] In this section of the book, Metropolitan Detroit, the most important economic-intensity region in Michigan, is presented as a regional case study. Besides being the population, industrial, and overall economic focus, Detroit illustrates most of the major political, economic, and social issues facing the state.

NOTES

1. Lawrence M. Sommers, "Distribution of Manufacturing in Norway: An Approach to the Delimitation of Economic Intensity Regions," *Journal of Geography* 61:5 (May 1962), pp. 196–204.

2. The reader is especially referred to the sections on "Landform Regions" (Chapter 4), "Major Agricultural Regions" (Chapter 8), and "Tourism and Recreation Regions" (Chapter 8).

CHAPTER 10

METROPOLITAN DETROIT

Joe T. Darden

Understanding the dominance of Detroit and the southeast Michigan region is of major importance in the geography of Michigan. It is the core region of the state, contains a large share of the population, industry, and income of the state, and has a great deal of political impact to go along with its economic importance. This chapter will highlight the significance of the highly diverse social and economic character of metropolitan Detroit. The Detroit area is a good example of the comingling and competition that occurs among the ethnic and racial groups that have been attracted to major midwestern industrial cities; it also exhibits many of the trends and problems of large-scale urbanization.

DETROIT AND ITS REGIONS

Detroit can be divided into five regions: (1) the central business district, (2) the central city, (3) the Standard Metropolitan Statistical Area, (4) the southeast Michigan region, and (5) the automotive region.

Central Business District

The Detroit central business district (CBD) is distinguished from other parts of the city by its concentration of commercial

References in this chapter are to "Sources and Selected References," Part Five.

activity and high land values. It contains large stores, company headquarters, and major office buildings; it also is a focus of urban transportation systems and congestion. More than any other part of the city, the central business district is responsible for Detroit's image to the outside world (Jenkins 1972, 141). Two major geographic features of the Detroit CBD are its location along the banks of a major commercial waterway and its closeness to Canada. It is a center for international trade because of its location and importance as a city; it also serves as a regional center for banking, legal services, government services, and utilities. Besides functioning as a regional center, the CBD is the focal point for many of the cultural, civic, and convention activities of residents of Detroit and the metropolitan region (Detroit Planning Department 1980a, IV-11). The central business district of Detroit is composed of census tracts 5172, 5173, 5206, and 5207 (Figure 10.1). It is bounded on the north by the Fisher Freeway; on the east, by the Chrysler Freeway; on the south, by Jefferson Avenue and the Detroit River; on the west, by the John C. Lodge Freeway.

Central City

The central city of Detroit is the corporate or political extent of the city. This area covers 139.6 sq mi (361.6 sq km) and

Detroit downtown area with Belle Isle in upper left and Windsor, Ontario, in upper right. (Courtesy Michigan Travel Bureau)

FIGURE 10.1. Census tracts of the central business district.

Intersection of Lodge and Fisher Freeways in downtown Detroit with Tiger Stadium in the center. (Courtesy Michigan Travel Bureau)

has the general shape of a right triangle. The Detroit River, which is also an international boundary between the United States and Canada, forms the southern boundary so Detroit lies north of Windsor, its twin city in Canada (Swartz et al. 1972, 17). Detroit's northern boundary is Eight-Mile Road, which also functions as the Wayne County boundary. Detroit is bounded on the west by a series of north-south arteries and on the east, by the suburb of Grosse

Point (Figure 10.2). In 1980, the population of Detroit central city was 1,203,339, making it the sixth largest central city in the United States.

Standard Metropolitan Statistical Area

The Detroit Standard Metropolitan Statistical Area (SMSA) comprises the six counties of Lapeer, Livingston, Macomb, Oakland, St. Clair, and Wayne—which in-

Detroit River with the Ambassador Bridge connecting Detroit and Windsor, Ontario. (Courtesy Michigan Travel Bureau)

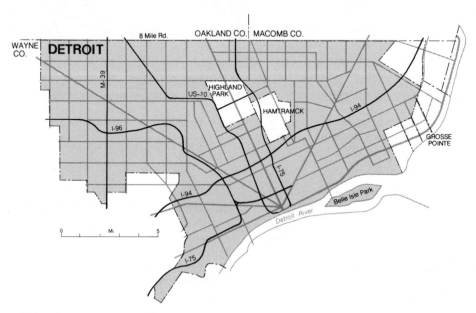

FIGURE 10.2. Map of the central city. The two blank areas in the center represent the municipal enclaves of Hamtramck and Highland Park, which are not a part of Detroit.

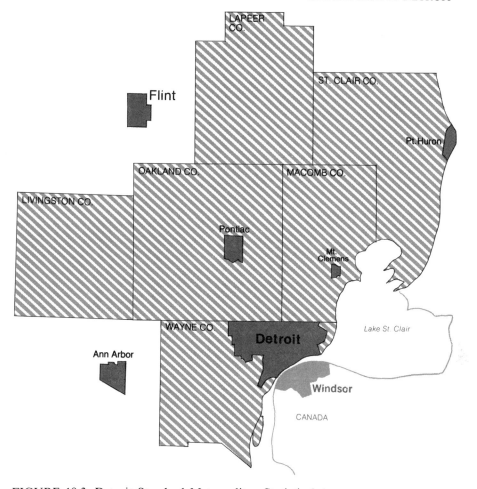

FIGURE 10.3. Detroit Standard Metropolitan Statistical Area.

cludes the Detroit central city (Figure 10.3). This area is the fifth largest SMSA in the United States with a population in 1980 of 4,342,000. The SMSA is the U.S. census unit on which most data are gathered and reported. According to the Bureau of the Census, it-expresses the spatial extent of the economic and social interaction and the interrelated network of human daily movement. Because of the international boundary, however, the actual extent of social, political, and economic interaction and human daily movement is not reported for the Detroit SMSA. Windsor, Ontario, is functionally a part of this SMSA, although it is not so counted. Even in the 1970s, the Greater Windsor Industrial Commission estimated that 11 percent of

Windsor's workers were employed in Detroit (Swartz et al. 1972, 21).

Southeast Michigan Region

Detroit is also the node for the southeast Michigan region, which consists of the seven counties of Livingston, Macomb, Monroe, Oakland, St. Clair, Washtenaw, and Wayne (Figure 10.4). This area had a total population of 4,682,131 in 1980 (U.S. Department of Commerce 1981c). This region was established as a planning area by the Southeast Michigan Council of Governments (SEMCOG), a voluntary council of governmental units formed for the purpose of providing coordinated guidance for the development of the region.

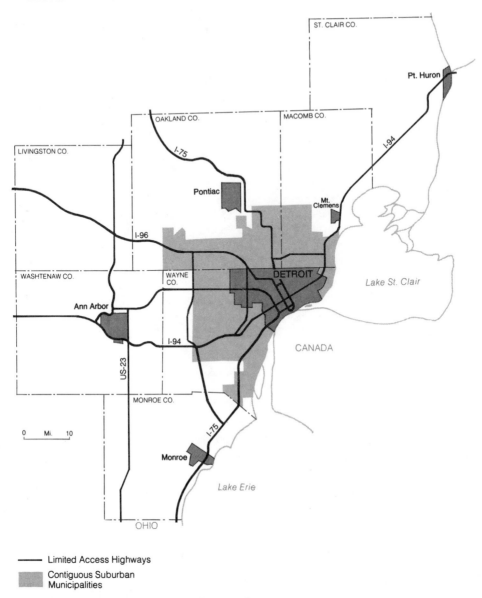

FIGURE 10.4. The southeast Michigan region.

Automotive Region

The Detroit automotive region is the nodal region of a vast midwestern manufacturing area, the node of which is focused on Detroit. The region is best defined in terms of spatial interaction involving flows of materials over highway networks, personnel over airways, and information movement over telecommunication lines (Swartz et al. 1972, 25). The Detroit automotive region is a large midwestern triangle in the heart of the North American manufacturing belt. The geographical apexes of this region are Oshawa, Ontario; Cincinnati, Ohio; and Milwaukee, Wisconsin (Figure 10.5). The decision-making node is in metropolitan Detroit, and within this triangle is contained about 90 percent of the automotive employment of both the United States and Canada (Swartz et al. 1972, 25). Connected to Detroit through transportation and communication networks are the rubber plants of Akron, Ohio, and Kitchener, Ontario; the metal foundries of Chicago and Cleveland; the machine tool shops of Cincinnati, Ohio, and Windsor, Ontario; the steel industries of Gary, Indiana, and Buffalo, New York; and the electronics and hydraulic research laboratories of Columbus and Dayton, Ohio (Hill 1978, 1). Apart from the cities in the southeast Michigan region, the triangle is close to such important automobile centers as Buffalo, Cleveland, Cincinnati, Toledo, Indianapolis, Chicago, Kenosha, Milwaukee, Windsor, Oakville, and Oshawa as well as many smaller centers (Hill 1978, 2; Swartz et al. 1972, 25).

In summary, there are many definitions of the Detroit area, each expressing a different spatial concept but each equally meaningful in understanding the entity that is Detroit. In this chapter, each of these spatial units or regions will be discussed.

GROWTH AND DECLINE OF THE CENTRAL CITY

Growth

The growth of any city is related to its site and situation. Site refers to the internal characteristics of the area in which a city is located, including physical characteristics; situation refers more to external characteristics and the relationship of the city to other areas. One of the important site factors in the growth of Detroit has been the Detroit River, which is located strategically in reference to the Great Lakes. It connects the lower lakes—Ontario and Erie—with the upper lakes—Huron, Mich-

FIGURE 10.5. Detroit automotive region.

Detroit Harbor Terminal on the Detroit River south of downtown business district. (Courtesy Michigan Travel Bureau)

igan, and Superior—and all traffic between those two sections of the Great Lakes passes through the Detroit River (Sinclair 1967, 357). The very name of the city stems from the French *d'étroit*—"of the strait."

In 1701, a French fur trader, Antoine de la Mothe Cadillac, founded the city of Detroit. The site at that time was ideal for his business as it lay on the short, straight stretch of water between Lake Erie and Lake Huron. He called the settlement Fort-Pontchartrain-du-Détroit; subsequently, the name was shortened to Detroit, and the strait was called the Detroit River (De Vito 1979, 3).

The river was important to the mercantile and military survival of the small settlement. Travel by land through the swampy peninsula of Michigan was hard, so trade was focused along the waterway. For more than a century, the river and the Great Lakes were the city's only connections with the outside world. The village-type settlement was located adjacent to the river between present-day Griswold and Wayne Streets and extended north to Jefferson Avenue (Glazer 1965, 11). It was composed of a security garrison, a mere handful of dwellings, and shops operated by bakers and skilled artisans. There was also a church.

Since the growth of any settlement is dependent upon the economic function that it performs, it is important to note that Detroit originally functioned as a garrison. The city's founder immediately took steps to change it from a fort into a major fur-trading center in order to strengthen the economy and, hence, increase population growth. Such growth was related to the location of the Detroit River. The river, Lake St. Clair, and the St. Clair River compose the southwest-northeast-trending "hinge" of southeast Michigan. Most physical and cultural features are oriented with regard to this hinge: Physical features parallel it, and human settlement has tended to develop at right angles to it (Hudgins 1945, 211).

The growth of Detroit has also been at right angles to the waterway hinge and can best be understood by examining the development of the area's road pattern (Swartz et al. 1972, 30). The first element of that pattern was the early Indian trails. These trails strongly influenced the pattern of the city's development as they became the main arteries of the city. They were the radial arteries that created the star-shaped pattern of Detroit's early suburban growth.

The second element of the area's road pattern had to do with the settlement of French farmers along the waterways of the Detroit River and Lake St. Clair. Their farms consisted of French long lots, which had narrow river frontages (400 to 900 ft [122 to 274 m]) and extended inland at right angles to the water as far as 3 mi (4.8 km) (Swartz et al. 1972, 31). The location of these farms influenced the local street patterns of Detroit as streets were laid out along the edges of the farms and city blocks grew accordingly.

In 1805, Michigan Territory was created, with Detroit as its capital; it was also the year that the village of Detroit was destroyed by fire (Glazer 1965, 20). Rebuilt, Detroit emerged as a true city between 1816 and 1865. In 1820, the city, exclusive of outlying areas, had 1,400 inhabitants and ranked forty-seventh in population among the cities of the nation. In 1830, its population numbered 2,200; by 1850, it ranked twenty-third, with a population of 21,000; by 1860, with 45,600 inhabitants, Detroit had become the eighteenth largest U.S. city (Glazer 1965, 25).

A continuing increase in the population and a shortage of space forced the city to annex new lands to accommodate new residences and businesses, and land was annexed three times between 1836 and 1855—in 1836, 1842, and 1849 (Gram et al. 1981, 7). The commercial center was at the foot of Randolph Street, and most businesses were located in the area enclosed by Jefferson Avenue on the north and Woodward Avenue on the east, although by this time, businesses had begun to move north (Gram et al. 1981, 18).

Factors in Detroit's Growth

Many factors contributed to the city's rapid growth, but the biggest factor was improvement in transportation technology. The completion of the Erie Canal in 1825 assured a relatively inexpensive water transportation route between New York City and Detroit, as well as to other cities on the Great Lakes. Detroit immediately became a major beneficiary of a new commerce, and as a result, migration to Detroit increased. The city also became the terminal and meeting place for settlers of Michigan, northern Ohio, and northern Indiana.

Improvement in transportation technology was not limited to the waterways. A network of highways radiating out from Detroit was constructed in the Michigan Territory. The Chicago Road ran to Ypsilanti and through the southern tier of present-day counties; the Gratiot Road linked Detroit and Huron; the Saginaw Road, connecting with the city of Saginaw, paved the way for the settlement of Oakland County (Glazer 1965, 27); and the Territorial Road ran through what is now Washtenaw County. Stagecoach service added to the commercial importance of the highways. Prospective settlers of the interior of Michigan made Detroit their headquarters for shopping and supplies. Thus, Detroit changed—because of transportation technology—from being a mere fur-trading center to being a major commercial center for many wholesale products. The designation of Detroit as a city with a federal land office and as a port of entry did much to enhance its commercial importance. Detroit was not yet considered an industrial city, but the establishment of railroad lines between Detroit and Chicago very gradually enlarged the market for products manufactured in Detroit.

Still a commercial center in 1850, Detroit

exported primarily flour, hides, lumber, beef, pork, and fish (Glazer 1965, 30), but the decade of the 1850s brought significant changes. In 1852, a railroad-car factory was founded, and during the decade, shipbuilding made great strides, and the tobacco industry grew. These developments were the beginning of the transformation of Detroit into a major industrial city. The population was already cosmopolitan. Of its 21,000 residents in 1850, 11,000 had been born in the United States and 10,000 were foreign-born. The largest number of the native-born gave the state of New York as their place of birth. The Irish were the largest group of foreign-born, but the German and English groups were also numerous (Glazer 1965, 36).

By 1865, Detroit's economic function had been transformed as new industries crowded out the old small shops, and by 1880, Detroit was the eighteenth largest U.S. city in population, with 116,300 inhabitants. It had ceased to be the small commercial city of the 1850s, but it had not yet become the giant manufacturing metropolis with large industrial zones and neat patterns of residential segregation (Warner 1972). Detroit in 1880 was spatially small despite some previous annexations. The distance from the river in the south to the northern boundary was only 3.5 mi (5.6 km) along Woodward Avenue (Zunz 1977, 446), but the declining population density from the center to the periphery was evidence that space within the city was only half used. Up to 1.3 mi (2.1 km) from the river, the city was somewhat thickly populated (60 people per acre [24 per ha]); beyond this distance, there was a dramatic decline in the density (Zunz 1977, 446). Most of the nonresidential structures, as well as hotels and boarding houses, were concentrated in the center of the city, and the central zone was surrounded by a mostly residential area. Beyond this residential zone was the underutilized land, a very large, low-density zone with many vacant spaces. There was no suburban settlement at the time.

The city was populated mainly by Yankees and members of earlier immigrant groups, including Canadians, English, Irish, and Germans. The Poles had started to move in, but very few people from other ethnic groups lived in Detroit, and only 2.4 percent of the population was black. There was a strong pattern of ethnic concentration in 1880, especially in the areas inhabited by four groups—Americans, Irish, Germans, and Poles—as 37 to 70 percent of their populations were concentrated in one area (Zunz 1977, 453). Of the native-born—i.e., American—families, 37 percent lived on the west side in Corktown (Glazer 1965, 53; Zunz 1977, 453). Fifty-two percent of the German families lived on the east side, as did most of the Poles (70 percent). The near east side also contained a strong mixture of immigrants from Austria, Belgium, the Netherlands, Luxembourg, Switzerland, and France as well as a small black population. Elsewhere the city was more Anglo-Saxon. Because of the large supply of unused available land within the city limits, there was not much crowding, but this fact did not keep the city from being spatially differentiated. Ethnic and class differences were pervasive (Zunz 1977, 464).

The primary industries in 1880—those employing 1,000 or more—were clothing, lumber, tobacco, food, transportation, and iron and steel products, and Detroit ranked nineteenth among U.S. cities in the number of workers employed in manufacturing establishments. Although Detroit was the location of some 825 establishments, the production of tobacco and cigars ranked first in value of manufacture (Glazer 1965, 50).

By 1900, Detroit had a population of 285,000, and its industries were highly diversified. There were over seventy-four foundries and machine shops, employing 15,900 workers, and 200 tobacco establishments, employing 4,500 workers. Such rapid growth can be attributed to several factors—for example, the availability of capital and improvements in the railroad network in Michigan (Glazer 1965, 51).

Many thousands of people migrated to Detroit because of its economic opportunities. Although the native-born came from all parts of the United States, a large number moved from rural Michigan into Detroit. About 96,000 of Detroit's residents were of foreign birth. The 32,000 Germans composed the largest group of foreign-born; there were 24,400 English Canadians and 3,500 French Canadians; and there were also 14,000 Polish immigrants as well as several thousand English, Scotch, Irish, and Russians (Glazer 1965, 53).

Continuing the late-nineteenth-century pattern of ethnic concentration, people still lived in identifiable neighborhoods. Some neighborhoods were ethnic, others were economic, and a few were ethnic-economic. Although Germans were found in various areas throughout the city, the most distinct German neighborhoods were located around Gratiot Avenue. A definite Jewish neighborhood had its center at Gratiot and Hastings, at the point where the Chrysler Freeway now intersects Gratiot (Glazer 1965, 53).

Detroit was at the threshold of an unprecedented industrial expansion. Between 1900 and 1910, the population increased from 285,000 to 465,000, and it more than doubled in the next decade to 993,000, which made Detroit the fourth largest city in the United States. Of the 993,000 inhabitants, about 41,000 were blacks, and 289,000 were foreign-born whites. In 1920, the Poles constituted the largest ethnic group (56,624), followed by the non–French Canadians (55,216), the Germans (30,238), and the Russians (27,278). The Armenians were the smallest European ethnic group with only 1,361.

The Russians were the least segregated from the blacks of all the ethnic groups, but there also was much sharing of residential space between blacks and Yugoslavians, Italians, Rumanians, and Greeks. There was moderate sharing of residential areas between blacks and Lithuanians, Austrians, and Syrians but little between blacks

Street lined with Greek shops and restaurants. (Courtesy Michigan Travel Bureau)

and the remaining white groups in Detroit (Table 10.1). The least sharing of residential space was between blacks and Belgians.

A tremendous increase brought Detroit's population to 1.6 million by 1930, making it the largest factory town in the world (De Vito 1979, 3), and the city annexed 60 sq mi (155.4 sq km) of land in the 1920s (Workers Education Local n.d., 4). The automotive industry, of course, was the major force behind this growth.

Detroit's automotive growth had begun when Ransom E. Olds of Lansing, Michigan, established his factory in Detroit in 1899. Detroit was a strategic location for the evolution of the automobile. It was halfway between the iron-ore fields of Minnesota and the coalfields of Appalachia, and its strategic location on the Great Lakes made it possible to transport these two basic elements to the city at low cost. Michigan's forests and copper mines attracted entrepreneurs, and they soon amassed large fortunes from lumber, iron, and copper. Their capital, in turn, bankrolled a wide range of metalworking industries in Detroit—shipbuilding, marine engines, and railroad cars—and each of these industries attracted large numbers of skilled workers. Therefore, abundant capital, skilled labor, weak unions, and cheap raw materials all made Detroit an ideal place to locate the early auto factories (Workers Education Local n.d., 3). Gathering vast quantities of raw materials and

TABLE 10.1. Residential segregation between blacks and ethnic groups in Detroit, 1920 (N = 21)

Origin of Group	City Population	Index of Segregation
	Low	
Black America	40,838	
Russia	27,278	24.9
Yugoslavia	3,702	35.2
Italy	16,205	36.7
Rumania	4,668	36.9
Greece	4,628	37.2
	Moderate	
Lithuania	2,653	40.8
Austria	10,674	42.8
Syria	1,877	46.8
Other countries	6,705	48.2
	High	
French Canada	3,678	58.3
France	1,740	61.1
Hungary	13,564	61.9
Germany	30,238	62.3
Ireland	7,004	62.6
Non-French Canada	55,216	62.8
Scotland	6,933	63.8
England	17,169	63.9
Czechoslovakia	3,351	66.1
Finland	1,785	66.2
Poland	56,624	66.3
Sweden	2,659	66.5
Denmark	1,505	67.0
Armenia	1,361	68.8
Netherlands	1,861	70.4
Belgium	6,219	81.9

N = number of wards.

Source: Computed by the author from data obtained from U.S. Bureau of the Census, Fourteenth Census of the United States Population, Vol. 3, Composition and Characteristics of the Population by States (Washington, D.C.: Government Printing Office, 1922). The formula for computing the segregation indexes above can be found in Joe T. Darden, "Residential Segregation of Blacks in the Suburbs: The Michigan Example," Geographical Survey 5:3 (July 1976), pp. 7-8.

semifinished products and converting them into finished, heavy, durable goods to be distributed throughout the country and the world, Detroit became the hub of one of the world's greatest manufacturing complexes (Hill 1978, 3).

The 113 percent growth of the population between 1910 and 1920 resulted in a large increase in the membership of many craft unions, including building trades, and organized labor came to be directly concerned with national, state, and city legislation. However, the Great Depression of the 1930s had an immediate impact upon automotive employees, and Detroit seems to have suffered more than any other large U.S. city because of its dependence on heavy industry and capital-goods production (De Vito 1979, 3). Traditionally, both of these sectors of economic activity have experienced the quickest declines during periods of depression and/or recession.

In the late 1930s, and continuing through World War II, the specialized demands of national rearmament led to large-scale industrial expansion and retooling in the city. New industrial facilities were also being constructed outside the city at this time, extending the industrial base beyond the confines of the older industrial areas. These war plants, when converted to producing peacetime goods, became the nuclei for suburbs that had mostly been farmland only a few years before (De Vito 1979, 3). The expansion of war-related industry continued to attract many people, so the population continued to grow to its peak, in 1950, of 1.8 million (Table 10.2).

Decline

The population of the central city of Detroit declined 9.7 percent during the decade of the 1950s, dropping from 1.8 million to 1.6 million. This decline coincided with the expansion of the suburbs brought about by industrial decentralization, Federal Housing Administration and Veterans Administration mortgage pro-

TABLE 10.2.   Population growth of Detroit, 1830–1980

	Total		Black		
Year	Population	Percentage Change	Population	Percentage Change	Percentage of Total Population
1830	2,200	--	73	--	3.3
1840	9,700	340.9	121	65.8	1.2
1850	21,019	116.7	587	385.1	2.8
1860	45,619	117.0	1,403	139.0	3.1
1870	79,517	74.3	2,231	59.0	2.8
1880	116,340	46.3	2,821	26.4	2.4
1890	205,853	76.9	3,431	21.6	1.7
1900	285,704	38.8	4,111	19.8	1.4
1910	465,766	63.0	5,741	39.6	1.2
1920	993,678	113.3	40,838	611.3	4.1
1930	1,568,662	57.9	120,066	194.0	7.7
1940	1,623,452	3.5	149,119	24.2	9.2
1950	1,849,568	13.9	300,506	101.5	16.2
1960	1,670,144	-9.7	482,229	60.5	28.9
1970	1,511,482	-9.5	660,428	37.0	43.7
1980	1,203,339	-20.4	758,939	14.9	63.0

Source: U.S. census figures published between 1830 and 1980.

grams, additions to the sewer and water systems, and interstate highway construction (De Vito 1979, 3).

Federal Housing Administration (FHA) mortgage insurance revolutionized home financing by guaranteeing payment of mortgages on properties that met the agency's standards. With all risk eliminated, lending institutions were willing to accept lower interest rates and much longer periods of repayment. Thus, home building doubled in the suburbs, and mortgage costs were very low. The FHA insurance program, which subsidized the growth of Detroit's suburbs, primarily benefited white middle- and working-class residents, because the FHA adopted a segregationist policy and refused to insure projects that did not comply. The common belief of white appraisers was that racial integration of the suburbs would lower property values. Although there was no evidence for this assumption, official FHA policy was based on it until 1948 (Orfield 1978, 80). White appraisers were told to look for physical barriers between racial groups, or to find and honor racially restrictive covenants, and race was officially listed as a valid reason for rejecting a mortgage (Helper 1969, 202). Thus, although the FHA provided an important service for young white families, blacks were viewed as a liability and denied equal access to the suburbs. At the same time, the FHA discouraged investment in predominantly black neighborhoods in the central city or in racially integrated neighborhoods generally (Orfield 1978, 81).

The Veterans Administration mortgage insurance program also shaped and reinforced the racial and economic segregation of the suburbs. This program allowed families of veterans to become homeowners with virtually no down payment, but non-white veterans held only 2 percent of these guaranteed mortgages in 1950. Thus, those veterans were rarely offered the same opportunity as white veterans to obtain new housing in the suburbs and thus build their equity.

At the same time, the federal government also subsidized the preparation of comprehensive plans for the emerging suburbs, and under these programs, there was usually no requirement for balanced growth of all income groups in the metropolitan region. Thus, competition was rampant among suburban communities for the most effective combinations of public and private actions to insulate themselves from the less affluent and racially different people living in the city (De Vito 1979, 4).

The population declines of the fifties, sixties, and seventies were largely the result of an out-migration of white families to the suburbs. By the sixties, however, new economic and social factors had come into play to attract people not only away from the city of Detroit, but also away from the older adjacent suburbs and farther out into newer suburbs, or exurbs. Exurbs are rural or nonmetropolitan areas by definition, but they still function as part of the metropolitan system (Roseman 1980, 51). By 1970, Detroit's population had decreased another 9.5 percent to 1.5 million, and between 1970 and 1980 the city experienced its greatest population decline in its history—decreasing 20.4 percent to 1.2 million—while the populations of the suburban counties (with the exception of Wayne) increased (see Table 2.2).

The average population loss for Detroit accelerated from an average of 0.7 percent per year in the 1960s to about 2 percent per year in the 1970s (Detroit Planning Department 1980b, 2). Most of this loss was due primarily to white out-migration and, to a lesser degree, to white natural decrease since the black population continued to increase. Thus, if there had been no out-migration, the population of Detroit would have continued to increase, because total births exceeded deaths by about 6,000 a year. However, since 1973, the white population of Detroit has not only moved out of the central city, but the population has experienced a "natural decrease," i.e., deaths have exceeded births by about 2,000 per year (Detroit Department of Planning 1980b, 4).

Factors Related to the Decline

Some factors causing the flight from the city and some of the older suburbs have been, first, the movement of industrial and commercial employers to the outer suburbs where there are large tracts of relatively inexpensive land for expansion. However, such movement outward has a negative and cumulative effect on sales. From 1972 to 1977, for example, the percentage of retail sales in Detroit either increased less than in the Detroit SMSA or declined absolutely—the percentage increase in the city of Detroit was only 9.7 percent; the increase in sales in the Detroit SMSA was 52 percent. Furthermore, Detroit experienced an absolute decline in sales by general merchandise stores, apparel and accessory stores, and furniture and equipment stores during the five-year period, 1972–1977, whereas there was no decline in sales in the SMSA (Table 10.3).

Second, the high cost of rehabilitating older housing relative to the apparent lower costs of, and lower taxes on, new housing in suburban municipalities also contributes to out-migration. Sixty-five percent of the housing units in the Detroit central city were built in 1939 or earlier, compared to only 17 percent in the suburbs of Detroit. Fifty-six percent of the owner-occupied housing in Detroit was built in 1939 or earlier, compared to 14 percent in the Detroit suburbs. And finally, 75 percent of the rental housing in the city was built in 1939 or earlier, compared to 25 percent in the suburbs (U.S. Department of Commerce 1980).

In Detroit, as in most large U.S. cities, the quality of residential areas tends to be related to distance from the city center. The oldest, poorest, and most congested areas are found in the central parts of the city; moving outward from the city center, housing gets newer and of higher quality, densities get lower, and neighborhood quality increases (Hill 1978, 10).

A third factor in the decline of the Detroit central city is the erosion of the city's tax base as wealthier citizens migrate disproportionally to the suburbs, along with industries. Thus, residents remaining in the city must bear a higher proportion of the total cost of providing social services, which results in a vicious cycle (Detroit Planning

TABLE 10.3.   Percentage change in sales from 1972 to 1977 in Detroit central city and SMSA

Kind of Business	Central City	SMSA
Retail stores	9.7	52.0
Building materials, hardware, garden supply, and mobile home dealers	26.7	48.7
General merchandise stores	-37.2	26.2
Food stores	12.7	45.4
Automotive dealers	33.9	70.2
Gasoline service stations	47.4	81.2
Apparel and accessory stores	-16.1	44.8
Furniture and equipment stores	-18.9	46.3
Eating and drinking places	11.2	60.6
Drug and proprietary stores	0.3	37.8
Miscellaneous retail stores	17.4	66.3

Source: U.S. Bureau of the Census, 1977 Census of Retail Trade (Washington, D.C.: Government Printing Office, 1978), Michigan-- Detroit SMSA (23-55).

Department 1980b, 2). This is an example of what may be called "negative circular causation and cumulative effects" (Fusfeld 1981, 148).

Associated with population decline is a continual drain of resources out of the area and into other more-progressive sectors of the suburbs. Although largely unmeasured, the drain includes human resources and capital. As a result, the declining area is left without the most important resources needed for development and growth, and the economic infrastructure is seriously deficient (Fusfeld 1981, 143).

The drain of human resources happens because professionals, managers, and administrators often leave declining areas first, followed by many of the most capable and most educated people. The drain of capital is equally striking. A substantial portion of the savings of the declining central city goes into financial institutions such as banks and savings associations whose investment policies often drain funds out of the central city area and into business loans, mortgages, and other investments in the suburbs. Perhaps one of the most important aspects of the flow of capital out of the central city takes place in housing. One deteriorated building draws down the value of surrounding property, and often leads to even less investment in the neighborhood in which the building is located. As housing deteriorates in one area, the remainder of the neighborhood soon begins to run down in a self-perpetuating cycle of decay. Home-improvement loans are often denied in a declining area, which leads to poor maintenance and, eventually, even further abandonment of housing (Darden 1980, 97). Just as growth breeds growth, decline breeds decline (Pred 1965).

Other factors have facilitated the migration process and, thus, have contributed to Detroit's decline. One such factor has been the construction of the interstate highways that connect Detroit to other areas and thus enable people to move farther away and still be within thirty-minutes' commuting time from the city center. There

has also been the desire by some residents to live at a distance from the poor who now disproportionally occupy the central city. Finally, Detroit is located in the "frost belt," and cities now losing population are generally located in this region of the Midwest and Northeast. On the other hand, growing cities are generally located in the Sun Belt where growing industries like oil and electronics are located, where the central cities have some undeveloped areas for expansion, and where northerners go to retire. Most large cities in the Northeast and Midwest have declining populations, mainly because of a movement of industries to the South, to the suburbs, and to other countries where wages are lower (Detroit Planning Department 1980b, 2).

Detroit's Decline in the Context of National Trends

As the Sun Belt states continue to grow economically and demographically, an axis is forming in the southwestern United States similar to the one that was created by New York and Chicago a century ago. In the industrial era, railroads, wheat, and heavy industries linked Chicago to New York, and Detroit benefited by being near the path between the two cities. Today, petrochemicals, oil, space-age technology, and the migration of people to the Southwest are undermining the advantages once held by the north-central and northeastern regions. Between 1970 and 1979, 40 percent of the population growth in the United States was in California, Texas, and Florida.

Population growth and employment expansion in the Sun Belt have attracted highly skilled workers, and the growth of the population has fed growth in service industries, which means even more job opportunities, which, in turn, have attracted more population. In other words, growth breeds growth—an example of "positive circular causation and cumulative effects." The growth in the Southwest is the result of dynamic industries such as energy and high technology, but Detroit and other older industrial cities in the

North continue to be heavily dependent on mature or declining industries (Detroit Planning Department, 1980a, III-9). The loss of population and industry, the decline of retail trade, and the subsequent erosion of the municipal tax base are problems that are common to cities like Detroit.

There are those people who believe, however, that recent demographic changes and economic changes will stabilize Detroit's population—and may even bring about a return of population to the central city. The demographic changes include the trend toward smaller households. Of the households in Detroit, 54 percent in 1976 were composed of only one or two persons, an increase from 48 percent in 1970 (Detroit Planning Department, 1980b, 5). In addition, divorce rates are higher, and there is a greater tendency for young adults to move out of the family household at an earlier age. Thus, the demand for housing by single people is expected to increase. Declining family size has reduced the number of years in which adults choosing housing must consider amenities that are child related; good schools, open space for children to play, and fear of congested streets are of less concern to people without children (Lipton 1977, 40). The greater number of single households, caused by deferring or postponing marriage and by divorce, creates a greater supply of people who may not desire suburban living. The absence of children negates many of the reasons why middle-class residents have preferred suburban locations so that many of them now at least consider living in the central city (Cybriwsky 1980, 25).

Economic changes include the drastic increase in the cost of gasoline, the increase in the cost of automobiles, and the difference in price between new suburban houses and other older houses of the central city. The cost of most suburban houses has escalated beyond the reach of many first-time buyers, thus increasing the demand for housing in Detroit. As the energy situation worsens, close-in locations are expected to become more and more advantageous, in part because reliance on the automobile will be lessened (Goldfield 1976, 83). However, experts disagree on the potential impact of energy considerations on residential-location decisions. Although some argue that the energy crisis can only favor central cities, others point to studies that suggest that Americans are not energy-price conscious and simply absorb the higher gasoline costs by cutting back in other areas (Muller 1978; Cybriwsky 1980, 26). Nevertheless, there is evidence that the downtown areas of many central cities in the United States experienced a remarkable revitalization during the 1970s. In some cities, this change has been massive and has resulted in an almost total physical and social transformation of the central area, which has led some experts to proclaim that a major shift in the basic sociogeographic structure of U.S. metropolitan areas is in the making (Cybriwsky 1980, 21). Are we now witnessing a "swing of the pendulum" away from suburban life toward living in the central cities, and will the big-city downtown areas become increasingly desirable as places to work, shop, and most important, live? These questions (as they relate to the city of Detroit) will be discussed in a later section in this chapter, but first another important aspect of urban geography is discussed—the character of racial and ethnic patterns.

RACIAL AND ETHNIC PATTERNS

The study of racial and ethnic groups in U.S. cities has a long history as the Chicago School of Urban Sociology has been focusing on racial and ethnic groups since the 1920s (Burgess 1928). Most studies emanating from the Chicago school have viewed racial and ethnic groups from the perspective of human ecology, and from this point of view, the population of a city competes for space and social position—that is, all individuals are rivals and compete for residential space (Hawley 1944). Past studies have informed us that the black population and foreign-born whites often have been in competition for the same "shabby tenements and back-street houses" (Clark 1981, 60).

An important consequence of the differences between racial and ethnic groups in their ability to compete is the propensity for human populations to locate unevenly— that is, to concentrate in some parts of the city and to avoid other parts (Lieberson 1963, 4). Insofar as the ensuing patterns of location are a function of the differences between racial and ethnic groups in their social positions, these patterns tell us something about the nature of the populations involved. Therefore, Park (1952, 177) concluded that social relations are inevitably correlated with spatial relations and physical distance with social distance.

Following this assumption, most past studies of racial and ethnic groups have viewed the residential patterns of the groups as a significant element in the study of their assimilation. The studies have, therefore, assessed the extent to which each group was living in the same residential areas as the native white population (Lieberson 1963, 11).

Gordon (1964, 27) has defined an ethnic group as a people set off by race, religion, or national origin sharing a sense of common origin and a common fate that gives meaning for the present and future to group traditions inherited from the past. For some individuals or groups, this feeling of attachment may not be strong enough to make them feel part of an "ethnic community," but the larger society may nevertheless define them as members of a particular ethnic group (Agocs 1974, 390–391).

Detroit, like many northern, industrial U.S. cities, is composed of numerous racial and ethnic groups. Such groups have come from Europe, Asia, and the Middle East, and some have come from various regions in the United States. Such groups once lived in well-defined, segregated areas of the city and the southeast Michigan region. Despite observable signs that ethnicity is still alive and well, Detroit and other large U.S. cities are regarded by many people as "melting pots" in which racial and ethnic groups are losing their separate identities and blending into a homogeneous, middle-class, American mainstream.

Blacks, Asian Americans, American Indians, and Hispanics are frequently viewed as more-recent immigrants to Detroit who have mostly remained lower-class residents and have retained a strong ethnic identity, partly because they lack the necessary education or skills to assimilate and to become upwardly mobile. But the melting-pot theory holds that these ethnic groups will acquire the education and skills, given sufficient exposure to urban and middle-class life-styles, and that they will find more opportunities open to them as their political power grows and as discriminatory practices in employment and housing decline (Handlin 1959, 120–121; Hauser 1965).

The melting-pot theory fails to recognize that the large and growing black population of Detroit, together with the other nonwhite and Hispanic population groups, has experienced prejudice and discrimination that far exceeds that experienced by white ethnic groups. This factor, more than recent migration, explains why there is a lack of spatial mobility from the segregated areas and a lack of movement into the mainstream of urban and suburban Detroit. This section focuses on some of the more recent immigrants to Detroit and on those groups that still have highly observable ethnic and racial concentrations—blacks, Poles, Hispanics, and Arab-Muslims. Emphasis is on their migration to Detroit and their residential patterns over time.

Blacks

Detroit ranks third behind New York and Chicago in the number of blacks in the city, 758,939 in 1980 (Figure 10.6), and Philadelphia and Los Angeles bring the number of cities with over 500,000 blacks to five. Detroit, which is 63 percent black, is the largest city in the United States in which the majority of the total population is black (U.S. Bureau of the Census 1981b).

FIGURE 10.6. Percent black population in Detroit, 1980. (Source: U.S. Bureau of the Census, *1980 Census of Population and Housing: Michigan*, "Final Population and Housing Unit Counts," PHC 80-V-24 [Washington, D.C.: Government Printing Office, 1981].)

Within the seven-county southeast Michigan region, blacks are concentrated primarily in Detroit and the rest of Wayne County (Table 10.4). The six remaining counties combined have only 91,022 blacks, or 9.9 percent of the region's total (Figure 10.7), and most of those, 84 percent, live in Oakland and Washtenaw Counties—Livingston, Macomb, Monroe, and St. Clair Counties combined have only 14, 737 blacks. Thus, except for Wayne County, few blacks live in suburban Detroit (Figure 10.8). In fact, 46, or 19.5 percent, of the 235 municipalities outside of Detroit are all white (Table 10.5). In those areas outside of Wayne County where blacks do live in large numbers, racial residential segregation remains high, although there were some changes between 1960 and 1980.

Black Residential Segregation. The level of black residential segregation remained virtually unchanged from 1970 to 1980 in the twenty-six suburban municipalities as a whole, as the mean level was 58.9 percent in 1970 and 58.4 percent in 1980, a reduction of only −0.5 percentage points (Table 10.6).[1] More significant changes, however, did occur in individual suburbs (Figure 10.9). Residential segregation declined in eighteen, or 69 percent, of the twenty-six suburban municipalities, with the index change ranging from −0.9 (Birmingham and Livonia) to −24.4 (Troy). The increase in segregation in the remaining municipalities ranged from 0.6 (Lincoln Park) to 41.8 (Oak Park)—the latter up from a very low 7.4 in 1970.

In 1980, the Detroit SMSA was expanded to include not only Wayne, Oakland, and Macomb Counties, but also Lapeer, Livingston, and St. Clair Counties (see Figure 10.3). Municipalities with five or more census tracts were chosen for analysis, and forty-seven municipalities met this crite-

Text resumes on page 192

TABLE 10.4. Racial composition of Detroit and the southeast region, 1980

Unit	White	Black	Indian	Asian and Pacific Islander	Other	Hispanic*
Livingston County	98,808	478	411	271	321	781
Macomb County	675,135	9,142	1,942	5,616	2,765	6,638
Monroe County	131,025	2,313	255	280	786	1,803
Oakland County	942,067	47,962	2,737	11,720	7,307	14,478
St. Clair County	134,109	2,804	558	302	1,029	2,066
Washtenaw County	227,091	28,323	720	5,631	2,983	4,055
Wayne County	1,457,409	829,868	6,667	15,164	28,132	46,301
Detroit City	(413,730)	(758,939)	(3,420)	(6,621)	(20,629)	(28,970)

Percentage Distribution

Unit	White	Black	Indian	Asian and Pacific Islander	Other	Hispanic*
Livingston County	98.5	0.5	0.4	0.2	0.3	0.8
Macomb County	97.1	1.3	0.3	0.8	0.3	1.0
Monroe County	97.3	1.7	0.2	0.2	0.5	1.3
Oakland County	93.1	4.7	0.3	1.1	0.7	1.4
St. Clair County	96.6	2.0	0.4	0.2	0.7	1.5
Washtenaw County	85.7	10.7	0.3	2.1	1.1	1.5
Wayne County	62.3	35.5	0.3	0.6	1.2	2.0
Detroit City	(34.3)	(63.0)	(0.2)	(0.5)	(1.7)	(2.4)

*The census includes Hispanics in either the white or black totals. Therefore, they are included in those two columns in this table, but they also appear as a separate group for purposes of reference.
Note: Percentages do not add to 100 because of rounding.

Source: Computed by the author from data obtained from U.S. Bureau of the Census, 1980 Census of Population and Housing: Michigan, Advance Reports, PHC 80-V-24 (Washington, D.C.: Government Printing Office, 1981).

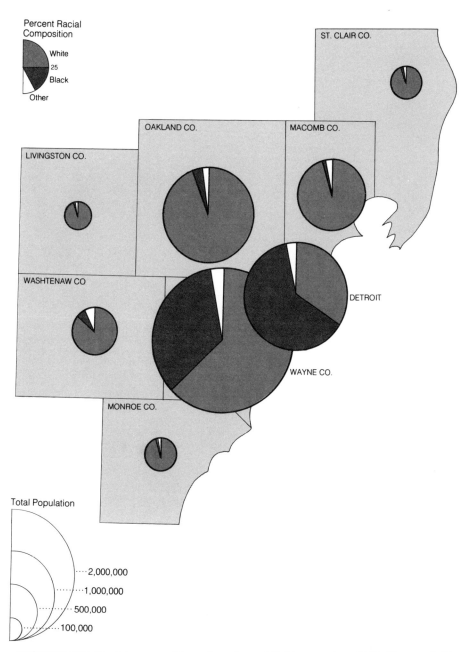

FIGURE 10.7. Racial composition of southeast Michigan region, 1980. (Source: U.S. Bureau of the Census, *1980 Census of Population and Housing: Michigan,* "Final Population and Housing Unit Counts," PHC 80-V-24 [Washington, D.C.: Government Printing Office, 1981].)

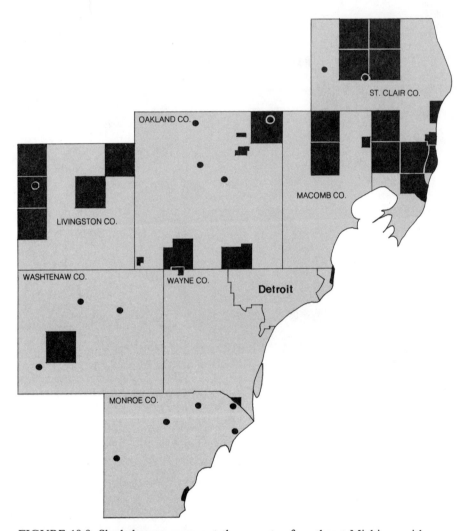

FIGURE 10.8. Shaded areas represent those parts of southeast Michigan with zero percent black population in 1980. (Source: U.S. Bureau of the Census, *1980 Census of Population and Housing: Michigan*, "Final Population and Housing Unit Counts," PHC 80-V-24 [Washington, D.C.: Government Printing Office, 1981].)

TABLE 10.5. Municipalities in the southeast region, by county, that were zero percent black in 1980

Livingston	Macomb	Monroe	Oakland	St. Clair	Washtenaw	Wayne
Conway Township	Armada	Carleton	Addison Township	Brockway Township	Barton Hills	Northville
Fowlerville	Armada Township	Estral Beach	Clarkston	Capac	Dexter	Rockwood
Handy Township	Grosse Pointe Shores	Luna Pier	Lake Angelus	Casco Township	Freedom Township	
Iosco Township	Ray Township	Maybee	Lake Orion	China Township	Manchester	
Oceola Township	Richmond	Petersburg	Leonard	Cohreville Township		
Tyrone Township		South Rockwood	Novi Township	Columbus Township		
			Ortonville	East China Township		
			Oxford	Emmett		
			Southfield Township	Emmett Township		
			South Lyon	Greenwood Township		
				Kenockee Township		
				Marysville		
				St. Clair		

Source: U.S. Bureau of the Census, 1980 Census of Population and Housing: Michigan, Advance Reports, PHC 80-V-24 (Washington, D.C.: Government Printing Office, 1981).

TABLE 10.6. Changes in black residential segregation in Detroit and its suburbs, 1970–1980[a]

| City | 1970 | | 1980 | | Index |
	Rank	Index	Rank	Index	Change
Roseville	2	92.1	1	89.7	−2.4
Allen Park	3	90.0	2	88.4	−1.6
Lincoln Park	6	81.7	3	82.3	0.6
Madison Heights	13	57.8	4	79.0	21.2
St. Clair Shores	5	84.3	5	78.7	−5.6
Westland	1	93.3	6	77.4	−15.9
Dearborn	20	50.2	7	72.8	22.6
Inkster	4	84.4	8	68.4	−16.0
DETROIT	7	78.2	9	67.4	−10.8
Warren	8	77.6	10	65.9	−11.7
Taylor	14	57.5	11	65.2	7.7
Dearborn Heights	18	52.8	12	60.5	7.7
Pontiac	10	68.1	13	60.0	−8.1
Southgate	11	61.4	14	59.1	−2.3
Livonia	16	54.7	15	53.8	−0.9
Oak Park	27	7.4	16	49.2	41.8
East Detroit	19	50.5	17	48.5	−2.0
Wyandotte	9	70.5	18	47.8	−22.7
Garden City	25	26.1	19	47.6	21.5
Southfield	24	31.5	20	46.6	15.1
Hamtramck[b]	15	55.3	21	40.9	−14.4
Royal Oak	26	25.9	22	36.1	10.2
Sterling Heights	12	58.4	23	35.9	−22.5
Birmingham	23	36.1	24	35.2	−0.9
Highland Park[b]	22	47.7	25	33.7	−14.0
Troy	17	53.6	26	29.2	−24.4
Ferndale	21	50.0	27	26.3	−23.7
Mean		58.9		58.4	−0.5

[a]Detroit's SMSA consisted of Wayne, Oakland, and Macomb Counties in 1970. The suburbs included the municipalities outside the city of Detroit that had a 1970 population of at least 25,000 total population. The segregation indexes were computed for 1970 and 1980 on the same municipalities for comparative purposes.

[b]Municipal enclave.

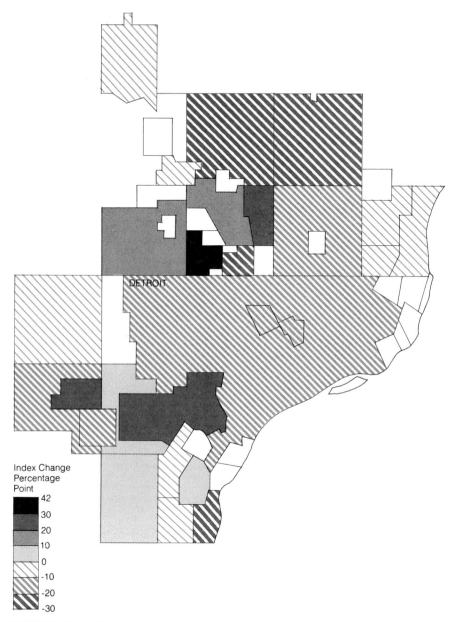

Index Change
Percentage
Point

- 42
- 30
- 20
- 10
- 0
- -10
- -20
- -30

FIGURE 10.9. Changes in black residential segregation in Detroit and its suburbs, 1970–1980. (Sources: U.S. Bureau of the Census, *1970 Census of Population and Housing*, "1970 Census Tracts, Final Report, Detroit SMSA" [Washington, D.C.: Government Printing Office, 1972] and U.S. Bureau of the Census, "Population and Housing Summary Tape File 1-A, Michigan" [Washington, D.C.: Data User Services Division, 1982].)

rion. The level of residential segregation in those municipalities ranged from a high of 90.6 percent in Plymouth Township to a low of 20.3 in Canton Township (Table 10.7). Eleven, or 23 percent, of the municipalities had levels of segregation above that in the city of Detroit.

For the purpose of evaluation, the suburbs within the Detroit SMSA are classified (according to level of segregation) into three categories. There are suburbs with high levels of segregation (above 50 percent), moderate levels (40 to 50 percent), and low levels (below 40 percent). Twenty-two, or 47 percent, of the suburbs have high levels of segregation; thirteen, or 28 percent, have moderate levels, and twelve, or 25 percent, have low levels of segregation (Figure 10.10). The mean level of segregation for all Detroit's suburbs is 53 percent, or 14.4 percentage points lower than the level in the city of Detroit.

In summary, the highly segregated suburbs tend to vary by size, number, and percentage of blacks. However, the common feature is the limited spatial distribution of the black population as most blacks are restricted to only a few neighborhoods or census tracts. If this trend continues, the ghetto pattern that characterized the city of Detroit at the turn of the century will emerge in the suburbs. Little suburban ghettos (where blacks constitute the majority in particular census tracts) are already developing.

Considerable debate has centered around identifying the factors that are related to black segregated housing patterns, but the discussion has focused on the relative roles of the complex forces of housing cost, discrimination, and residential choice (Clark 1980, 96). Is housing cost the primary reason so few blacks live in the suburbs of Detroit compared to the high concentration of blacks in the city? This question was answered by Hermalin and Farley (1973). Using 1970 census data, these authors examined each suburb of 25,000 or more in the Detroit urbanized area. They looked at the total number of occupied dwelling units and the actual and expected units occupied by blacks. Looking at the actual numbers first, they saw that more than 96 percent of the 17,000 black households in the twenty-six Detroit suburbs were in four municipalities: Hamtramck, Highland Park, Inkster, and Pontiac. Twenty of the twenty-six suburbs had fewer than fifty black households.

The authors then determined the proportion of housing units in each economic category throughout the Detroit urbanized area that was occupied by blacks. They next considered the distribution of owned and leased housing by value in each suburb and ascertained how many blacks would be in that particular suburb if they were in each value of housing in the same proportion that they were throughout the entire Detroit urbanized area. Similarly, the authors ascertained how many whites would be expected in each suburb if whites in each economic bracket occupied housing there in the same proportion that they did throughout the entire area. In all twenty-six suburbs combined, fewer than 4 percent of the total households were black, but the proportion expected on the basis of housing value was 12 percent. In nineteen of the twenty-six suburbs, 0.1 percent or less of the households were black even though 5 percent was the minimum expected. In most suburbs, the proportion expected to be black was between 9 and 18 percent (Hermalin and Farley 1973, 606). Similar calculations were made using family income as the criterion. In every suburb, the expected proportion of black families was within the range of 12 to 23 percent, yet the actual proportion of black families was 0.1 percent or less in eighteen of the twenty-six suburbs.

The implication of these results is that the cost of housing, or the inability of blacks to pay for housing outside of Detroit, is not the primary reason so few blacks live in the suburbs of Detroit. The data seem to suggest that racial discrimination in housing is by far the stronger explanation.

The fact that discrimination in housing

TABLE 10.7. Levels of black suburban residential segregation in Detroit and its suburbs, 1980[a]

High		Moderate		Low	
Plymouth Township	90.6	Oak Park	49.2	Royal Oak	36.1
Roseville	89.7	East Detroit	48.5	Sterling Heights	35.9
Allen Park	88.4	Wayne City	48.1	Grosse Pointe Farms	35.7
Lincoln Park	82.3	Wyandotte	47.8	Birmingham	35.2
Madison Heights	79.0	Garden City	47.6	Highland Park[b]	33.7
St. Clair Shores	78.7	Chesterfield Township	47.3	Farmington Hills	32.8
Clinton Township	77.5	Southfield	46.6	Avon Township	32.2
Westland	77.4	Waterford Township	45.6	Berkley City	30.7
Mount Clemens	75.5	Brownstown Township	44.7	Troy	29.2
Dearborn	72.8	Bloomfield Township	41.8	Ferndale	26.3
Inkster	68.4	Redford Township	41.8	West Bloomfield Township	20.4
DETROIT	67.4	Hamtramck[b]	40.9	Canton Township	20.3
Harrison Township	65.9	Fraser	40.4		
Warren	65.9				
Taylor	65.2				
Dearborn Heights	60.5			Mean	53.0
Pontiac	60.0				
Southgate	59.1				
Shelby Township	58.5				
Port Huron	57.8				
Romulus	56.1				
Livonia	53.8				
Trenton	51.1				

[a]Places with five or more census tracts.
[b]Municipal enclave.

Source: Computed by the author from data obtained from the U.S. Bureau of the Census, "Population and Housing Summary Tape File 1-A, Michigan" (Washington, D.C.: Data User Services Division, 1982).

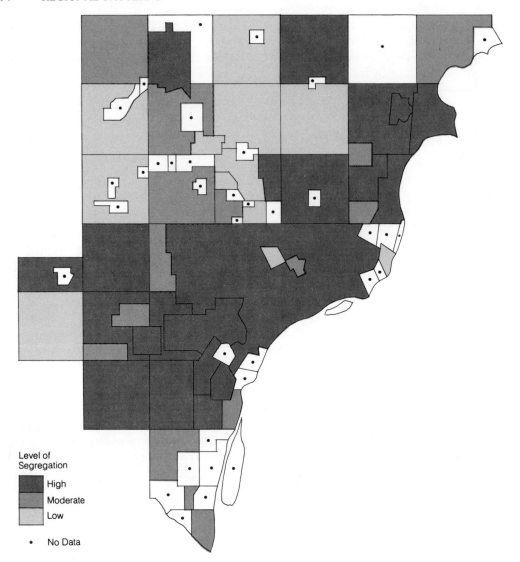

FIGURE 10.10. Level of segregation in Detroit and its suburbs, 1980. (Source: U.S. Bureau of the Census, "Population and Housing Summary Tape File 1-A, Michigan" [Washington, D.C.: Data User Services Division, 1982].)

has existed for a long time in Detroit has been well documented (Butler 1964; Katzman 1973; Deskins 1981, 108). As early as 1830, Detroit's 73 blacks lived in the midst of a hostile white social climate, and race riots were common. As a result, blacks were concentrated in a single area, only .06 sq mi (.15 sq km) in size, that had taken shape just to the east of the city's center (Deskins 1981, 100). By 1850, the black core area continued to be a single

cluster covering .5 sq mi (1.3 sq km) and occupying about 8.5 percent of the city's total area. Within this limited area, 587 blacks lived, representing a 385 percent increase in the black population in two decades (Deskins 1981, 100). In 1860, the black area expanded to cover an area of .88 sq mi (2.3 sq km).

Until 1910, the black population of Detroit grew rather slowly, but between 1910 and 1920, the greatest growth was in the black population (611.3 percent). To reduce the likelihood of black expansion into white residential areas, restrictive real estate covenants were established, which allowed certain houses in specific areas to be sold to whites only (Black 1947). The prevailing attitude of the whites in Detroit was best stated by the U.S. Federal Housing Administration in 1938 and again in 1947. In 1938 the FHA stated: "Areas surrounding a location are investigated to determine whether incompatible racial and social groups are present, for the purpose of making a prediction regarding the probability of a location being invaded by such groups. If a neighborhood is to retain stability, it is necessary that properties shall continue to be occupied by the same social and racial classes" (U.S. Federal Housing Administration 1938, par. 937).

The enforcement of these covenants by the state of Michigan obviously restricted the movement of blacks west of Woodward Avenue, which was an unbreached barrier to black residential expansion until 1950 (Deskins 1981, 109). In 1948, the U.S. Supreme Court declared that restrictive covenants designed to prevent the sale or resale of real property to persons of specified race, color, religion, national origin, or ancestry were unenforceable by either state or federal courts on the grounds that such enforcement would constitute governmental action in furtherance of racial discrimination—see *Shelly* v. *Kraemer,* 334 (U.S.) 1 (1948) and *Hurd* v. *Hodge* 334 (U.S.) 24 (1948). In denying the enforceability of racially restrictive covenants, however, the Supreme Court did not specify that those covenants were illegal or void.

It is apparent that historically, blacks have been excluded from most white neighborhoods in Detroit through various discriminatory means, and there is also evidence that such discriminatory tactics have persisted in the form of "racial steering" by white real estate brokers. In a study of ninety-seven randomly selected real estate agents in the Detroit SMSA between 1974 and 1975, it was found that blacks, more often than whites, were shown houses *not* located in the city where the agent's office was located; that is, they were steered out of town. Also, where and whether houses were shown to blacks depended upon the location of the real estate office within the suburban municipality. Moreover, when whites were steered out of a suburb, about four-fifths of the municipalities where they were shown houses were nearby white suburbs. In contrast, when blacks were steered out, two-thirds of the houses they were shown were in the racially mixed municipalities of Inkster and Detroit (Pearce 1979, 335). Detroit alone accounted for almost a third of the homes shown to blacks, although only 13 percent of the real estate firms were located in Detroit. Not only did blacks see a disproportionate number of houses in Inkster and Detroit, but they were steered there by firms located in the western, southern, and eastern-shore suburbs. Clearly, then, the study revealed a consistent pattern of racially differentiated treatment of homeseekers. The data showed that these were not isolated instances of individual racism; instead, there was a high level of consistency across the entire metropolitan area. There was a clear existence of practices that excluded three-fourths of the black families from ever seeing homes and steered out many of the few that did see homes.

The existence of racial steering and/or racial discriminatory treatment in providing housing information was also revealed by a national study conducted by the U.S. Department of Housing and Urban Development. Of the forty SMSAs studied, Detroit ranked first in discriminatory treatment of blacks in the rental housing market and third—behind Cincinnati and Columbus, Ohio—in discrimination in housing sales. In the rental market in Detroit, whites were favored 67 percent of the time and blacks only 10 percent—a statistically significant difference of 57 percentage points. In the sales market, whites were favored 64 percent of the time, and blacks 22 percent—a statistically significant difference of 42 percentage points. If there were no racial discrimination, one could expect there would be no difference in the percentage of whites and of blacks favored by real estate brokers, and hence, the discriminatory treatment index would be zero. The greater the difference in treatment on the basis of race, the greater the discriminatory treatment index (U.S. Department of Housing and Urban Development 1979, 180–181).

The third factor often advanced to explain black residential segregation is choice, or a preference by blacks to remain segregated (Wolf 1981, 34–39). In other words, despite the evidence presented here, some people continue to argue that the blacks in Detroit do in fact have freedom of spatial mobility and that the blacks who remain in black segregated areas are there by choice (Coleman 1979, 11). It is conceivable that some blacks might desire to live only with other blacks even if they had total freedom to choose their living space, but explanation for this preference cannot be totally divorced from past and present forces of racism and discrimination (Darden 1973, 64). Since blacks have never had total freedom to live in any area of the Detroit SMSA they wanted, the influence of personal preference cannot be adequately measured, and the case for personal preference as a factor in racial residential segregation remains hypothetical.

Within this hypothetical context, the black self-segregation or black-preference issue has been addressed with surveys of black attitudes toward racially integrated housing, and such surveys conducted in Detroit and other cities have provided little support for the voluntary segregation hypothesis (Brink and Harris 1967, 232–233; Campbell and Schuman 1968; Pettigrew 1973; Farley et al. 1978). Most blacks surveyed in the study of Detroit by Farley et al. were willing to live in racially mixed neighborhoods, whereas the whites were reluctant to remain in neighborhoods blacks were moving into and would not buy houses in already integrated areas. Taken as a whole, the message of the testimony on

residential patterns in the Detroit school desegregation case of *Bradley* v. *Milliken* in 1971 was this:

> Segregation is measured as concentration, but this concentration is caused by exclusion and discrimination motivated by racial prejudice. Economic factors are of minor importance, and since blacks are not an ethnic group in the way in which foreign-born families once were, voluntary congregation is unlikely except as a response to intimidation. Thus, racial concentration is largely compelled, and government has been such a potent force in this compulsion that its outcome can be described as *de jure* segregation, the product of state action. The outlook for housing integration is bleak. Racial separation in residence is severe, widespread, unresponsive to economic improvement, worsened by the passage of time, and impervious to the assimilative processes that dispersed other groups. [Wolf 1981, 26]

The empirical evidence suggests that the voluntary segregation proposition in Detroit is a myth. Why, then, does the argument that "blacks prefer to live among their own kind" continue to be advanced? Two factors are probably responsible. First, some groups have advanced such an argument as a rationale for maintaining the status quo and for preventing or delaying any efforts toward decreasing black residential segregation (Myrdal 1944, 619–621; Wallace 1953, 25; Darden 1973, 64). Second, other people are merely unaware of the differences in the historical development of racial and ethnic groups in U.S. cities. They are unaware that unlike white ethnic—i.e., European—immigrant groups, blacks clustered together not necessarily to enjoy a common linguistic, cultural, and religious tradition, but because a systematic pattern of racial discrimination left them no alternative (Spear 1967, 228). Blacks have been tied together less by a common cultural heritage than by a common set of grievances. Thus, the clustering of blacks in Detroit can best be described as not primarily by choice, but as an involuntary adaptation to white discrimination (Spear 1967, pp. 228–229).

Poles

Although there is evidence of a steadily rising rate of spatial dispersion of the Polish population accompanied by a high degree of cultural assimilation, the Poles remain an identifiable, spatially concentrated, white ethnic group in Detroit (Mackun 1964). According to the 1970 census, there were 165,736 Polish residents in the seven-county southeast Michigan region, and they composed the second largest white ethnic group in the region—the Canadians made the largest. In 1970, 41 percent of the Poles lived in the central city, where they remained the largest white ethnic group—20 percent of the total population of foreign stock (Wrobel 1979, 32). The suburban city of Warren, not Hamtramck, had the second largest concentration of Poles, with 6.2 percent. Hamtramck, still called Little Poland because of its historical dominance by Poles, had 5.5 percent of all the Poles in the seven-county region and was followed by Dearborn, Dearborn Heights, Southfield, Oak Park, and Wyandotte as centers of Polish concentrations (Michigan Ethnic Heritage Center 1971, 118).

Some of the Poles who settled in Detroit in the nineteenth century had emigrated from Prussian-held former Polish territories (Orton 1981, 12), and they generally arrived with a modest sum of money, acquired from the sale of their property in the Old Country, which they used to build houses (*Detroit Free Press* 1873, 1). Although many of the emigrants were from rural areas, they had a rudimentary education and often had learned a trade besides farming. The Prussian Polish immigrants of the late 1850s were not the first Poles in Detroit, but they were the first ones who came primarily for economic betterment and eventually united to establish an ethnic community (Orton 1981, 12).

During the 1860s, Polish immigration to Detroit mounted steadily so that by 1870, there were close to 300 families. These Prussian Poles, most of whom understood and spoke German, clustered in or near the east-side German neighborhood that was expanding along Gratiot Avenue toward Mt. Elliott, then Detroit's eastern boundary. They gradually moved northward, and by the 1880s, the Poles formed the most distinctive ethnic settlement on the city's then northeast side, characterized by the local press as Little Poland (Orton 1981, 162). From an estimated 300 Polish families in 1870, the community had grown to about 14,000 persons by 1885 (*Detroit Tribune* 1885, 9). By the turn of the century, the Polish population was estimated at 40,000, about 16 percent of Detroit's population (Curwood 1904, 4). This figure, however, cannot be confirmed since many Poles indicated either Germany, Austria-Hungary, or Russia as their country of origin to the federal census takers (Orton 1981, 162).

Many of the Polish immigrants had been drawn to Detroit by reports of its expanding industries and the availability of unskilled work. More often than not, however, the Poles' choice of Detroit was influenced by the presence of relatives, friends, or people from the immigrants' villages in the Old Country (Napolska 1946). After 1900 and with the emergence of the automobile plants, fewer Poles arrived directly from Poland; increasingly, they came from the mining regions of Pennsylvania or other U.S. cities where employment opportunities were fewer (Orton 1981, 169).

The territorial concentration of Polish Americans in the Detroit area started in the mid-1800s in an area immediately adjacent to St. Albertus Church. The influence of the parish was very important for the location and spread of the Poles, and the new parish soon became the center of an expanding Polish-American settlement. The Polish church, in other words, exerted a centripetal, or concentrating, force on the growth of the settlement.

As the Polish community expanded between two main thoroughfares—Woodward Avenue to the west and Gratiot Avenue to the east—it had a definite effect on the spatial distribution of many other ethnic groups in the city. In addition to St. Albertus Parish, the core settlement of Polish immigrants on the east side of Detroit, St. Casimir Parish attracted Poles on the west side.

The first decades in Detroit were not easy for the Polish immigrants as ignorance of local ways, periodic economic adversity, and religious division, exacerbated by the uncomprehending and sometimes intolerant majority population of Detroit, posed severe hurdles to their adjustment. However, the twentieth century brought great changes to Detroit's Polish community. Both the native language and the traditional values and customs of a rural, agrarian society were modified by the novel environment of urban, industrial Detroit. The 1920 census showed the Poles to be the single largest European ethnic group in Detroit, and their movement outward from the original east-side and west-side Polish neighborhoods continued and speeded up. By World War II, the locus of Polish Detroit had become the municipal enclave of Hamtramck, still considered one of the most Polish cities in the United States. After World War II, Poles on Detroit's east side increasingly relocated beyond Six-Mile Road and in the suburban communities of Macomb County (Orton 1981, 195). Many of the original Polish homes on the east side were occupied by new waves of migrants, especially blacks from the rural South, and a similar pattern of out-migration occurred on the west side. As economic conditions improved, Poles moved in large numbers to Warren, Dearborn, and downriver suburban communities in Wayne County (Mackun 1964). Today, the Poles are no longer clustered in and around St. Albertus Parish as they have expanded so their center of population is closer to the northern suburb of Warren than to downtown Detroit. Still, Polish parishes continue to serve clearly identifiable ethnic neighborhoods (Wrobel 1979, 35).

The Poles are often steered by real estate brokers into the suburb of Warren and away from the city of Detroit (Wrobel 1979, 130), but while the brokers have encouraged the Poles to move to some Detroit suburbs, they used to keep them out of others. Grosse Pointe, for example, kept non-white and white ethnic groups out of the area through a point system that remained in force until the mid-1960s. This point system was an attempt to prevent entry into the area, not only of blacks, but of Poles, Mexicans, and other selected ethnic groups (Sengstock 1974).

Hispanics

The population of Spanish origin—Hispanics—includes Mexicans, Cubans, Puerto Ricans, and other Latin American peoples. In 1980, this population in the seven-county southeast Michigan region stood at 76,122 (U.S. Department of Commerce, 1981c). Most Hispanics are concentrated in Wayne County, and within Wayne County, most live in Detroit (see Table 10.4).

Within the city of Detroit, Hispanics live primarily in a few areas (Figure 10.11). They are not only segregated from non-Hispanic whites in Detroit, but segregation is even higher between the Hispanics and the blacks. The index of segregation in 1980 between the Hispanics and non-Hispanic whites was 56.7 percent; the level of segregation between Hispanics and blacks was 69.1 percent. Thus, Hispanics are not evenly distributed in the city, and they are isolated from both whites and blacks.

Detroit has the second largest Hispanic community in the Midwest—only Chicago has a larger concentration—and most of them are of Mexican stock. Therefore, the remainder of this discussion of Hispanics will focus on the Mexican Americans in Detroit.

Factors in Mexican Immigration to Detroit. The first Mexicans to arrive in Detroit were attracted by the same thing that had drawn countless other ethnic groups—jobs. Three reasons were the most important in the Mexican migration to Detroit: (1) The railroads, which had employed Mexican

FIGURE 10.11. Percent Hispanic population in Detroit, 1980. (Source: U.S. Bureau of the Census, "Population and Housing Summary Tape File 1-A, Michigan" [Washington, D.C.: Data User Services Division, 1982].)

track hands in other states, began to transfer them as far north as Detroit (Meier and Rivera 1972); (2) the Ford Motor Company's announcement of a five-dollar workday lured thousands of immigrants, including Mexicans, to work in the automobile and related industries (Salas and Salas 1974); and (3) some came to escape working in the sugar-beet industry, which had heretofore employed Mexican workers in the Southwest, Michigan, and other midwestern states (Baba and Abonyi 1979, 39). This last factor brought by far the largest numbers of Mexican migrants to the state of Michigan. Although the 1900 census showed only 8 foreign-born Mexicans in Detroit, the Mexican community had grown to 1,268 by 1920.

In most cases, Mexican Americans came from economically and socially deprived rural backgrounds and had little knowledge of English, a limited education or formal training, an inadequate knowledge of urban, middle-class United States, and a different set of values and attitudes (Knoll 1974). Other factors exacerbating the Mexican Americans' adjustment to Detroit included their deeply dependent ties to the mother country or state, which resulted in frequent trips between Detroit and Mexico or Texas. This tendency disrupted the children's school adjustment and often affected the job stability of the parents. It also was related to feelings of hopelessness and alienation, and that alienation was further reinforced by the immigrants' subsequent rejection by both their state or country of origin and their local Detroit community (Knoll 1974, 263).

Residential Patterns. Mexicans were scattered throughout the city during the early 1900s, but noticeable Spanish-speaking communities, or barrios, gradually became evident as the Mexicans were excluded from certain sections of Detroit. One such barrio was on the near east side of downtown Detroit in the vicinity of Lafayette and Congress Streets (Baba and Abonyi 1979, 51). A Mexican restaurant, barbershop, bar, pool hall, and several other establishments that catered primarily to Mexicans attested to the ethnic flavor of the barrio, which became a permanent feature of the cultural landscape of Detroit. It was, in part, a reminder that there was indeed discrimination in housing against the Mexicans in Detroit. There were homeowners who refused to rent to Mexicans, and there were many barbershops, restaurants, bars, and other public places that either segregated or completely barred Mexicans (Baba and Abonyi 1979, 56). Such discrimination did not prevent or discourage Mexican settlement in Detroit, but by the end of the 1920s, most of the growth was in Corktown, a neighborhood on the near west side surrounding Tiger Stadium—which had been named after the Irish immigrants who had settled there in earlier years.

In 1940, there were 1,565 foreign-born Mexicans in Detroit. Almost a third of them lived in three census tracts next to Holy Trinity Church (Baba and Abonyi 1979, 62), and most of the remainder lived in contiguous census tracts along Michigan Avenue (U.S. Bureau of the Census 1941). The Catholic Church was a factor in influencing the settlement sites of the foreign-born Mexicans, but the location of industry was more important.

In time, significant numbers of the Mexican Americans settled outside the Detroit central city. Some settled near the Dodge plant in Hamtramck (a municipal enclave); others settled in South Dearborn near the Ford River Rouge plant and in the downriver communities of River Rouge, Ecorse, Wyandotte, and Lincoln Park where employment opportunities were numerous, particularly at the Great Lakes steel plant in River Rouge (Baba and Abonyi 1979, 63).

In 1970, there were 2,914 Mexicans in the city of Detroit according to the U.S. Census, but the Mexican-American community was seriously undercounted by the Census Bureau (Salas and Salas 1974, 374). Nevertheless, the 1970 statistics showed that the Mexican-American residential pattern in southwestern Detroit had remained relatively stable, although the extreme eastern edge of the 1940 settlement had shifted west. A new site was also evident on the west side, stretching south across the city limits into Dearborn. By 1970, several other areas in the seven-county region had also become important settlement sites for Mexican Americans (Baba and Abonyi 1979, 66).

In summary, most of the Mexican-American settlement sites have been directly linked to the availability of industrial jobs in the region, and despite the wide dispersion of Mexican Americans throughout the seven-county region, the barrio remains. According to the 1980 census statistics, one census tract, 5212, was 52.2 percent Hispanic even though the Hispanic population represents only 2.4 percent of the total Detroit population (U.S. Department of Commerce 1981a). This tract is located west of the central business district and is bounded by Grand Boulevard on the west, Fisher Freeway on the south and east, and a railroad track on the north. Adjacent census tracts 5211, 5233, and 5234, which are already more than 36 percent Hispanic, are expected to have a Hispanic majority by 1990.

Although Europe no longer provides great numbers of immigrants to the United States, immigration from Mexico is high and continues to rise. Thus, the Mexican Americans will continue to have a significant impact on the state of Michigan and especially on the Detroit area (Baba and Abonyi 1979, 77).

Arab-Muslim Americans

The Arab-Muslim population in the Detroit area numbers about 7,000 and is concentrated primarily in Dearborn, a suburb of Detroit (Figure 10.12). Within Dear-

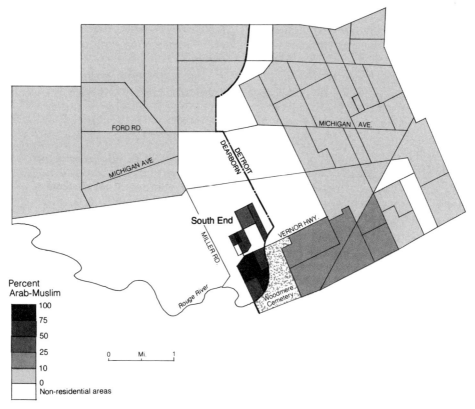

FIGURE 10.12. Percent Arab-Muslim population in Detroit, 1977. (Source: Mohammad Siryani, "Residential Distribution, Spatial Mobility, and Acculturation in an Arab-Muslim Community" [Ph.D. dissertation, Michigan State University, 1977].)

born, the Arab population is restricted to a single area known as the South End (Siryani 1977, 4), which is located between the city limits of Detroit on the east and the Ford River Rouge plant on the west; the northern boundary of the area is John Kronk Avenue, and West Fort bounds it on the south. The South End is geographically isolated from the rest of Dearborn, and the neighborhood is often not even associated with that city as many people think the area is a part of Detroit (Siryani 1977, 4). The South End is directly tied to the development and expansion of the Ford River Rouge Complex. Initially, the South End was settled by European immigrants, and while some of these Europeans and their decendants remain, the area today is basically composed of Arabic-speaking immigrants from Lebanon, Yemen,

and Palestine (Wigle and Abraham 1974, 280).

The Lebanese, for the most part, are permanent residents. Originating mainly from southern Lebanon, many of them have been residents of the South End for two, three, or four generations. The Yemeni are recurrent migrants, returning to Yemen frequently. They have been arriving only since 1948 and come from both North and South Yemen. Finally, the Palestinians must be separated into two groups: those who arrived as displaced persons as a result of the Israeli expansion and occupation of their land, and those who came before direct Israeli penetration of the West Bank in 1967 (Wigle and Abraham 1974).

Arab Immigration to the Area. The first Arab-Muslim immigration consisted of ten people who arrived in Detroit in 1914 to work at the Ford Highland Park plant (Wasfi 1964, 80), but the numbers increased gradually. Most of the newcomers were Syrians of Lebanese origin and were either related to the first immigrants or from the same village (Siryani 1977, 48). The pioneers came with the intention of making money and returning to the Old Country. They were concentrated in a small community in Highland Park, and another group of Arab-Muslim immigrants that came between 1918 and 1922 constituted the nucleus of the Dearborn Arab-Muslim community (Siryani 1977, 49). Available work in the Ford River Rouge plant was the prime reason for this latter settlement.

Most of the Arab- Muslim immigrants came to Dearborn after World War II (Siryani 1977, 50), and this big flow consisted of either relatives or friends of the already existing Lebanese community. In fact, most of them were from two or three villages in southern Lebanon. Prior to 1948, the majority of Arab immigrants was of Lebanese origin, but Palestinians and Yemeni came to Dearborn in waves after the three Arab-Israeli wars of 1948, 1967, and 1973, and recently immigrants have come from the occupied territories of the West Bank of Jordan (Aswad 1974).

The majority of the Arab immigrants came from rural villages in the Middle East. As a class, they were middle-and lower-middle peasants, either small landowners or landless (Wigle and Abraham 1974, 280).

Residential Patterns. In 1926, there were twelve Arab residences in Dearborn, and seven of them were located on Wyoming and Salina Streets, south of Dix Avenue. By 1930, there were twenty-eight households identified with Arab surnames, and the Arab population was starting to cluster in the South End area just south of Dix Avenue along Wyoming, Salina, Ferenez, and Canterbury Streets (Siryani 1977, 60). Between 1930 and 1940, Dearborn's Arab-Muslim population grew from twenty-eight to sixty-five households, and during the next three decades, the Arab-Muslim population increased rapidly, and segregation intensified. Today, the South End is generally referred to as an Arab-Muslim ghetto (Siryani 1977; Wigle and Abraham 1974).

The South End is physically as well as culturally distinct. Along Dix Avenue, the main street bisecting the area, traditional Middle Eastern customs are evident. Numerous coffeehouses are interspersed with Middle Eastern restaurants and grocery stores that import much of their food from the Old Country. Advertisements are written in Arabic, and Arabic is the main language spoken (Wigle and Abraham 1974, 280). There are five distinct coffeehouses that cater to the Lebanese, Yemeni, and Palestinians. Divisions among the groups are firmly rooted and are not only based on nationality differences but also follow regional or village differences. Within the coffeehouses themselves, tables are frequently arranged according to village (Wigle and Abraham 1974, 289).

The immigration of racial and ethnic groups to the Detroit area has been strongly linked to the economy of the Detroit area. When the economy is on the rise, immigrants flock to the area in search of employment, and economic problems have a negative impact on new population movement into the area.

ECONOMY

Detroit's economy, as well as that of the entire southeast Michigan region, is in transition. Manufacturing is still the primary economic force in the area, but, consistent with national trends, the service sector and office-oriented employment have been growing (Detroit Planning Department 1979, 5). Because of a strong reliance on the manufacture of durable goods, particularly auto production, Detroit has been especially vulnerable to national business cycles. In April 1980, the business activity index reported each month by the Manufacturers National Bank reached its lowest level since December 1975. The index measures employment, volume of financial ac-

General Motors headquarters in Detroit.

tivity, steel output, electric power consumption, automobile and truck production, and automobile sales (Detroit Planning Department 1980a, III-5). The auto industry is now a mature industry with saturated markets, and growth is due largely to replacement.

Historically, despite the severe effects of recessions, Detroit always has weathered the downturns, but the current slowed economy across the United States has resulted in several different, serious factors in Detroit. There is a combination of the severe slump in the auto industry, the long-term decline in manufacturing jobs in general, and a declining population.

Political pressure, labor differentials, and new market potentials have encouraged firms to locate operations in the South and in foreign countries. An increasing number of countries are instituting local-content laws that require foreign sellers to establish production facilities in the host country if they wish to enter that market. Although this policy helps the seller penetrate new markets, it tends to create unemployment in the home country.

International plant relocation from Detroit and other industrial cities has occurred as a response to several other factors as well. Firms are seeking to minimize costs by locating in areas that have low wages and few costly strikes (Detroit Planning Department 1980a, III-7). Firms are also seeking to maximize their profits by locating in high-productivity, politically stable regions or in areas that will provide a new market. Although this pattern of spatial mobility helps producers, it tends to create further unemployment in the home city and country—in this case, Michigan and Detroit.

Patterns of Unemployment in the Detroit Area

Detroit became one of the largest industrial cities in the United States because of the heavy manufacturing and durable goods industries, particularly the production of automobiles. Since the 1960s, the manufacturing sector in general has declined somewhat, and the city has acquired some of the problems typically associated with older industrial regions. These problems center around the impact that a changing technology and a cyclical economy have on the worker as an individual, the industry, and the city as a whole.

Since the 1960s, manufacturing employment has declined from 40 percent of Detroit's residents to 34 percent. In the process, the work force has become more professional and service oriented with fewer sales workers, clerical workers, craftsmen, and laborers (Detroit Planning Department 1980a, III-3). The largest group, i.e., the skilled workers, has remained fairly constant as a percent of the total work force, although the absolute number has declined. Retail and wholesale trade employment here also dropped. In 1980, government employees composed 17 percent of Detroit workers, compared to 10 percent in 1960 and 14 percent in 1970. This growth in the government sector is not expected to continue, as county and city governments lay off employees during fiscal crises, and the federal and state governments are not expanding (Detroit Planning Department 1980a, III-3).

The three major elements that affect the Detroit area employment rates are national growth trends, industry mix, and regional competition. Even though manufacturing employment is declining, the service industries in Detroit are expanding at a faster rate than in the nation as a whole. The move to an economy that is less dependent upon heavy industry has meant high unemployment in the manufacturing sector of Detroit, and service-oriented employment increases in education, medical services, and government have not been large enough to offset the manufacturing job losses. Also, many of the unemployed lack the required skills to make the change from durable goods manufacturing to the service sector (Detroit Planning Department 1979, 5).

The Detroit labor force is characterized as 42 percent white collar, 38 percent blue collar, and 20 percent service workers. Because of the high concentration of blue-collar workers in the central city, Detroit incurs greater economic adjustment hard-

ships than the suburban municipalities in the southeast Michigan region do, especially among the large nonwhite population in Detroit. Thus, in the 1970s, the central city consistently had a higher unemployment rate than the SMSA, the state of Michigan, or the United States as a whole (Table 10.8). In fact, the central city had an unemployment rate that was 2.3 times the rate of the United States in 1980.

Of the 7.4 million unemployed people in the United States in 1980, a disproportionate share were residents of central cities. Although central city residents made up 28 percent of the labor force, they accounted for 33 percent of the unemployed (U.S. Department of Labor 1981, 1). This disparity is related to the fact that nonwhites, who constitute a disproportionately large number of the total unemployed, are much more likely than whites to live in the central cities. Blacks, however, have consistently higher rates of unemployment than their white counterparts regardless of area of residence. In both suburbs and nonmetropolitan areas, the ratio of black-to-white unemployment rates was 2.0 to 1 in 1980; the difference was even greater in the central cities where it was 2.3 to 1. The Hispanic

TABLE 10.8. Annual average unemployment rates, 1970–1980

Year	Detroit City	Detroit SMSA	Michigan	United States
1970	8.1	6.4	6.7	4.9
1971	9.4	7.5	7.6	5.9
1972	8.9	6.9	7.0	5.9
1973	6.9	5.4	5.8	4.9
1974	8.5	6.8	7.4	5.6
1975	14.5	11.7	12.5	8.5
1976	11.1	8.9	9.4	7.7
1977	9.9	7.9	8.2	7.0
1978	8.3	6.6	6.9	6.0
1979	10.1	7.8	7.8	5.8
1980	16.4	13.4	14.0	7.0

Source: Michigan Employment Security Commission; U.S. Department of Labor, Bureau of Labor Statistics, Geographic Profile of Employment and Unemployment Annual Reports (Washington, D.C., 1971–1981).

TABLE 10.9. Estimated unemployment rates in Detroit by age, race, and sex, FY 1980

Age	Total Unemployed	White Unemployed	Nonwhite Unemployed	Ratio of Whites and Nonwhites
Total, Male and Female				
16+	10.5	7.0	14.2	2.0
16-19	39.5	16.7	60.0	3.5
20+	8.7	6.4	11.1	1.7
Male				
16+	10.3	7.3	13.5	1.8
16-19	31.8	13.0	54.5	4.1
20+	9.0	6.9	10.9	1.5
Female				
16+	10.8	6.5	15.3	2.3
16-19	50.0	23.1	66.7	2.8
20+	8.3	5.7	11.7	2.0

Source: Michigan Employment Security Commission.

population, too, had consistently higher rates of unemployment in 1980 than white workers, but, as in the past, the Hispanic rates were consistently lower than those of black workers (U.S. Department of Labor 1981, 2).

In 1980, Detroit's unemployment rate reached 16.4 percent, the highest since the 1975 recession when unemployment was 14.5 percent. In the city of Detroit, the unemployment rates varied by age, race, and sex. White women 20 years of age and over had the lowest unemployment rate, 5.7 percent; the highest unemployment rate (66.7 percent) was among nonwhite women 16-19 years old (Table 10.9).

The racial difference ratio makes the variation in unemployment clear. Nonwhite males 20 years old and over had the lowest gap in unemployment when compared to whites of the same age group. Nonwhite teenagers, on the other hand, had four times the unemployment rate of whites of the same age.

Detroit faces several problems as a result of the economic transition that is occurring. Like many aging industrial cities, Detroit is a victim of federal programs of tax incentives, loan guarantees, and government contracts that have promoted the outward flow of capital from mid-central and northeastern cities to the suburbs, to the Sun Belt metropolitan areas of the South and West, and to the low-wage countries of the Third World. The challenge to Detroit is multifaceted, and the success of the city is dependent upon its ability to adapt to national and international trends.

URBAN REVITALIZATION AND DETROIT'S FUTURE

Detroit became seriously concerned about its future following the civil disorders of the late sixties. Consequently, a group called New Detroit was formed to tackle the social problems of the city and another group, Detroit Renaissance, was formed to deal

New Center Commons in downtown Detroit, an example of urban renovation.

Detroit Renaissance Center, focal point of Detroit Renaissance efforts, with the tunnel-to-Canada facilities in the foreground. (Courtesy Michigan Travel Bureau)

with economic revitalization and development.

In 1973, the board members of Detroit Renaissance realized that any downtown development would have to be on a scale large and diverse enough to create its own environment. Henry Ford II took the lead position through his Ford Land Development Company and launched the Renaissance Center Project, a $600-million riverfront hotel-office complex that was meant to symbolize the rebirth of Detroit and signal to the investment community that Ford and his backers were committing themselves to the central city's future. With confidence born of conviction rather than marketing studies, Ford encouraged over fifty major Detroit-based companies to share the risk. As a result, a hotel with 1,400 rooms, 300,000 sq ft (27,900 sq m) of commercial space, and four office towers—

for a total of 6 million sq ft (558,000 sq m)—became new additions to downtown Detroit (De Vito 1979, 4). Only eighteen months after the center's dedication, Ford announced plans for Phase Two—a joint venture with David Rockefeller to construct two more office towers at a cost of approximately $70 million.

The short-range future of downtown Detroit will also include development of the West Riverfront Area, Washington Boulevard, Cadillac Center, and a Downtown People Mover. The West Riverfront Project, located west of Cobo Hall (see Figure 10.1), is the second area along the river where development activity is currently in progress and includes 2,500 units of the Riverfront West Housing Project. The Washington Boulevard area includes a major pedestrian mall and 380 residential units. Cadillac Center is located in the heart of downtown and will include 600 sq ft (55.8 sq m) of retail space. Finally, the planned Downtown People Mover, a fully automated 2.92-mi (4.7-km) loop, will link most activity areas, proposed and existing, in the downtown sector. These developments are expected to create new jobs—the Renaissance Center, for example, is projected to eventually employ some 40,000 people— but the success of all these programs could be seriously hampered by a major or persistent national economic downturn that affects the automobile industry. Most of the new jobs coming into the city will accommodate primarily service and white-collar workers (De Vito 1979, 11). This trend will eventually be a stabilizing force, but presently it is doing little to reduce the structural unemployment caused by the continuous reduction of low- and medium-skilled factory jobs.

Detroit has, however, the necessary resources for a productive future. It is located near energy supplies; it has abundant water, large markets, and a skilled labor force. These resources must be used to the maximum if the city is to be productive in the future. Detroit must take advantage of possible alternatives within its existing capacity to diversify and expand in order to compete with the regional demographic shifts in population growth and economic power (Detroit Planning Department 1980a, 111–112). To become competitive, however, Detroit must adapt to change.

A New Vision of Detroit

Because Detroit is a declining manufacturing city and must complete the transition to an advanced-services center or to a world-class industrial city, a new vision is necessary. Although Henry Ford and other investors can initiate the process of building a new city, they must gain the support and imagination of the citizenry at large in order to succeed. If enlightened private investment is to sustain momentum, the general public must become even more supportive of Detroit's future (Knight 1979, 13). There is some evidence that such support does exist. A survey of attitudes about Detroit conducted by the Market Opinion Research Corporation in 1978 found that residents, irrespective of race or residential location in the Detroit metropolitan area,

expressed greater faith in the city's future than they had in 1976 and 1977. Only 47 percent of those polled in 1976 felt optimistic about the city's future, compared to 71 percent in the later survey (De Vito 1979, 11).

The people who are the most optimistic about Detroit's future view the city not as a declining industrial city, but as a city in transition and in the process of becoming a world city whose institutional base is automobile technology. Without a vision of Detroit as a new type of city, the Renaissance Center and other redevelopment projects are likely to be perceived as unsuccessful rather than as the precursors of the "new Detroit" (Knight 1979, 14). These new structures are merely the tip of the iceberg, i.e., the only visible part of a much larger development that will continue to grow in the decades ahead.

Detroit's future as an international advanced-services center or world city is limited only by the role that locally based, advanced-service organizations seek to play in international development and by the constraints that are placed on these operations by the home environment. The term "advanced" implies high-level decisions, new knowledge, new management methods, automation, and a new application of expertise (Knight 1979, 25). To a large degree, the future of the advanced-services center depends on the quality of the talent it can attract. Talent will attract clients, but if the talent required cannot be recruited because these professionals do not wish to live and work in the Detroit area, then the future of Detroit as an advanced-services center will be jeopardized. That future will also be jeopardized if there are not enormous public investments in human resources programs to identify the unemployed, discouraged workers, and workers in the labor force with obsolete, or soon-to-be-obsolete, skills. New skills required in the local economy must be identified and—through contractual services with Detroit and Michigan educational institutions—learned in order to meet the demands of the new economy (Hill 1978, 16). To supplement private employment, human services programs will also have to be supported by large-scale public service employment of central city residents in the areas of health care services, schools, youth services, public safety, recreation, housing, environmental reconstruction, and community agencies and organizations (Detroit 1975).

The transition to a high-technology, advanced-services economy will provide Detroit with an alternative to a continuation of the long-term decline of production activities, and Detroit already has the foundation for building an advanced-services economy. In 1977, Detroit had the third largest concentration of industrial corporations in the United States; only New York and Chicago had more. In other words, outside New York City, which is a special case, Chicago and Detroit have the largest concentrations of corporate administrative organizations in the nation, more than twice those of the next largest centers such as Pittsburgh, Cleveland, Minneapolis, and Philadelphia (Stephens and Holly 1980).

There is some concern, however, that corporations will follow their factories and not remain in the city. If company headquarters do follow their factories and leave the Detroit region altogether, other advanced services would be severely affected. New York has had an exodus of corporate headquarters in recent years, so there is some basis for concern, but in Detroit, the commitments and efforts of the major automobile firms seem stronger (Knight 1979, 30). For instance, the Ford Motor Company was instrumental in the building of the Renaissance Center, and other firms have also been involved in the building and rebuilding process.

Future Detroit Industries

Modernization of industrial processes is already occurring in Detroit and this, of course, means automation. Robots and computers will replace people in the advanced-services postindustrial economy, but they will also create new types of jobs. Workers will be needed to make and maintain the new robots and computers so until robots make robots, or make the robots that make the robots, former auto workers and blue-collar workers will still be in demand. But they must be retrained for the jobs in Detroit's future industries. These industries will consist of the following:

Robotics. Industrial robots and other automated production equipment will provide Detroit with one of its most significant opportunities to create high-technology manufacturing jobs. Although applicable to a wide range of production processes in a number of industries, the largest and most rapidly developing market for robots is the automotive industry (Hanieski 1981, 5).

Plastics. The target market effort for plastic products is related to the long-term conversion by the auto industry to lightweight materials in order to reduce vehicle weight and conserve fuel.

Electronics. Detroit's potential to attract high-technology electronic firms is based on both market proximity and the presence of technical support systems. The installation of sophisticated electronic control systems in new vehicles is a significant market for electronic components.

Alternate (Solar) Energy Equipment. The term "alternate energy equipment" covers the entire range of industrial and consumer solar and wind energy devices and biomass conversion processes and equipment. Detroit has a long history in the mass production of durable goods.

Metalworking Machinery. Metalworking machinery manufacture includes industries that produce machine tools, tools and dies, and accessory equipment and constitutes the production backbone of all durable goods manufacturing. Detroit is one of the largest markets for metalworking machinery in the world (Hanieski 1981, 6).

Detroit has tremendous potential for building an advanced-services center in a postindustrial world, but this aim will not be accomplished unless the vision is shared by the people who are to invest in its development—the people who are presently living in the city, the Detroit metropolitan area, and the southeast Michigan region. The future of Detroit is in their hands.

NOTES

1. In 1970, census tract data existed for twenty-six municipalities that were outside the city of Detroit but within the Detroit SMSA, which then consisted of Wayne, Oakland, and Macomb Counties. The analysis of the change in black suburban residential segregation is made using these same counties and municipalities. Residential segregation is defined as the overall unevenness in the spatial distribution of blacks and whites over census tracts within each suburban municipality, and an index of dissimilarity is used to measure the degree of segregation for each. The formula can be stated as follows:

$$D = 100(\tfrac{1}{2} \sum_{i=1}^{k} \mid x_i - y_i \mid).$$

where x_i = the percentage of the suburban municipality's black population living in census tract i;

y_i = the percentage of the suburban municipality's white population living in the same census tract i;

D = the index of dissimilarity, or one-half the sum of the absolute differences (positive and negative) between the percentage spatial distribution of blacks and whites in each suburban municipality (Darden and Tabachneck 1980, 228).

The index may range from zero, indicating no segregation on the basis of race, to 100, indicating total segregation.

PART 6

THE FUTURE

Michigan has rapidly changed in the twentieth century, and that trend seems likely to continue in the future. Population growth is giving way to population stagnation overall with some areas, like Detroit, losing population and others, like the oil-boom counties in the northern Lower Peninsula, growing very rapidly in relative numbers of people. The overdependence on the automobile, the increasing use of fuel-efficient smaller vehicles, the intense world competition in the automotive industry, and the impact of increasing costs of energy are major problems for Michigan in the decade of the 1980s. The automobile is closely identified with energy shortages, rising energy costs, and the inefficient sprawl of human settlements over the landscape. The amount and quality of land, food, air, and water resources are growing areas of concern and offer challenges for present and future generations. Urban areas are suffering from rising crime rates and many other problems associated with age and congestion. All of these developments threaten the ability of residents to maintain a high quality of life in the future years—the theme of the next chapter.

CHAPTER 11

SOME MAJOR QUALITY OF LIFE ISSUES

ENVIRONMENTAL POLLUTION

Michigan is fortunate in having a diverse natural environment consisting of a variety of lakes, rivers, forests, soil types, minerals, and landforms. These natural resources of the state have been increasingly utilized by the growing population and the increasing range of economic activity. Cities, roads, factories, and other aspects of the cultural environment and activities of people have disrupted the ecosystem balance and decreased the quality of the basic resources through various kinds of pollution. As technology has increased the ability of people to change their natural environment, the rate of pollution and misuse of Michigan's air, land, and water resources has accelerated.

The degree of environment change and the character of the resulting problems vary considerably in the state. The overall environment quality is particularly serious in the densely populated southeastern parts of Michigan due to the extreme population pressure on the air, land, and water resources. The situation is also serious in the more sparsely populated areas where industries are dumping raw sewage into bodies of water or manufacturing plants like chemical companies are allowing toxic substances to pollute surface water and groundwater supplies in areas surrounding an industrial site. A special problem developed in Michigan when PBB, a fire retardant chemical, was accidentally mixed into cattle feed and consumed by thousands of dairy animals in the state. The consequences for the animal and human populations have been far reaching. A number of animals had to be destroyed, a number of people consuming dairy products from affected animals have suffered various illnesses, and because of diffusion of the contaminated products, it is now estimated that all residents of Michigan probably have a small percentage of the PBB chemical in their body.

Water, a major natural resource in Michigan, generally is good in quality. It is subject to contamination, however, from urban concentrations, industrial pollutants, agricultural fertilizers and wastes, and sediments from the water erosion process. The control of toxic and hazardous materials is the major problem in maintaining high water-quality standards. In 1979, the Department of Natural Resources identified over 268 sites where there is known groundwater contamination, over 281 sites where contamination is suspected, and over 50,000 sites where there is potential contamina-

Power plant at the mouth of the Saginaw River. (Courtesy Michigan Department of Natural Resources)

tion.[1] The distribution of the potential groundwater contamination sites correlates quite closely with the density of population (Figure 11.1). Certain industries such as iron and steel, mining, paper and pulp, oil production and refining, and chemical manufacturing accentuate the pollution problem where these industries are dominant—such as in the case of the chemical industries in Muskegon County.

In general, the poorest water is found in the streams of the Lake Erie drainage basin (Figure 11.2). This fact is closely related to the population density patterns, the concentrations of industry, and the intensity of agriculture in the area. The best water quality is found in the sparsely populated Lake Superior and northern Lake Michigan drainage basins. The water flowing into southern Lake Michigan and Lake Huron is of medium to good quality.

The location of Michigan in the western Great Lakes area makes the quality of water

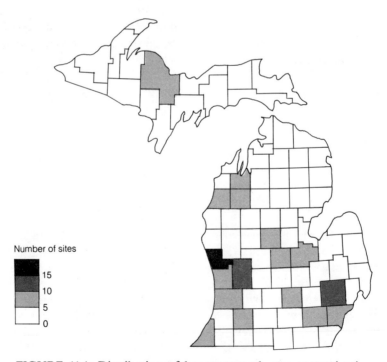

Number of sites

15
10
5
0

FIGURE 11.1. Distribution of known groundwater contamination, by county, 1979. (Source: Michigan Department of Natural Resources, Environmental Services Division, *Water Quality and Pollution Control in Michigan, 1980* [Lansing, 1980].)

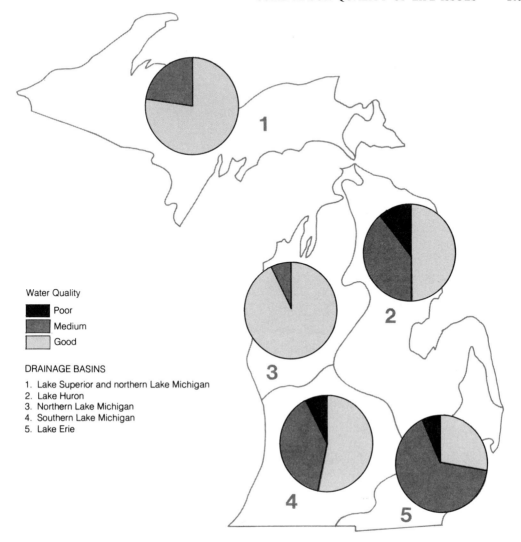

FIGURE 11.2. Regional water quality, water year 1979. (Source: John H. Hartig and Michael E. Stifler, *Water Quality and Pollution Control in Michigan* [Lansing: Department of Natural Resources, 1980], pp. 2–3.)

in the adjoining lakes significant. About 40 percent of Michigan's surface is covered by freshwater, and it is estimated that about 30 million people and a quarter of the nation's manufacturing work force live in the Great Lakes Basin. Thus, pollution is possible from the large number of manufacturing, waste treatment, agricultural, mining, and transportation activities found in that basin. Pollution also results from the activities along the immediate shorelines of the Great Lakes as well as from tributaries entering the lakes. The large size

of these water bodies means that they can regenerate themselves from minor concentrations of toxic substances, but in some areas, the degree of pollution, the shallowness of the water, or the lack of water movement in small bays causes severe pollution problems. Examples of such areas in Michigan are the outer portions of Green Bay, Saginaw Bay, the western shore of Lake St. Clair, and western Lake Erie (Figure 11.3). Also, small local areas may have poor-quality water because of thermal pollution from power plants or sewage or

Example of visual and water pollution on Lake Michigan, near Michiana in the extreme southwestern corner of the state. (Courtesy Michigan Department of Natural Resources)

industrial contamination from a local settlement or activity. Lake Superior, northern Lake Huron, and northeastern Lake Michigan have high-quality water, the rest of Lake Michigan and southern Lake Huron have water of medium quality, and Lake Erie has the poorest quality of water.

Acid precipitation is not yet a serious problem in Michigan, but the concentrations have increased in the last thirty years, apparently because of the rapid increase in the use of fossil fuel. Some of this problem arises from a greater consumption of coal and petroleum in the state, but some is also brought in by the southwesterly winds bringing contamination from the industries of the greater Milwaukee and Chicago metropolitan and industrial areas. Excess concentrations may affect life in the

freshwater lakes, decrease crop production, and potentially cause erosion of metal structures and buildings. The eastern tip of the Upper Peninsula and the area south of a line from Muskegon to Rogers City have the highest concentrations of sulfur in the rain; the density decreases westward (Figure 11.4). The alkalinity of the soil tends to neutralize sulfur, and thus, the thick glacial debris and soil cover in certain parts of the state may have some positive impact on this problem.

Michigan has an active state pollution-control program and has also implemented federal legislation such as the Clean Air Act. Water, land, and air quality management programs have resulted in the reduction of the pollution levels of a number of toxic substances (Figure 11.5). Efforts

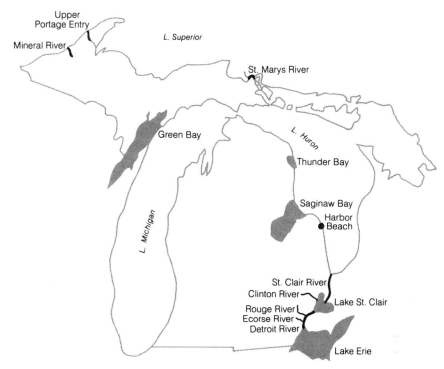

FIGURE 11.3 (*above*). Water quality problems in Great Lakes and connecting channels. FIGURE 11.4 (*below*). Acid precipitation increases north to south, 1979. (Source for both figures: Adapted from Michigan Department of Natural Resources, Environmental Services Division, *Water Quality and Pollution Control in Michigan, 1980* [Lansing, 1980].)

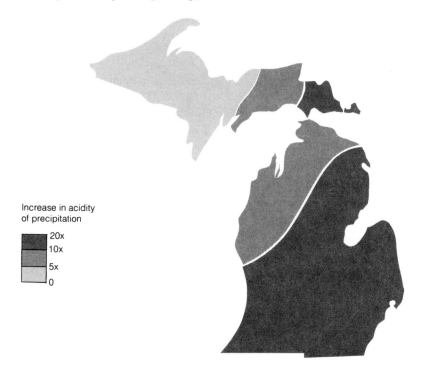

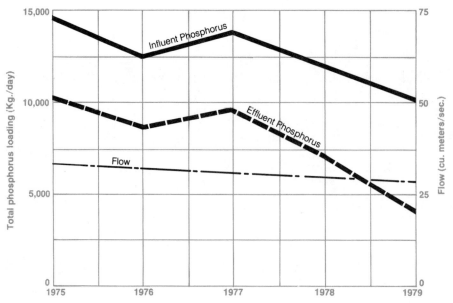

FIGURE 11.5. Phosphorous trends from Detroit wastewater treatment plant, 1975–1979. (Source: Michigan Department of Natural Resources, Environmental Services Division, *Water Quality and Pollution Control in Michigan, 1980* [Lansing, 1980], p. 106.)

have been largely directed toward point sources of pollution such as waste treatment plants, electrical power plants, and industrial facilities, but effort is also being turned toward nonpoint sources such as runoff from agricultural areas, storm water, and occasional accidents such as oil and chemical spills.

ENERGY AND URBAN SPRAWL

Inexpensive fossil fuels have fostered large-scale industrialization and the use of the automobile for transportation during the present century. The automobile facilitated mobility, which resulted in the spread of human settlements over the U.S. and Michigan landscapes. People from the central cities spread into suburbs and satellite cities and then into the nonmetropolitan areas so that now it is difficult to find strictly rural areas, only various degrees of urbanization. The national Interstate Highway System, begun in 1956 and largely completed in Michigan, has provided an even further impetus for the sprawl and splatter of urban functions and settlements in a loose, unnucleated pattern.

The rapid increase of liquid fossil fuel prices since the Arab embargo of 1973 and the occasional shortages of gasoline since that time have called into question the continued unmanaged spread of people over the landscape. In order to conserve fossil fuels, driving distances are being shortened, car and van pools are being utilized, the use of mass transportation is increasing, and more-fuel-efficient automobiles are being introduced. More-nucleated human settlement patterns would facilitate the use of such fuel-conserving innovations as district heating (use of both energy and heat from power development by utilities) and mass transportation.

During the coming decades, the people of Michigan need to reorganize their human settlement patterns to make them more energy, transportation, resource, and food-chain efficient, and the citizens will have to make significant choices in the face of population, economy, resource, and cost changes. Adaptations in Michigan will most

Midland, Michigan, is dominated by a Dow Chemical Company plant and the Consumers Power nuclear plant (under construction), which are shown in the center and lower left of the photograph. (Courtesy Michigan Department of Natural Resources)

Intersection of Interstates 90, 275, 696, and Michigan 102 in Oakland County. Note the amount of land consumed by the highways and how they foster settlement. (Courtesy Michigan Department of Natural Resources)

likely take place within the framework of a stable or declining population, at least through the 1980s, because of a net out-migration to the Sun Belt and a declining birth rate. Rising fossil-fuel energy costs and shifts to renewable resources will tend to curtail urban sprawl and redirect urban growth toward multinucleated cities. The Urban Land Institute interim report entitled *Development Choices for the 80s* indicates that Americans must soon consider some combination of the following choices: (1) increasing the compactness of metropolitan and nonmetropolitan fringe development, (2) accelerating the process of infill and redevelopment of vacant and poorly used land in existing communities, (3) increasing the mixture of land uses in order to diversify the character of the opportunities available in a community, (4) increasing transportation choices, especially mass transportation, (5) providing an adequate supply of energy efficient housing, and (6) organizing existing and newly developing areas into "urban villages," which would be compact and allow easy access to many daily necessities by walking or bicycling.[2]

The following major adaptations are likely to take place in future organizational patterns of human settlements in Michigan:

1. more nucleation of suburbs and non-metropolitan areas in the highly urbanized southern one-third of the state to permit energy efficiencies,
2. reorganization of sections of existing cities so that energy-saving innovations such as mass transportation and district heating can be implemented,
3. decentralization of people and urban functions from larger cities to smaller, compact, energy-efficient communities in the urban south, and
4. an increase in the number and size of urban settlements in the sparsely populated northern two-thirds of Michigan where renewable sources of energy such as wood, wind, solar thermal, and low-head hydro are available and employment opportunities that are largely based on these kinds of energy alternatives may be developed (Figure 11.6).[3]

Figure 11.7 presents a model of the nature of the contemporary and future metropolis and summarizes the character of current urban sprawl and some indicated future changes that need to take place to achieve energy efficiency. The present highly specialized and linear patterns of activity scattered along major thoroughfares, made possible by flexible automobile transportation, need to be replaced by a clustering of activities in community centers. These more

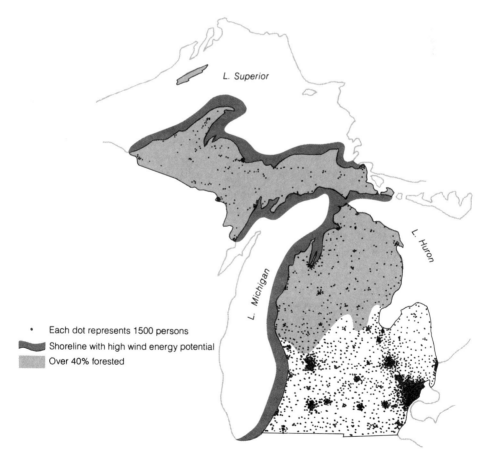

FIGURE 11.6. Population, wood biomass, and wind distributions. (Source: Adapted from Lawrence M. Sommers, "The Potential Impact of Increased Use of Renewable Energy Resources on Land Use Patterns and Policy: The Case of Michigan," *Proceedings of Applied Geography Conferences* 2 [1979], p. 66.)

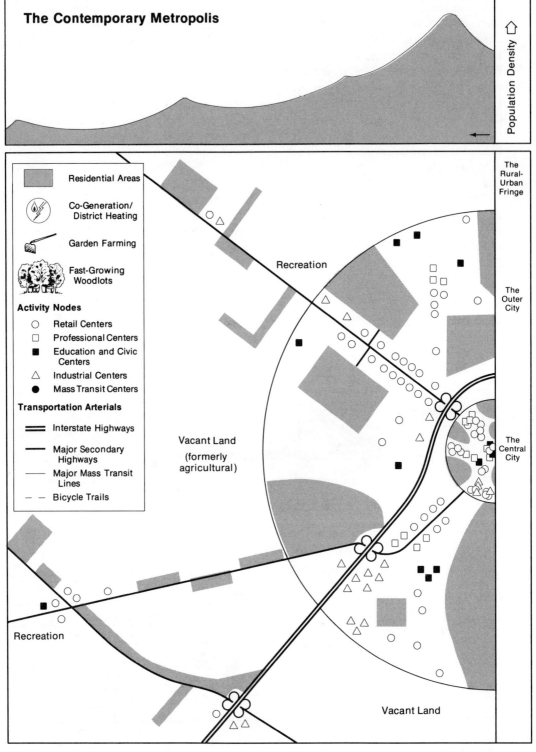

FIGURE 11.7. Contemporary and future metropolis. (Source: Lawrence M. Sommers and Herman E. Koenig, *Energy and the Adaptation of Human Settlements* [East Lansing: Michigan State University, 1980], pp. 16–17.)

223

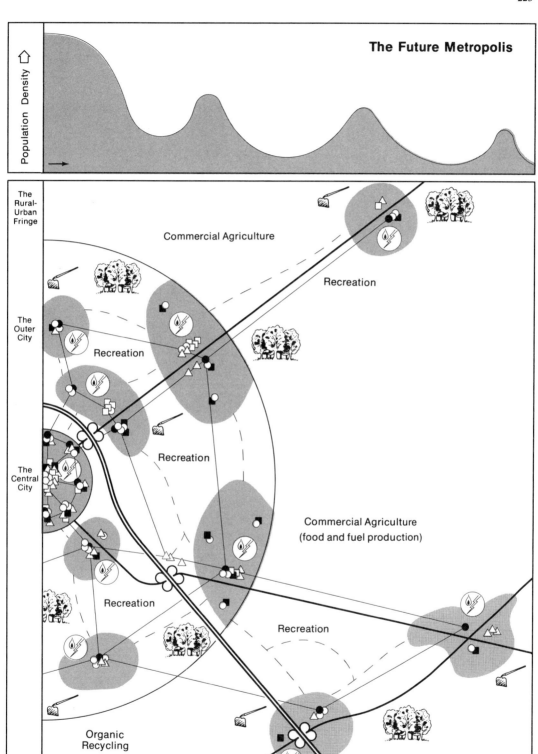

The Future Metropolis

Population Density

The Rural-Urban Fringe

Commercial Agriculture

Recreation

The Outer City

Recreation

Recreation

The Central City

Commercial Agriculture
(food and fuel production)

Recreation

Recreation

Organic Recycling

compact and economically diverse activity nodes in the central city would be, in large part, accessible by walking, bicycling, and public transportation as well as by motorized vehicles. Outside the central city, urban functions should become more concentrated at points of maximum accessibility by mass-transit lines and nonautomobile transportation.

In the nonmetropolitan areas, urban nodes should become more diversified, more compact, and centered on transportation crossing points such as road intersections. Prime agricultural land near the cities would be retained for food production, and other areas could be reserved for such uses as recreation, growing wood for energy, and market gardening. Small industries based on local resources such as food processing may develop. The net result would be a clearer separation between rural and urban land uses with the major objectives of greater energy efficiency, increased nucleation of human settlements, and the maintaining or improving of the quality of life standards.

SOME FUTURE QUALITY OF LIFE INDICATORS

Michigan enjoys a variety of physical environments and cultural heritages that form the background and context for the activities of the citizens of the state. Contrasts in life-style are extreme—from the totally urban environment of the central city to the forested and wilderness areas of certain northern portions of Michigan. It is difficult to generalize about the future quality of life as the state is so diverse, but certain indicators can be used to make generalizations. Quality of life is closely allied to economic and social standards of living so that factors such as total income, disposable income, unemployment rates, and crime rates become important. These indicators show great variability among regions of Michigan as well as within specific

large urban places such as Detroit.

The per capita personal income in Michigan averaged $10,758 in 1981 compared to $10,495 for the United States. The counties in Michigan ranged from an average high of $14,126 per capita personal income in Oakland County to a low of $5,183 in Oscoda County (Table 11.1). In general, incomes are considerably higher in the southeastern and urban counties than in the northern and more rural counties. The Bureau of the Census indicates that the mean, or arithmetic average, income of families in the Detroit SMSA was $25,278 in March 1979 compared to $21,431 for all SMSAs in the United States, and the disposable income average was $7,822 per capita in Michigan in 1979 compared to $7,399 for the United States. These income figures reflect the generally high-wage rates of Michigan's industry. In the Detroit SMSA, 45 percent of the families had an income of over $25,000 in 1979, but 5.3 percent were below the poverty level. Thus, overall, Michigan has high living and quality of life standards, but there are many areas of urban and rural poverty.

Unemployment is another indicator of quality of life, and the rates vary widely over the state. The average for Michigan in 1980 was 12.6 percent compared to 7.1 percent for the United States. The county unemployment rate averages in that same year ranged from 25.7 percent in Montmorency County to a low of 8.2 percent in Washtenaw County (Table 11.2). The unemployment rate varies from year to year and season to season, but in general, the proportional number of people looking for work is higher in the counties of the northern two-thirds of Michigan and lower in the urban southern counties. The proportion of the state's unemployed is much higher in densely populated counties in the south, especially the southeast. The overdependence upon one industry, such as the manufacturing of automobiles, accentuates the unemployment problem when auto sales are down, and some major diversification

TABLE 11.1. Per capita personal income, by county, 1981

County	Per Capita Personal Income	Percent Change 1971-1981	County	Per Capita Personal Income	Percent Change 1971-1981
Oakland	14,126	151.2	Alpena	8,450	159.7
Wayne	11,486	145.5	Manistee	8,369	156.4
Washtenaw	11,462	158.3	Delta	8,357	166.3
Macomb	11,430	143.9	Sanilac	8,237	144.3
Genesee	11,296	154.4	Antrim	8,232	168.9
Ingham	11,062	157.4	Schoolcraft	8,230	191.7
Kalamazoo	10,852	156.9	Allegan	8,205	150.9
Midland	10,750	136.9	Menominee	8,060	182.2
Kent	10,586	150.9	Gogebic	8,022	153.8
Calhoun	10,497	144.3	Iosco	7,968	138.3
Saginaw	10,485	149.7	Barry	7,913	130.3
Monroe	10,163	159.4	Ionia	7,837	158.6
Grand Traverse	10,160	157.6	Wexford	7,768	150.5
Bay	10,048	159.1	Benzie	7,740	127.8
Clinton	9,850	150.1	Cheboygan	7,717	150.1
Dickinson	9,763	175.8	Isabella	7,687	176.2
Jackson	9,758	138.1	Keweenaw	7,657	190.1
Luce	9,698	235.3	Presque Isle	7,646	178.8
Ottawa	9,655	142.5	Baraga	7,568	135.9
Eaton	9,638	133.8	Chippewa	7,562	156.9
Shiawassee	9,574	149.4	Roscommon	7,514	135.5
Lenawee	9,525	145.1	Mason	7,505	123.4
Berrien	9,501	128.2	Montmorency	7,500	155.8
St. Clair	9,481	148.6	Kalkaska	7,369	165.1
Livingston	9,464	142.8	Houghton	7,301	165.7
Huron	9,356	183.3	Arenac	7,226	136.8
Cass	9,174	142.6	Newaygo	7,206	122.8
Gratiot	9,147	151.6	Oceana	7,170	132.4
Muskegon	9,123	154.7	Ontonagon	7,131	145.2
Emmet	9,099	149.1	Gladwin	7,037	135.5
Tuscola	9,007	152.7	Alcona	7,025	157.7
Lapeer	8,892	141.1	Clare	6,998	144.0
St. Joseph	8,869	129.6	Alger	6,934	164.5
Branch	8,844	161.9	Osceola	6,873	155.6
Marquette	8,752	169.6	Crawford	6,798	149.3
Otsego	8,723	170.1	Ogemaw	6,756	150.1
Montcalm	8,686	151.8	Lake	6,529	131.7
Leelanau	8,660	140.0	Missaukee	6,309	152.0
Charlevoix	8,636	170.1	Mecosta	5,929	144.8
Iron	8,601	194.3	Oscoda	5,183	110.4
Mackinac	8,507	189.1			
Hillsdale	8,479	144.4	Michigan	10,758	147.0
Van Buren	8,462	145.6	United States	10,495	151.9

Source: Michigan Department of Economics, Bureau of Economic Analysis, Regional Economics Information System (Lansing, 1982); reproduced in David I. Verway, ed., Michigan Statistical Abstract, 1982-83 (Detroit: Wayne State University, 1983), p. 214.

TABLE 11.2. Unemployment rates, by county or groups of counties, 1980

County or Group of Counties	Civilian Labor Force	Unemployment Number	Rate
Alcona, Iosco	12,675	2,065	16.3
Alger	3,800	550	14.5
Allegan	34,125	3,875	11.4
Alpena	15,675	2,225	14.2
Antrim	7,475	1,200	16.1
Arenac	6,000	900	15.0
Baraga	3,325	450	13.5
Barry, Calhoun	80,300	9,300	11.6
Bay	53,400	8,100	15.2
Benzie	4,425	725	16.4
Berrien	72,900	9,600	13.2
Branch	21,725	2,975	13.7
Cass	21,025	2,725	13.0
Charlevoix	9,450	1,425	15.1
Cheboygan	9,675	1,925	19.9
Chippewa	11,400	2,175	19.1
Clare	9,625	1,475	15.3
Clinton, Eaton, Ingham, Ionia	236,900	24,900	10.5
Crawford	3,475	600	17.3
Delta	17,025	2,000	11.7
Dickinson	12,625	1,075	8.5
Emmet	12,900	1,600	12.4
Genesee, Shiawassee	229,400	40,500	17.7
Gogebic	8,600	750	8.7
Grand Traverse, Kalkaska, Leelanau	42,725	3,900	9.1
Gratiot	16,275	2,275	14.0
Hillsdale	20,000	2,375	11.9
Houghton, Keweenaw	15,875	1,850	11.7
Huron	13,950	2,350	16.8
Iron	5,950	675	11.3
Isabella	26,375	2,200	8.3
Jackson	66,100	7,700	11.6
Kalamazoo, Van Buren	134,900	11,400	8.5
Kent, Ottawa	313,200	26,300	8.4
Lake	2,650	425	16.0
Lenawee	38,650	5,625	14.6
Livingston, Lapeer, Macomb, Oakland, St. Clair, Wayne	2,030,500	266,800	13.1
Luce	3,075	400	13.0
Mackinac	6,425	1,075	16.7
Manistee	9,775	1,275	13.0
Marquette	29,975	4,075	13.6
Mason	12,750	1,675	13.1
Mecosta	14,750	1,375	9.3
Menominee	10,800	1,000	9.3
Midland, Gladwin	37,250	4,175	11.2
Missaukee, Wexford	14,600	2,300	15.8

TABLE 11.2 (continued)

County or Group of Counties	Civilian Labor Force	Unemployment Number	Unemployment Rate
Monroe[a]	62,500	7,275	11.6
Montcalm	20,100	2,900	14.4
Montmorency	2,725	700	25.7
Muskegon, Oceana	78,100	10,500	13.4
Newaygo	13,125	2,075	15.8
Ogemaw	7,475	1,050	14.0
Ontonagon	3,375	425	12.6
Osceola	7,850	1,075	13.7
Oscoda	2,375	450	18.9
Otsego	9,050	800	8.8
Presque Isle	4,500	900	20.0
Roscommon	5,700	875	15.4
Saginaw	101,800	14,700	14.4
St. Joseph	25,550	2,975	11.6
Sanilac	15,695	2,950	18.8
Schoolcraft	3,625	550	15.2
Tuscola	25,425	4,300	16.9
Washtenaw	144,500	11,900	8.2
Upper Peninsula (15 counties)	135,875	17,050	12.5
Michigan[b]	4,297,945	540,740	12.6

[a]Monroe is part of the Toledo, Ohio, labor-market area. Separate data for place of work are not compiled.

[b]All 83 counties, including Monroe.

Source: Michigan Employment Security Commission; reproduced in David I. Verway, ed., Michigan Statistical Abstract (Detroit: Wayne State University, 1981), pp. 160–177.

in the state's economy is necessary to alleviate this problem.

Crime rates are another indicator of quality of life, and they vary with the total population, unemployment rates, ethnic composition of the population, and other factors. The total number of crimes is much higher in the inner cities of metropolitan areas, but the ratio of crimes per 10,000 inhabitants varies widely over the state. In 1980, Detroit had a ratio of 1,059 index crimes (murder, manslaughter, rape, robbery, aggravated assault, burglary, larceny, and motor vehicle theft) compared to 890

in Grand Rapids, 992 in Cadillac, 1,478 in Muskegon, 819 in Traverse City, 508 in Alpena, and only 296 in East Lansing (Table 11.3). The ratio of the more serious crimes per total population is thus not necessarily better in the smaller urban places in northern Michigan.

Quality of life is a difficult factor to measure accurately. It varies with the aspirations of individuals, the opportunities of individuals, and the living potential of different places and regions. In terms of available disposable income and diversity of environments, both physical and human

TABLE 11.3. Index crimes in selected cities, 1980[a]

	Total Population	Total Index Crimes	Index Crimes Per 10,000 People
Benton Harbor	14,407	3,515	2,440
Muskegon	40,823	6,035	1,478
Flint	159,611	21,201	1,328
Harper Woods	16,361	1,984	1,213
Pontiac	76,715	8,736	1,139
Saginaw	77,508	8,607	1,110
Jackson	39,739	4,313	1,085
Detroit	1,203,339	127,420	1,059
Hamtramck	21,300	2,212	1,038
Ypsilanti	24,031	2,489	1,036
Cadillac	10,199	1,012	992
Battle Creek	35,724	3,536	990
Grand Rapids	181,843	16,185	890
Port Huron	33,981	3,012	886
Traverse City	15,516	1,270	819
Ann Arbor	107,316	8,587	800
Niles	13,115	982	749
Sault Ste. Marie	14,448	1,079	747
Grand Haven	11,763	855	727
Bay City	41,593	2,875	691
Novi	22,525	1,533	681
Marquette	23,288	1,423	611
Escanaba	14,355	791	551
Holland	26,281	1,425	542
Mt. Pleasant	23,746	1,235	520
Alpena	12,214	621	508
Livonia	104,814	5,238	500
Menominee	10,009	492	492
Big Rapids	14,361	610	425
East Lansing	48,309	1,432	296

[a]Index crimes include murder, manslaughter, rape, robbery, aggravated assault, burglary, larceny, and motor vehicle theft.

Source: U.S. Bureau of the Census, 1980 Census of Population and Housing, Advance Reports (Washington, D.C.: Government Printing Office, March 1981).

or cultural, Michigan provides an opportunity for a variety of modes of life.

NOTES

1. John H. Hartig and Michael E. Stifler, *Water Quality and Pollution Control in Michigan* (Lansing: Department of Natural Resources, Environmental Services Division, 1980), p. IV.

2. Council on Development Choices for the 80s, *Development Choices for the 80s,* interim report prepared by the Urban Land Institute (Washington, D.C.: Department of Housing and Urban Development, 1980).

3. Lawrence M. Sommers, "The Potential Impact of Increased Use of Renewable Resources on Land Use Patterns and Policy: The Case of Michigan," *Applied Geography Conference* 2 (1979), pp. 61–70.

CHAPTER 12

MICHIGAN TOMORROW

The geography of the state of Michigan is constantly changing. The economy is rapidly entering a postindustrial era, which means that a higher and higher proportion of the population will be earning a living from the tertiary sector of the economy—retail and wholesale trade, government services, various professions, transportation and communication, recreation, and research and development. The nature of this change is illustrated by the nonmanufacturing and government job increases during the thirteen-year period from 1968 to 1980 (Table 12.1). The nonmanufacturing and government sectors accounted for 71 percent of the jobs in 1980 and will likely total well over 75 percent by the turn of the century. This situation will undoubtedly affect the life-styles, aspirations, and work patterns of the citizens of Michigan.

The recession of 1981–1982 demonstrated the problems that accompany an overspecialized economy. The overdependence upon the automotive and related industries caused unemployment to be excessively high, especially in cities like Detroit and Flint. The automobile industry is unlikely to return to its former levels of employment or production, so people employed in this sector must find employment in other industries or migrate to other states. Both reactions are taking place, and

this trend will undoubtedly continue.

Population trends indicate that Michigan will have stable or slow growth in the 1980s and early 1990s. Net out-migration to the Sun Belt and other states will continue, and within Michigan, the large cities will lose population, and the sparsely populated counties in the northern two-thirds of the state will gain. Despite these trends, Michigan will continue to be a highly urban state. The metropolitan cities in the south will grow in size, as will the smaller centers in the nonmetropolitan areas. The desirable lake, forest, and hilly areas of the west and north will continue to draw retired and vacationing people as well as people seeking a life-style other than that of the big city. Thus, it is likely that the area north of the Muskegon–Bay City line will continue to grow relatively faster than the remainder of the state. The bulk of the population will still live, however, in the urban areas of southern Michigan.

The higher costs and changing forms of energy are going to have a major impact on the way Michiganians live in the coming decades. The regional organization of population distribution, energy resources, food production, and employment opportunities will have to be taken much more into consideration in individual, group, and political decisions in the future. Urban space

TABLE 12.1.   Civilian nonfarm wage and salary jobs, 1968 and 1980

| | 1968 | | 1980 | |
| | Thousands | | Thousands | |
Industry	of Jobs	Percent	of Jobs	Percent
Manufacturing	1,162.0	39.2	1,007.2	29.2
Nonmanufacturing[a]	1,330.7	44.9	1,819.1	52.7
Government	470.6	15.9	627.8	18.1
Total	2,963.3		3,454.1	

[a]Excludes domestic work and agricultural employment; includes construction, transportation, communication, public utilities, wholesale and retail trade, finance, mining, and other services.

Source: David I. Verway, ed., Michigan Statistical Abstract (Detroit: Wayne State University, 1981), pp. 178-179.

will have to be reorganized so as to conserve and reduce the amounts and costs of energy required. The resources of regions will have to be better utilized for the benefit of the people in the region, which, in densely populated regions, will mean managing and preventing further uncontrolled urban sprawl and agglomerating existing scattered human habitats into nucleated settlements so the use of energy and other resources can be maximized. The food-chain needs to be shortened by increasing the amount of market gardening in the vicinity of urban settlements (see Figure 11.7), which will involve policy changes on various levels to get people to accept a society that consumes less energy and other resources per capita while maintaining or improving upon the existing quality of life.

Michigan, as do all the states in the United States, faces a major challenge in maintaining its economy and way of life in the coming decades. A thorough knowledge of the geography of the state and its regions is mandatory in gaining the understanding necessary to develop local and statewide policies to bring about desirable and needed changes. The better utilization and development of the physical and human resources of cities, counties, and the state will be the key to future success. People with a good background in the geography of Michigan will make better decisions for the future of their state.

SOURCES AND SELECTED REFERENCES

GENERAL

Catton, Bruce. *Michigan, A History*. New York: W. W. Norton and Company, 1976.

Davis, Charles M. *Readings in the Geography of Michigan*. Ann Arbor, Mich.: Ann Arbor Publisher, 1964.

Dunbar, Willis F. *Michigan: A History of the Wolverine State*. Grand Rapids, Mich.: Wm. B. Eerdmans Publishing Co., 1973.

Hudgins, Bert. *Michigan: Geographic Backgrounds in the Development of the Commonwealth*. 4th ed. Ann Arbor, Mich.: Edwards Brothers, 1961.

Morrison, Paul C. "Geographer's Mirror of Michigan: A Bibliography of Professional Writings." *Michigan Academician* 50 (1965), pp. 493–518.

Santer, Richard A. *Michigan: Heart of the Great Lakes*. Dubuque, Iowa: Kendall/Hunt Publishing Co., 1977.

Senninger, Earl J., Jr. *Atlas of Michigan*. 3rd ed. Flint, Mich.: Flint Geographical Press, 1970.

Sommers, Lawrence M., ed. *Atlas of Michigan*. East Lansing: Michigan State University Press, 1977.

Verway, David I., ed. *Michigan Statistical Abstract*. 16th ed., *1981*. Detroit: Wayne State University, 1982.

————. *Michigan Statistical Abstract*. 17th ed., *1982–83*. Detroit: Wayne State University, 1983.

Warner, Robert, and Vanderhill, C. Warren, eds. *A Michigan Reader: 1865 to the Present*. Grand Rapids, Mich.: Wm. B. Eerdmans Publishing Co., 1974.

Wood, L. H. *Geography of Michigan: Physical, Industrial, and Sectional*. Kalamazoo, Mich.: Horton-Beimer Press, 1914.

Young, Gordon; Amos, James L.; and Rogers, Martin. "Superior-Michigan-Huron-Erie-Ontario—Is It Too Late?" *National Geographic* 144 (1973), pp. 147–185.

PART 1

Michigan. Department of State Highways and Transportation. State Highway Commission. "Official Michigan Highway Map." Lansing, 1983.

Romig, W. *Michigan Place Names*. Grosse Pointe, Mich.: W. Romig and Co., 1973.

U.S. Department of the Interior. Geological Survey. *Index to Topographical Maps of Michigan*. 1975. (Available from the Geological Survey, Department of Natural Resources, State of Michigan, Lansing.)

PART 2

Beegle, J. A.; Wang, Ching-li; and Lepper, Carol. *Michigan Age-Sex Composition, 1970*. Rural Sociology Studies no. 5. East Lansing: Agricultural Experiment Station, Michigan State University, July 1974.

234   SOURCES AND SELECTED REFERENCES

Hart, John F. "A Rural Retreat for Northern Negroes." *Geographical Review* 50:2 (April 1960), pp. 148–167.

Heller, C. F.; Quandt, E. C.; and Raup, H. A. *Population Patterns of Southwestern Michigan.* Kalamazoo: New Issues Press, Institute of Public Affairs, Western Michigan University, 1974.

Michigan. Department of Education. *Michigan Educational Statistics, 1980–81.* Lansing, 1982.

Michigan. Department of Management and Budget. Planning and Policy Analysis Division. "Population Projections for the Counties of Michigan." Lansing, 1974.

Michigan. Department of Public Health. *Michigan Health Statistics, 1978.* Lansing, 1981.

———. *Michigan Vital Statistics by County, 1978.* Lansing, 1979.

Michigan. Department of State Police. *Uniform Crime Report.* East Lansing, annually 1973–1980.

Michigan Health Council. "Health Manpower in Michigan." Newsletter. East Lansing, Mich., Spring 1975.

O'Hare, W. P.; Rathje, Richard; and Beegle, J. Allan. *Recent Trends in Growth of Michigan Municipalities.* Agricultural Experiment Station, Rural Sociology Studies no. 8. East Lansing: Michigan State University, May 1979.

Peters, Bernard C. "Settler Attitudes Toward the Land as Revealed in the Pioneer Poetry of Kalamazoo County." *Michigan Academician* 6:2 (Fall 1973), pp. 209–217.

Poles in Michigan. Vol. 1, *Detroit.* Detroit: Poles in Michigan Associated, 1953.

Schnell, G. A., and Monmonier, M. A. "U.S. Population Change 1960–70." *Journal of Geography* 75:5 (May 1976), pp. 280–291.

Sommers, Lawrence M., and Lounsbury, John L. "Impact of Population Growth Trends on State and Local Land Use Policy: The Examples of Michigan and Arizona." *Proceedings of Applied Geography Conferences* 5 (1982), pp. 116–136.

Thaden, J. F. "Ethnic Settlements in Rural Michigan." *Michigan State University Agricultural Experiment Station Quarterly Bulletin* 29:2 (1946), pp. 102–111.

———. "The Farm People of Michigan According to Ethnic Stock." Map. East Lansing: Agricultural Experiment Station, Michigan State College, 1945.

U.S. Bureau of the Census. *Census of Housing.* U.S. summaries for the years 1930, 1940, 1950, 1960, 1970, and 1980. Washington, D.C.: Government Printing Office, various years.

———. *Census of Population: 1970.* Vol. 1, *Characteristics of the Population.* Pt. 1, "U.S. Summary." Washington, D.C.: Government Printing Office, 1972.

———. *Census of Population: 1970.* Vol. 2, *Subject Reports.* Report PC(2)-2B, "Mobility for States and the Nation." Washington, D.C.: Government Printing Office, 1973.

———. *Current Population Reports.* Series P-25, no. 903. Washington, D.C.: Government Printing Office, 1981.

———. *1980 Census of Housing: Selected Housing Characteristics by States and Counties.* Washington, D.C.: Government Printing Office, 1981.

———. *1980 Census of Population and Housing.* Advance Reports. Washington, D.C.: Government Printing Office, March 1981.

———. *1980 Census of Population and Housing, Michigan.* Washington, D.C.: Government Printing Office, 1981.

———. *Statistical Abstract of the U.S.* Washington, D.C.: Government Printing Office, 1981.

U.S. Department of Health, Education and Welfare. Office of Education. Bureau for Education Personnel Development. "Detroit Area Ethnic Groups 1971," by Bryan Thompson. Grant no. OEG-0-70-2030(725). Washington, D.C., 1971.

Vanderhill, C. W. *Settling the Great Lakes Frontier: Immigration to Michigan 1857–1924.* Lansing: Michigan Historical Commission, 1970.

PART 3

Braun, E. Lucy. *Deciduous Forests of Eastern North America.* New York: Hafner Publishing Co., 1964.

Brown, Claudeous J.D. *Michigan Streams.* Ann Arbor: Institute for Fisheries Research, University of Michigan, 1944.

Buckler, W. R., and Winters, H. A. "Rates of Bluff Recession at Selected Sites Along the Southeastern Shore of Lake Michigan." *Michigan Academician* 8:2 (Fall 1975), pp. 179–186.

Dorr, John A., and Eschman, Donald F. *Geology of Michigan.* Ann Arbor: University of Michigan Press, 1970.

Eichenlaub, Val. *Weather and Climate of the Great Lakes Region.* Notre Dame, Ind.: Notre Dame Press, 1979.

Farrand, W. R., and Eschman, D. F. "Glaciation of the Southern Peninsula of Michigan: A Review." *Michigan Academician* 7:1 (Summer 1974), pp. 31–56.

Flint, Richard F. *Glacial and Pleistocene Geology.* New York: John Wiley and Sons, 1957.

Flint, Richard F., et al. "Glacial Map of the U.S. East of the Rocky Mountains." Scale 1:1,750,000. Boulder, Colo.: Geological Society of America, 1959. (2 sheets)

Gifford, A. R., and Humphrys, C. R. "Lake Shore Classifications—Southern Peninsula of Michigan." Mimeographed. East Lansing: Department of Resource Development and the Agricultural Experiment Station, Michigan State University, 1966.

Harman, Jay R. *Troposphere Waves, Jet Streams, and United States Weather Patterns.* Association of American Geographers, Resource Paper no. 11. Washington, D.C., 1971.

Hough, J. L. *Geology of the Great Lakes.* Urbana: University of Illinois Press, 1958.

Kelley, Robert W. *Guide to Michigan Fossils.* Lansing: Michigan Department of Conservation, n.d.

Merz, Robert W. *Forest Atlas of the Midwest.* Rev. ed. St. Paul, Minn.: North Central Forest Experiment Station, U.S. Department of Agriculture, 1979.

Michigan. Department of Natural Resources. "The Glacial Lakes Around Michigan." Bulletin 4, by R. W. Kelley and W. R. Farrand. Lansing, 1967.

———. *Michigan Mineral Producers.* Lansing, annually.

———. *Michigan's Oil and Gas Fields.* Lansing, annually.

Michigan. Department of Natural Resources. Fisheries Division. "Michigan's Twenty Largest Inland Lakes." Lansing, 1974.

Michigan. Department of Natural Resources. Geological Survey Division. "Bedrock of Michigan." Map. Lansing, 1968.

———. "Map of the Surface Formations of the Southern Peninsula of Michigan." Publication 49, by H. Martin. Lansing, 1957.

Michigan. Department of Natural Resources. Resources Planning Division and Water Resources Commission. "Water Holding Capacity and Infiltration Rates of Soils in Michigan." Michigan Agricultural Extension Project 413, by I. F. Schneider and A. E. Erickson. Lansing, n.d.

Pawling, J. W. "Morphometric Analysis of the Southern Peninsula of Michigan." Ph.D. dissertation, Michigan State University, 1969.

Rieck, Richard. "Morphology, Structure, and Formation of Eskers with Illustrations from Michigan: A Bibliographical Index to Esker Literature." M.A. thesis, Wayne State University, 1972.

Rieck, Richard L., and Winters, Harold A. "Characteristics of a Glacially Buried Cuesta in Southeast Michigan." *Annals of the Association of American Geographers* 72:4 (December 1982), pp. 482–494.

———. "Lake, Stream, and Bedrock in South-central Michigan." *Annals of the Association of American Geographers* 69:2 (June 1979), pp. 276–288.

Sommers, Lawrence M.; Thompson, Cymbria; Tainter, Suzanne; Lin, Leslie; Colucci, Thomas W.; and Lipsey, J. Michael. *Fish in Lake Michigan: Distribution of Selected Species.* Ann Arbor: Michigan Sea Grant Advisory Program, 1982.

Thatcher, Charles. "Pigeon River Perspectives." *Michigan Natural Resources* (May–June 1976), pp. 2–9.

U.S. Army Corps of Engineers. Department of Agriculture. North Central Forest Experiment Station. "The Growing Timber Resource of Michigan—1966." Resource Bulletin NC-9. St. Paul, Minn., 1970.

U.S. Bureau of Mines. *Minerals Yearbook—Metals, Minerals, and Fuels.* Washington, D.C., annually.

U.S. Department of Commerce. National Oceanic and Atmospheric Administration. *Climatological Data—Michigan Annual Summary, 1980.* Vol. 95, no. 13. Asheville, N.C., 1981.

U.S. Department of Commerce. National Oceanic and Atmospheric Administration in cooperation with the Michigan Weather Service. *Climate of Michigan by Stations.* by N. D. Strommen. Asheville, N.C., 1974.

U.S. Department of Commerce. National Oceanic and Atmospheric Administration. National Ocean Survey. *Great Lakes Water Levels, 1860–1970; Great Lakes Water Level, 1971-1982.* Detroit: Lake Survey Center, annually.

U.S. Department of the Interior. Geological Survey. "General Availability and Quality of Groundwater in the Bedrock Deposits in Michigan. Map, by F. R. Twenter. 1965.

_____ . "General Availability of Ground-water in the Glacial Deposits in Michigan." Map, by F. R. Twenter. 1967.

_____ . *Pleistocene of Indiana and Michigan and the History of the Great Lakes.* Monograph no. 53, by F. Leverett and F. B. Taylor. Washington, D.C., 1915.

_____ . "State of Michigan Map." Washington, D.C., 1970.

_____ . *Water Resources Data for Michigan.* Okemos, Mich., 1980.

Veatch, J. O. "Presettlement Forest in Michigan." Map. East Lansing: Department of Resource Development, Michigan State University, 1959.

Whiteside, E. P.; Schneider, I. F.; and Cook, R. L. *Soils of Michigan.* Special Bulletin 402. East Lansing: Soil Science Department, Michigan State University, 1956.

Wieber, J. M. "A Billion Tons of Iron Ore." *Michigan Natural Resources* (November–December 1975), pp. 16–17.

PART 4

Automobile Club of Michigan. *Michigan Outdoor Guide.* Dearborn, Mich.: Touring Department and Motor News, 1983.

Automotive News. 1981 Market Data Book issue.

Barlowe, Raleigh. "Project '80: Land and Water Resources." Research Report no. 52. East Lansing: Agricultural Experiment Station and the Cooperative Extension Service, Michigan State University, 1970.

Boas, Charles W. "Locational Patterns of the Michigan Passenger Automobile Industry." In *Readings in the Geography of Michigan,* ed. C. M. Davis, pp. 259–263. Ann Arbor: Ann Arbor Publishers, 1964.

Chubb, Michael, and Chubb, Holly R. *One Third of Our Time? An Introduction to Recreation Behavior and Resources.* New York: John Wiley and Sons, 1981.

Detroit Free Press. "Winter Scene." October 26, 1975.

Dice, Gene. "Supply-Demand in Michigan Campgrounds." Extension Bulletin E-895. East Lansing: Cooperative Extension Service, Michigan State University, September 1975.

Fridgen, Joseph D., and Allen, David J., eds. *Michigan Tourism: How Can Research Help?* Department of Park and Recreation Resources, Agricultural Experiment Station, Sp. Report no. 6. East Lansing: Michigan State University, 1981.

Gardner, Philip D., and Kimball, William J. "Michigan's Land Use Picture." East Lansing: Department of Resource Development, Agricultural Experiment Station, and the Cooperative Extension Service, Michigan State University, 1976.

Gogebic Community College. "1973–74 Michigan Snowmobile Survey." Mimeographed. Ironwood, Mich., 1974.

Hill, Elton B. and Mawby, Russell G. *Types of Farming in Michigan.* Special Bulletin 206. 2d rev. East Lansing: Agricultural Experiment Station, Michigan State College, 1954.

Hodgson, Ronald W. *New Leisure Patterns to Revolutionize Rural Land Use by 1985.* Research Report 191. East Lansing: Agricultural Experiment Station, Michigan State University, April 1973.

Lowenstein, Bill. "Hunting in Michigan: The Early Eighties." *Michigan Natural Resources* (September–October 1981), pp. 40–49.

McKee, Russell. "Seeing Elk." *Michigan Natural Resources* (September–October 1981), pp. 9–18.

Manthy, Robert S.; James, Lee M.; and Huber, Henry H. "Michigan Timber Production—Now and in 1985." Research Report no. 192. East Lansing: Agricultural Experiment Station and the Cooperative Extension Service, Michigan State University, 1973.

Michigan. Department of Agriculture. "Michigan Agricultural Land Requirements: A Projection to 2000 A.D." Mimeographed. Lansing, 1973.

_____ . *Michigan Agricultural Statistics 1981.* Lansing, 1981.

_____ . *Michigan Agricultural Statistics 1982.* Lansing, 1982.

_____ . *Michigan County Statistics—Field Crops, 1972–1977.* Lansing, 1978.

Michgan. Department of Conservation. Research and Development Division. *History of Michigan Deer Hunting.* Report no. 85, by C. L. Bennett, Jr., et al. Lansing, 1966.

Michigan. Department of Labor. Michigan Employment Security Commission. Office of Research and Statistics. *Civilian Labor Force Estimates, Michigan by County.* Lansing, annually.

Michigan. Department of Management and Budget. *Economic Report of the Governor.* Lansing, annually.

Michigan. Department of Natural Resources. *Coastal Effects of Coal Transshipment in Michigan: An Evaluation Strategy.* Lansing:

Great Lakes Basin Commission, October 1980.

———. "Michigan's Natural River System." Map. Lansing, n.d.

Michigan. Department of Natural Resources. Office of Planning Services. *Michigan Recreation Plan, 1979.* Lansing, 1979.

Michigan. Department of State Highways and Transportation. "545 Zone Statewide Transportation Modeling System Instate Zone Map." Lansing, 1974.

———. "Official Railway Map of the State of Michigan, January, 1976." Lansing, 1976.

———. "Traffic Flow Map." Lansing, 1973.

Michigan. Department of State Highways and Transportation. Bureau of Transportation Planning. Aviation Planning Section. *Air Carrier Statistics: Fiscal Year 1974-75; Aviation Statistics; and Registered Aircraft by State Planning and Development Regions, 1970–75.* Lansing, 1975.

Michigan. Department of State Highways and Transportation. Railway Planning Section. "Rail FRA Density Bandwidth Plot." Lansing, 1975.

Michigan. Employment Security Commission. *Civilian Labor Force, Unemployment, and Employment in Michigan Counties.* Lansing, annually.

Michigan. Employment Security Commission. Bureau of Research and Statistics. *Motor Vehicle and Related Industries in Michigan.* Lansing, Summer 1981.

Michigan. Waterways Commission and Department of Natural Resources. "Michigan Harbors Guide, 1975." Lansing, 1975.

Michigan State Economic Record. Bureau of Business Research, Michigan State University, bimonthly, 1959–1981. Issued by Wayne State University beginning in 1982.

Michigan State University. Cooperative Extension Service. "Natural Resources in Michigan's Economic Future." Mimeographed. East Lansing. October 1981.

Motor Vehicle Manufacturers Association. *Automobile Facts and Figures.* Detroit, various years.

Patrick, Michael, and Ferres, Bernie. "Railroad Reorganization in Michigan." *Michigan Farm Economics* no. 401. East Lansing, June 1976. Includes map.

Saint Lawrence Seaway Development Corporation. "1974 U.S. Great Lakes Ports Statistics for Overseas and Canadian Waterborne Commerce." Washington, D.C., 1975.

Schenker, E.; Mayer, H. M.; and Brockel, H. C. *The Great Lakes Transportation System.* Technical Report 230. Madison: University of Wisconsin Sea Grant College Program, January 1976.

Thompson, Donald C. "Grand Rapids: A Furniture Legend." *Chronicle* (Historical Society of Michigan) 2:3 (1975), pp. 3–10.

U.S. Bureau of Economic Analysis. *Regional Economics Information System, 1979.* Washington, D.C., 1979.

U.S. Bureau of Labor Statistics. *State Profile of Employment and Unemployment, 1977, Employment and Earnings.* Washington, D.C., January 1980.

U.S. Bureau of the Census. *Census of Agriculture: 1950.* Vol. 2, *General Report,* Chapter 2. Washington, D.C.: Government Printing Office, 1952.

———. *Census of Agriculture: 1964.* "Statistics for the State and Counties, Michigan." Washington, D.C.: Government Printing Office, 1967.

———. *Census of Agriculture: 1969.* Vol. 1, Pt. 13, "Michigan." Section 1, "Summary Data." Washington, D.C.: Government Printing Office, 1972.

———. *Census of Manufactures: 1972.* Vol. 4, *Area Series,* "Michigan." MC72(3)-23. Washington, D.C.: Government Printing Office, 1975.

———. *Census of Population: 1970.* Vol. 1, *Characteristics of the Population.* Pt. 24, "Michigan." Washington, D.C.: Government Printing Office, 1973.

———. *1978 Annual Survey of Manufacturers.* Washington, D.C.: Government Printing Office, 1981.

———. *1977 U.S. Census of Manufactures. Area Series,* "Michigan." Washington, D.C.: Government Printing Office, 1979.

———. *1977 U.S. Census of Retail Trade. Area Series,* "Michigan." Washington, D.C.: Government Printing Office, 1979.

———. *Survey of the Origin of Exports of Manufacturing Establishments in 1972.* Industrial Reports, Series MA-161(72)-2. Washington, D.C.: Government Printing Office, 1974.

U.S. Department of Agriculture. North Central Forest Experiment Station. "Forest Area in Michigan, 1980." St. Paul, Minn., 1982.

U.S. Department of the Army. Corps of Engineers. *Waterborne Commerce of the United States.* Pt. 3, "Waterways and Harbors—

Great Lakes." Vicksburg, Miss., annually.

U.S. Department of the Interior. Fish and Wildlife Service. "Michigan Permanent Water Areas." Map. Washington, D.C., n.d.

U.S. Department of the Interior. Geological Survey. *National Atlas of the United States.* Washington, D.C., 1970.

U.S. Department of the Interior. National Park Service. "Isle Royale." Brochure. Denver, Colo.: Denver Service Center, 1968.

_____. "Pictured Rocks." Brochure. Denver, Colo.: Denver Service Center, 1975.

_____. "Pictured Rocks National Lakeshore General Development Plan." Denver, Colo.: Denver Service Center. 1975.

_____. "Sleeping Bear Dunes, National Lakeshore, Michigan." Denver, Colo.: Denver Service Center, n.d.

U.S. Federal Aviation Administration. *Airport Activity Statistics of Certified Route Air Carriers, 12 Months Ended 31 December 1979,* Tables 6 and 7. Washington, D.C., 1981.

U.S. Federal Communications Commission. "Statistics of Communication Common Carriers." Washington, D.C., February 1973.

Upper Peninsula Travel and Recreation Association. "Waterfalls Guide." Iron Mountain, Mich., 1975.

Ward's Communications, Inc. *Ward's Automotive Yearbook, 1958–80.* Detroit: Ward's Communications, Inc., annually 1958–1980.

Wright, Karl T. "Michigan's Changing Agriculture." *Michigan State Economic Record* 21:2 (1979), p. 1.

Wright, Karl T., and Dueweke, Daniel A. "The Changing Scene in Michigan Agriculture." Extension Bulletin E-1253, File 15-33. East Lansing: Michigan State University, October 1978.

Wright, Karl T.; Ferris, John N.; and Sorenson, Vernon L. "Growth in Michigan Agriculture: A Background Paper for the Michigan Governor's Conference, April 1 and 2, 1981." Agricultural Economics Staff Paper no. 81-8. East Lansing: Michigan State University, February 1981.

PART 5

Agocs, Carol. "Ethnicity in Detroit." In *Immigrants and Migrants: The Detroit Ethnic Experience,* ed. David Hartman, pp. 390–408. Detroit: Wayne State University, 1974.

Aswad, Barbara. "The Southeast Dearborn Arab Community Struggles for Survival Against Urban Renewal." In *Arabic-Speaking Communities in American Cities,* ed. Barbara Aswad, pp. 53–83. New York: Center for Migration Studies of New York, 1974.

Baba, Marietta, and Abonyi, Malvina. *Mexicans of Detroit.* Detroit: Wayne State University, 1979.

Black, Harold. "Restrictive Covenants in Relation to Segregated Negro Housing in Detroit." M.S. thesis, Wayne State University, 1948.

Bradley vs. *Milliken,* 338 F. Supp. 582 (1971).

Brink, William, and Harris, Louis. *Black and White.* New York: Simon and Schuster, 1967.

Burgess, Ernest W. "Residential Segregation in American Cities." *Annals of the American Academy of Political and Social Science* 140 (1928), pp. 105–115.

Butler, Broadus N. "The City of Detroit and the Emancipation Proclamation." In *Assuring Freedom to the Free: A Century of Emancipation in the U.S.A.,* ed. Arnold M. Rose, pp. 72–94. Detroit: Wayne State University Press, 1964.

Campbell, Angus, and Schuman, Howard. *Racial Attitudes in Fifteen Cities.* Ann Arbor, Mich.: Institute for Social Research, 1968.

Clark, Dennis. "Immigrant Enclaves in Our Cities." In *The Ghetto: Readings with Interpretations,* ed. Joe T. Darden, pp. 59–73. Port Washington, N.Y.: Kennikat Press, 1981.

Clark, W.A.V. "Residential Mobility and Neighborhood Change: Some Implications for Racial Residential Segregation." *Urban Geography* 1:2 (April–June 1980), pp. 95–117.

Coleman, James. "Destructure Beliefs and Potential Policies in School Desegregation." In *Detroit Metropolitan City-Suburban Relations,* ed. John W. Smith, pp. 5–12. Dearborn, Mich.: Henry Ford Community College, 1979.

Curwood, J. "An Ethnographical Study of Detroit." *Detroit-News Tribune,* August 21, 1904, p. 4.

Cybriwsky, Roman A. "Revitalization Trends in Downtown-Area Neighborhoods." In *The American Metropolitan System: Present and Future,* ed. Stanley D. Brunn and James O. Wheeler, pp. 21–36. John Wiley and Sons, 1980.

Darden, Joe T. *Afro-Americans in Pittsburgh: The Residential Segregation of a People.* Lexington, Mass.: D.C. Heath and Co., 1973.

_____. "Lending Practices and Policies Af-

fecting the American Metropolitan System."
In *The American Metropolitan System: Present and Future,* ed. Stanley D. Brunn and James O. Wheeler, pp. 93–110. New York: John Wiley and Sons, 1980.

─────── . "The Residential Segregation of Blacks in Detroit, 1960–1970." *International Journal of Comparative Sociology* 17 (1976a), pp. 84–91.

─────── . "Residential Segregation of Blacks in the Suburbs: The Michigan Example." *Geographical Survey* 5:3 (July 1976b), pp. 7–16.

Darden, Joe T., and Tabachneck, Arthur. "Algorithm 8: Graphic and Mathematical Descriptions of Inequality, Dissimilarity, Segregation, or Concentration." *Environment and Planning A* 12 (1980), pp. 227–234.

Deskins, Donald R. "Morphogenesis of a Black Ghetto." *Urban Geography* 2 (April–June 1981), pp. 95–114.

Detroit. *Moving Detroit Forward: A Plan for Urban Economic Revitalization.* Detroit, 1975.

Detroit Free Press. July 11, 1873, p. 1.

Detroit Planning Department. *Overall Economic Development Annual Report and Program Projection: 1980.* Detroit, 1980a.

─────── . *Population Trends in Detroit.* A report. Detroit, November 1980b.

─────── . *Proposed Master Plan Economic Capacity Section—Article 301.* Draft. Detroit. 1979.

Detroit Tribune. December 6, 1885, p. 9.

De Vito, A. P. "Urban Revitalization: The Case of Detroit." *Urban Concerns* (May–June 1979), pp. 3–13.

Durkin, Julie, and Cleland, Charles. *An Archival Assessment of the Archaelogical Resources That May Be Impacted by the Detroit People Mover Project.* A report prepared by Aurora Associates for the Southeast Michigan Transportation Authority. Detroit, 1981.

Farley, Renolds, et al. "Chocolate City, Vanilla Suburbs: Will the Trend Toward Racially Separate Communities Continue?" *Social Science Quarterly* 7 (1978), pp. 319–344.

Fusfeld, Daniel. "The Economy of the Urban Ghetto." In *The Ghetto: Readings with Interpretations,* ed. Joe T. Darden, pp. 131–155. Port Washington, N.Y.: Kennikat Press, 1981.

Glazer, Sidney. *Detroit: A Study in Urban Development.* New York: Bookman Associates, 1965.

Goldfield, D. R. "The Limits of Suburban Growth: The Washington D.C. SMSA." *Urban Affairs Quarterly* 12 (1976), pp. 83–102.

Gordon, Milton. *Assimilation in American Life.* New York: Oxford University Press, 1964.

Gram, John, et al. *A Literature Cultural Resource Survey and Field Inspection of the Detroit Downtown.* Bloomington, Ind.: Resource Analysts, 1981.

Handlin, Oscar. *The Newcomers: Negroes and Puerto Ricans in a Changing Metropolis.* Garden City, N.Y.: Anchor, 1959.

Hanieski, John F. "Diversifying the Michigan Economy." *Michigan State Economic Record* 23:2 (February 1981), pp. 1–8.

Hauser, Philip. "Demographic Factors in the Integration of the Negro." *Daedalus* (Fall 1965), pp. 847–877.

Hawley, Amos H. "Dispersion Versus Segregation: Apropos of a Solution of Race Problems." *Papers of the Michigan Academy of Science, Arts, and Letters* 30 (1944), pp. 667–674.

Helper, Rose. *Racial Practices of Real Estate Brokers.* Minneapolis: University of Minnesota Press, 1969.

Hermalin, Albert, and Farley, Reynolds. "The Potential for Residential Integration in Cities and Suburbs: Implications for the Busing Controversy." *American Sociological Review* 38 (October 1973), pp. 595–610.

Hill, Richard. "At the Crossroads: The Political Economy of Postwar Detroit." *Urbanism Past and Present* (Summer 1978), pp. 1–21.

Hudgins, B. "The Evolution of Metropolitan Detroit." *Economic Geography* 21 (1945), pp. 206–220.

Jenkins, Raymond. "Downtown: Keystone to the Future." In *Metropolitan America: Geographic Perspectives and Teaching Strategies,* ed. Robert D. Swartz et al., pp. 141–153. Oak Park, Ill.: National Council of Geographic Education, 1972.

Katzman, David M. *Before the Ghetto: Black Detroit in the Nineteenth Century.* Urbana: University of Illinois Press, 1973.

Knight, Richard V. "City Development in an Industrial Region: Detroit, A Case Study." In *Detroit Metropolitan City-Suburban Relations,* ed. John W. Smith, pp. 13–38. Dearborn, Mich.: Henry Ford Community College, 1979.

Knoll, Gaustina Ramirez. "Casework Services for Mexican Americans." In *Immigrants and Migrants: The Detroit Ethnic Experience,* ed. David Hartman, pp. 261–269. Detroit: Wayne State University, 1974.

Lieberson, Stanley. *Ethnic Patterns in American Cities*. Glencoe, Ill.: Free Press, 1963.

Lipton, Gregory. "Evidence of Central City Revival." *Journal of the American Institute of Planners* 43 (1977), pp. 136–147.

Mackun, Stanley. "The Changing Patterns of Polish Settlements in the Greater Detroit Area: Geographic Study of the Assimilation of an Ethnic Group. Ph.D. dissertation, University of Michigan, 1964.

Meier, Matt S., and Rivera, Feliciano. *The Chicanos: A History of Mexican Americans*. New York: Hill and Wang, 1972.

Michigan Ethnic Heritage Center. *Ethnic City: A Guide to Ethnic Detroit*. Vol. 2. Detroit: Ethnic Studies Division, Center for Urban Studies, Wayne State University, 1971.

Muller, P. O. "Suburbia, Geography, and the Prospect of a Nation Without Important Cities." *Geographical Survey* 7 (1978), pp. 4–5.

Myrdal, Gunnar. *An American Dilemma*. New York: Harper and Brothers, 1944.

Napolska, Mary R. *The Polish Immigrant in Detroit to 1914*. Chicago: Polish Catholic Union of America, 1946.

Orfield, Gary. *Must We Bus?* Washington, Brookings Institution, 1978.

Orton, Lawrence. *Polish Detroit and the Kolasinski Affair*. Detroit: Wayne State University Press, 1981.

Park, Robert E. *Human Communities*. Glencoe, Ill.: Free Press, 1952.

Pearce, Diana M. "Gatekeepers and Homeseekers: Institutional Patterns in Racial Steering." *Social Problems* 26:3 (February 1979), pp. 325–342.

Pettigrew, Thomas. "Attitudes on Race and Housing: A Social Psychological View." In *Segregation in Residential Areas*, ed. Amos Hawley and Vincent P. Rock, pp. 21–84. Washington, D.C.: National Academy of Sciences, 1973.

Pred, Allen. "Industrialization, Initial Advantage, and American Metropolitan Growth." *Geographical Review* 55 (1965), pp. 158–185.

Roseman, Curtis C. "Exurban Areas and Exurban Migration." In *The American Metropolitan System: Present and Future*, ed. Stanley D. Brunn and James O. Wheeler, pp. 51–58. New York: John Wiley and Sons, 1980.

Salas, Gumecindo, and Salas, Isabel. "The Mex-

ican Community in Detroit." In *Immigrants and Migrants: The Detroit Ethnic Experience*, ed. David Hartman, pp. 374–387. Detroit: Wayne State University, 1974.

Sengstock, Mary. "Southfield: The Ethnic Grosse Pointe." In *Immigrants and Migrants: The Detroit Ethnic Experience*, ed. David Hartman, pp. 339–344. Detroit: Wayne State University, 1974.

Sinclair, Robert. *The Face of Detroit—A Spatial Synthesis*. Detroit: Wayne State University, National Council for Geographic Education, U.S. Office of Education, 1970.

————. "Port-Hinterland-Foreland-Maritime Space Relationships of the Port of Detroit." *Wiener geographische Schrifter*, no. 24–29. Festschrift Leopold G. Scheidl, vol. 2. Vienna: Berger and Sohne, 1967.

Siryani, Mohammad. "Residential Distribution, Spatial Mobility, and Acculturation in an Arab-Muslim Community." Ph.D. dissertation, Michigan State University, 1977.

Southeast Michigan Council of Governments. *1970 Transportation Related Data SEMCOG Region*. Detroit, December 1972.

Spear, Allen H. *Black Chicago: The Making of a Negro Ghetto, 1890–1920*. Chicago: University of Chicago Press, 1967.

Stephens, John D., and Holly, Brian. "The Changing Patterns of Industrial Corporate Control in the Metropolitan United States." In *The American Metropolitan System: Present and Future*, ed. Stanley D. Brunn and James O. Wheeler, pp. 161–179. New York: John Wiley and Sons, 1980.

Swartz, Robert, et al. *Metropolitan America: Geographic Perspectives and Teaching Strategies*. Oak Park, Ill.: National Council of Geographic Education, 1972.

U.S. Bureau of the Census. *Annual Housing Survey: Housing Characteristics for Selected Metropolitan Areas*. Washington, D.C.: Government Printing Office, April 1980.

————. *Census of Population and Housing, 1980*. PL. 94-171, "Population Counts Michigan." Washington, D.C.: Government Printing Office, 1981a.

————. *Data User News 16* (October 1981b), pp. 4 and 9.

————. *Fourteenth Census of the United States Population*. Vol. 3, *Composition and Characteristics of the Population by States*. Washington D.C.: Government Printing Office, 1922.

————. *1980 Census of Population and Hous-*

ing: Michigan. Advance Reports, PHC 80-V-24. Washington, D.C.: Government Printing Office, March 1981c.

———. *16th Census of the United States: 1940 Population and Housing Statistics for Census Tracts in Detroit.* Table 3. Washington, D.C.: Government Printing Office, 1941.

———. *U.S. Census of Population and Housing General Demographic Trends for Metropolitan Areas, 1960 to 1970.* Final Report PHC (2) 24, "Michigan." Washington, D.C.: Government Printing Office, 1971.

U.S. Department of Housing and Urban Development. Office of Policy Development and Research. *Measuring Racial Discrimination in American Housing Markets: The Housing Market Practices Survey.* Washington, D.C., 1979.

U.S. Department of Labor. Bureau of Labor Statistics. *Employment in Perspective: Minority Workers.* Report 652. Washington, D.C., 1981.

U.S. Federal Housing Administration. *Underwriting Manual.* Washington, D.C.: Government Printing Office, 1938.

Wallace, David A. "Residential Concentration of Negroes in Chicago." Ph.D. dissertation, Harvard University, 1953.

Warner, Sam. *The Urban Wilderness.* New York: Harper and Row, 1972.

Wasfi, Afif A. "Dearborn Arab-Moslem Community: A Study of Acculturation." Ph.D. dissertation, Michigan State University, 1964.

Western Upper Peninsula Planning and Development Region. *Natural Resource Analysis.* Houghton, Mich., June 1974.

Western Upper Peninsula Regional Planning Commission. *Open Space and Recreation Inventory and Interim Plan.* Houghton, Mich., October 1972.

West Michigan Regional Planning Commission. *Recreation and Open Space Inventory and Analysis.* Grand Rapids, Mich., April 1976.

Wigle, Laurel, and Abraham, Sameer. "Arab Nationalism in America: The Dearborn Arab Community." In *Immigrants and Migrants: The Detroit Ethnic Experience,* ed. David Hartman, pp. 279–302. Detroit: Wayne State University, 1974.

Wolf, Eleanor P. *Trial and Error: The Detroit School Segregation Case.* Detroit: Wayne State University Press, 1981.

Workers Education Local 189, Michigan Chapter. *Union Town: A Labor History Guide to Detroit.* Detroit, n.d.

Wrobel, Paul. *Our Way: Family, Parish, and Neighborhood in a Polish-American Community.* Notre Dame, Ind.: University of Notre Dame Press, 1979.

Zunz, Oliver. "The Organization of the American City in the Late Nineteenth Century: Ethnic Structure and Spatial Arrangement in Detroit." *Journal of Urban History* 3:4 (August 1977), pp. 443–466.

PART 6

Brown, Allan S. "Caroline Vartlett Crane and Urban Reform." *Michigan History* 56:4 (1972), pp. 287–301.

C. A. Doxiadis Associates. *Emergence and Growth of an Urban Region, The Developing Urban Detroit Area.* Vol. 3. Detroit: Detroit Edison Co., 1970.

"Chemical Clean-up Paying Off." *Michigan Natural Resources* (July–August 1974), p. 20.

Commission on Population Growth and the American Future. *Population and the American Future.* Washington, D.C., 1972.

Hall, Dennis. "The Land Is Borrowed from Our Children." *Michigan Natural Resources* (July–August 1975), pp. 2–9.

Hartig, John H. *Highlights of Water Quality and Pollution Control in Michigan.* Lansing: Department of Natural Resources, Environmental Services Division, 1981.

Hartig, John H., and Stifler, Michael E. *Water Quality and Pollution Control in Michigan.* Lansing: Department of Natural Resources, Environmental Services Division, 1980.

Hepp, Ralph E., and Ott, Stephen L. "Farmland and Open Space Preservation Act." Extension Bulletin, E. 792, no. 40. East Lansing: Michigan State University, May 1975.

Michigan. Department of Management and Budget. "Population Projections for the Counties of Michigan." Lansing, 1974.

Michigan. Department of Natural Resources. *Michigan's Future Was Today.* Lansing: Office of Land Use, September 1974.

———. *Michigan: 1980 Annual Air Quality Report.* Lansing: Air Quality Division, 1980.

Morscheck, Richard. "Minding Our PCB's." *Michigan Natural Resources* (March–April 1976), pp. 4–7.

Reinking, R. L., and Zilinski, R. E. "Effect of Deicing Salt on Sodium Content of Lake Macatawa, Michigan." *Michigan Academician* 8:3 (1975), pp. 373–382.

Rummel, Walt. "Ghost Towns Are Everywhere." *Michigan Motor News,* September 1975.

Sheaffer, John R. "Reviving the Great Lakes." *Saturday Review,* November 7, 1970, pp. 62–65.

Sommers, Lawrence M. "The Potential Impact of Increased Use of Renewable Resources on Land Use Patterns and Policy: The Case of Michigan." *Applied Geography Conference* (Binghamton, N.Y., 1979), pp. 61–70.

————. "Regionalization: A Key Approach to Understanding Societal Issues." *Proceedings of Applied Geography Conferences* 4 (1981), pp. 179–186.

Sommers, Lawrence M., and Koenig, Herman E. *Energy and the Adaptation of Human Settlements: A Prototype Process in Genesee County, Michigan.* East Lansing: Michigan State University, 1980.

Sommers, Lawrence M.; Wood, Garland A.; Johnson, James H., Jr.; and Miller, Tracy C. *Household Energy Consumption in Oakland and Livingston Counties, Michigan.* East Lansing: Michigan State University, 1981.

Tanner, Howard. "Putting Waste in Its Place." *Michigan Natural Resources* (November–December 1972), pp. 2–7.

U.S. Department of Agriculture. Soil Conservation Service et al. "Prime Lands of Michigan." Map. Washington, D.C., 1973.

ABOUT THE CONTRIBUTORS

JOE T. DARDEN is professor of geography and urban affairs at Michigan State University in East Lansing. He is the author of *The Ghetto: Readings with Interpretations, Residential Segregation of Blacks in Detroit, 1960–1970* and numerous other publications in the areas of urban social geography and the geography of minority groups in the United States.

JAY R. HARMAN is professor of geography at Michigan State University in East Lansing. He is author of *Tropospheric Waves, Jet Streams, and United States Weather Patterns* and other articles on weather and forest geography in the eastern United States.

SHERMAN R. HOLLANDER is cartographer for Land Resource Programs, Department of Natural Resources, State of Michigan, in Lansing. He was formerly staff cartographer for the Department of Geography at Michigan State University and has been the cartographer for several geography books.

LAURIE K. SOMMERS is completing a Ph.D. in folklore at Indiana University in Bloomington. She was formerly employed as an assistant historian of the Michigan History Division in Lansing and as folklorist-consultant at Commonwealth Associates in Jackson. She is coeditor and contributor to *Discourse in Ethnomusicology II* and has published several articles, book reviews, and reports on various aspects of Michigan history.

INDEX